The World we have lost

This book is dedicated to Susan Ault,
now Susan Stewart,
Keith Allison and John Harrison,
who have spent so much of their leisure time
since 1962 voluntarily at work,
helping to bring into being
the systematic study of English
social structure in the past.

The World we have lost

by Peter Laslett

CHARLES SCRIBNER'S SONS

NEW YORK

Contents

Introduction

This essay has been six years in the making, and is on the way to being overtaken by events. It began as an attempt to write out in a straightforward way the introductory facts about the structure of English society as it was before the Industrial Revolution, and to make some comparison with its structure in the twentieth century. But the idea of an introduction to a subject of this kind turned out to be peculiarly elusive. Even the choice of the point at which to start is a problem, for it may determine the view of the whole which will be taken. Every descriptive remark after that may also mask the reality it aims to convey. Accordingly I have found that the task of working out an intelligible plan of a complete social structure is extraordinarily formidable; putting it down in clear, readable form has been even more so.

Hence a whole series of successive provisional drafts of the text over the six years, of which the one printed here is the last. The difficulties have not been entirely intellectual and literary. Since 1959, when a casual reference brought *The Rector's Book, Clayworth, Nottinghamshire*[1] up out of the vaults of the Library of Congress, sources for this study have been coming to light so rapidly that it has been almost impossible to decide when the time had come to pause and write down a summary of knowledge acquired to date. In this situation resort was had to the Third Programme of the British Broadcasting Corporation, and some of the material of *The World we have lost*, as well as its title, appeared as talks and in *The Listener* in the years 1960, 1962, and 1963.

It became clear quite early that two much more important things were wanted in addition to an introductory essay to the subject as a whole. One was an arrangement for collaborative research, which would make it possible to undertake tasks no man could hope to carry out on his own. The second was the fund of information and the necessary time to write a large and something like a definitive study of the social structure of pre-industrial England, and perhaps of Europe generally.

The first of these objects has been happily attained, and the *Cambridge Group for the History of Population and Social Structure* began its official life in 1964, with the generous support of the Calouste Gulbenkian Foundation of London.[2] This should secure the

[1] *For the importance of this apparently unpromising title to the historical study of social structure see note 9 on page 242 and the references in the text.*

[2] *This small research unit was jointly founded by E. A. Wrigley and Peter Laslett, and owes a great deal to the personal interest of Mr James Thornton, Secretary of the Foundation. Its work is described in an article appearing in December, 1965, in the* International Social Science Journal, *which also gives details of the accumulation of material referred to above, and of the organization of correspondence with volunteers all over England.*

second object as well. One of the titles in the series of works to be published by the Cambridge Group will be the full treatise of which the present essay is merely a foretaste. This wholly more academic work will print as much of the evidence as seems to be required, and others of the monographs which we are planning, together with various articles, will also contain instalments of the full facts and figures which have been used so sketchily here.

But though *The World we have lost* is in a sense a collaborative work, and could never have been written if only one man had been at work, it is emphatically not a publication of the *Cambridge Group for the History of Population and Social Structure* and does not appear under that imprint. The first of the series to be issued by the Group will in fact come out early in 1966, an *Introduction to English Historical Demography*, edited by E. A. Wrigley, with contributions from him, from the present author and others. That work, and other publications, will contain instalments of precisely those findings which are repeatedly mentioned in this book as being urgently needed and probably obtainable, since some of them have already been worked out in France, mainly statistics of population. In this sense it is possible to say that *The World we have lost* is fortunately about to be overtaken, in respect at least of the research results which it presents.

The rougher facts and figures used here belong to an earlier and less regular period in the initial stages of this departure in historical and social research. The present essay has been dedicated to three of the volunteers who undertook the wearisome tasks of working through the newly-found documents to find out if the newly-worked-out hypotheses were of any value. Several other volunteers should also be thanked for their part in the investigations and in the consultations which took place in Cambridge: Mr Newman Brown, Mr John Montgomery, Mrs Bessie Maltby and Mr F. G. Emmison. Nearly all these historians are still working in correspondence with the Cambridge Group, but in the more advanced and regular way which has now become possible.

It is understandable, nevertheless, that the rapid advance of these studies over the months since the last provisional version of this text was written has made the author feel that he would now like to write it even yet again, with certain differences. Many of the changes would be due to the extraordinarily interesting research on which Dr Wrigley has been engaged.

The first results of his reconstruction of families in the village of Colyton in Devon have turned out to be of the greatest importance to the views expressed here about population in relation to the means of subsistence. The correspondence in which he has been engaged with the hundreds of historians all over Britain, most of them amateurs, who have undertaken to make counts of entries in parish registers for the Cambridge Group, has made available a store of accurate information never before assembled for any country. All of it is relevant to the statements in this essay and when we come to analyse it systematically the whole subject will be given a fullness and a depth which must transform it. Perhaps these developments will finally alter the factual details set out here surprisingly little. But they have already had considerable effects on the overall view.

A summary of Dr Wrigley's own results from Colyton will be appearing very shortly in a learned article, and at greater length in one of the monographs to be published by the Cambridge Group. They must not be anticipated here. But one implication of what he is about to say cannot go unnoticed. His work will demonstrate that there is no such thing as a constant state of pre-industrial or traditional or peasant society in Europe, at least in respect of demographic characteristics. Traditional society showed a notable flexibility even in such fundamental arrangements as marriage, reproduction and family size. There were always mechanisms at work permitting communities of men and women to reduce or to expand the rate of formation of families. Family limitation, in fact, cannot any longer be looked upon as a phenomenon of advanced industrializing or industrialized society. Nor can it be thought of as associated with the appearance of rational attitudes, a permanent feature once those attitudes became established. It could apparently come and go, in generations which lived well before the Great Industrial Revolution.

This departure will make it necessary to think out again what is written in this book about births, marriages and deaths, about the problem of the starving peasantry and about personal discipline and social survival. Some of the provisional conclusions about number of children to a marriage, about illegitimacy and about the likelihood of peasant brides being pregnant at marriage may have to be modified. The whole view of the relationship between moral behaviour and social imperative may have to be shifted slightly too. But by and large it seems to me that most of the statements made here will be given an exact expression and a convincing context rather than shown to be seriously misleading.

Repeated revision of the text has introduced and elongated a theme which had very little part in the original plan. This is the discussion of the methods and outlook of the historians, which is particularly evident in Chapters 2, 7, 8 and 10. If the book were to be recast, these statements would also be somewhat modified, and the revision would likewise be due to some extent to the recent progress of the work at Cambridge and to discussions with Dr Wrigley about it.

There are frequent acknowledgements of the danger of using the expression 'industrialization' in a wholesale fashion, but it could still be the case that too much reliance has been placed here upon the word and upon the unity of the process which it stands for. This is perhaps understandable in the presentation of a theme which is one of heightened contrast between a before and an after, where the point of division is made to come at the time when a society took an 'industrial' character upon itself. But this might only too easily be held to imply that all industrialized societies have more in common with each other than any has with a pre-industrial society, or even with itself as it was in the pre-industrial era.

This is an uncomfortable claim. It could only be shown to be true if our detailed knowledge of societies were very much greater than it now is, and our means of describing them very much more exact than they could ever be. Moreover, it tends to confirm historians in their tendency to think too readily in terms of watersheds, since it turns industrialization into a watershed of a universal kind. This may obscure just those features and tendencies which should be most eagerly sought out and shown up.

We may take an example in class-conflict. It is one thing to argue, as it is argued in Chapter 2, that England before industrialization is best called a one-class society where overall, nation-wide class conflict could scarcely arise. But it is quite another thing to allow this to persuade us to believe that before industrialization all instances of quarrels over capital, rent, wages or access to the land were in some sense out of their time, exceptional, anachronistic. The facts are, of course, that differences, conflict, even outright fighting over such things have been a constant and consistent feature of economic organization, and are in no way peculiar to large-scale, factory-organized production. Mr J. O. Foster, of St Catharine's College, Cambridge, has evidence to illustrate what may seem a remarkable paradox, that the growth of factory production was actually associated with the subsidence of particularly acute conflict between workers and employers in certain Lancashire cotton towns. He insists that many other features of the social situation than the mere organization of work and the distribution of ownership have to be taken into account; the presence or absence of the capitalists, the perception of the social structure by the workers, and so on.

There is a strong tendency to suppose that overall social changes were more coherent, uniform and consistent than they could possibly have been. Only if we slip into this way of thinking about industrialization could we be led into the associations just described. There is of course another source of the desire to describe as 'anticipations' or as 'survivals' those events which we would like to believe are untypical of the general historical situation as it was when they occurred. This is the Hegelian or Marxian mode of interpretation which wishes to lay it down that an epoch is in an essential way different in order from its predecessor. It would be very unfortunate if the concept of industrialization and of the differences it makes were to come to be looked on in this way.[1] The extraordinary variations between locality and locality, industry and industry, which our evidence is beginning to show up in the structural changes which took place in England over the period of 'industrialization' should we hope correct this possible obliquity of view.

We can now begin to look upon industrialization as a series of modifications which took place in the lives of very large numbers of individual communities, a different process in every particular case, different in content, in the succession of events, in the time taken up. Now this is not a single process at all. Strictly speaking it did not happen to 'England' or 'English society', and questions about the stage reached by a whole country at a particular time are abstract questions about *averages* rather than about events.

How deceptive it may be to think of our country as a whole in which a unitary process occurred during a given number of years is shown by the work of another Cambridge researcher, Mr M. Anderson of Queens' College. Economic interplay between industrial and commercial centres and the rural hinterland was no doubt extensive, but he finds indications that the social structure of the English countryside changed much less than might be expected until late in the progress of industrialization. Traditional England got smaller in relation to industrial England and was finally reduced to an insignificant fringe. The succession of events was much more intricate than this of course, but a point of great interest is that the familial structure discussed here seems to have shown a remarkable persistence in the countryside right into 'industrial' times. The large family of resident children, and of residing in-laws and relatives seems to have been characteristic of the expanding urban and industrial areas as early as the 1840's and 50's, but had not yet become characteristic of agricultural society.

So much for the little that can now be said of the directions in which the interpretative doctrine of the present preliminary study may have to be recast. The discussion raises the whole insistent and complex problem of the correct relationship between what is economic change, and what is social structural change. The reader

[1] *Though it has to be said that Marx himself, in this respect as in so many others, is a very different person from his followers. The quotation from the* Communist Manifesto *for example printed on page 16, in a sense contains the very point which the argument there is trying to make, that exploitation is no product of capitalism. Feudalism was exploitation, but 'veiled by political and religious illusions' (i.e. patriarchalism or something very like it).*

will very soon see for himself that there is little discussion of economic history and development in this essay. He may even find instances of an occurrence or a change which is interpreted here as a modification of the social structure, when a much more straightforward and convincing explanation would be that it was a response to economic necessity. This possibility is present in much of the general, static analysis as well, especially in Chapter 2. The writer can only frankly confess that this weakness is to be expected in an intellectual historian attempting sociological analysis, in past time.

The same attempt at a disarming of criticism is all that is open to him in response to the professional demographers and statisticians who find holes in the numerical arguments. The dubious figures and conclusions which some of them may still contain, in spite of the strenuous efforts of friends and associates, will not perhaps worry these critics as much as the failure to see the significance of things which a better trained worker could never have overlooked. I hope it is justifiable to ask them to remember that this is a first brash attempt, an essay in suggestive hypothesis, and pretends to be nothing more.

In addition to the general modifications of the argument of this book there are as might be expected a large number of individual points which might have been revised if the works containing ·the evidence had been known to me when the relevant passages were composed for this volume. The work of Philippe Ariès on childhood originally published in France in 1960 and translated into English as *Centuries of Childhood* in 1962, has made it clear that some of my assertions about authoritarianism, educational practices and the unchanging nature of familial structure and attitudes could well be a little simple-minded. A corresponding exercise in English sources, used but of course only in passing by Ariès, would no doubt lead to much illumination and considerable revision of these early impressions. The appearance this year of complete works on topics important to the discussion by my two friends Lawrence Stone (*The Crisis of the Aristocracy*) and T. H. Hollingsworth (*The Demography of the British Peerage*) has also modified my opinion on certain points, as well as noticeably extended the evidence. There are important articles by W. G. Hoskins, whose help and friendliness has been crucial, and by others too numerous to name. An appreciable difficulty of attempting to create what seems to be a different type of study, however slight in consequence the effort may be, is· the sense of abysmal ignorance which it creates and which seems never to grow less.

The list of those to whom I owe thanks and acknowledgements is so long that it could only be unreadable in full. There are first of all the French scholars, without whose achievements and example many of the activities reported here could never have gone forward. I hope Louis Henry and Pierre Goubert will accept this tribute to their pre-eminence, and my thanks for their friendliness and forbearance with an awkward English visitor. M. Alfred Sauvy, the *doyen* (now in the English sense only) of the Institut National d'Études Démographiques and of demographic studies all over the world, has been very obliging, and I owe much to J. N. Biraben (now in Montreal) and other members of the staff of the Institut.

Almost no County Record Office in this country has failed to assist these researches in some way or other, and I should like their officials to know how much their help has been appreciated; there is Miss Holmes at Dorchester, Mr Stitt at Stafford, Miss Macpherson at Kendal, Mr Hull at Maidstone, Mr Walne at Hertford, Mr Wood at Warwick, Miss Sinar at Matlock, Mr Jones at the Guildhall in London, amongst all the rest. Advice, encouragement, criticism and help has reached me in some quantity from my American friends and I should particularly like to thank Richard Schlatter, Jack Hexter, Bernard Bailyn, Edmund Morgan, George Homans, Page Smith, Allan Nevins, Karl Deutsch, Vann Woodward, John Krause, James Birren and David Potter, but there is a very long list of others. Dan Boorstin has advised me from a closer quarter, and good company it has been.

The social scientists nearer home who have been good enough to guide me are also a large company, and I wish that I had been a better pupil. David Glass, Tom Marshall, Max Gluckman, Meyer Fortes, Jack Goody, Audrey Richards, David Lockwood, John Goldthorpe and Edmund Leach are some of them, and I owe a great deal to Edward Shils, my caustic mentor now for nearly twenty years. David Eversley has been an unfailing source of help and friendliness. Many people have given quite unlooked for assistance far in excess of what a researcher has a right to expect; there are Mr and Mrs Gooder of the Birmingham Extra-Mural Board as one instance, or the many clergy of the English Church who have responded to queries and given access to the documents in their care. A number of literary scholars have assisted too; there is Mrs Florence Trefethen, of Lexington, Massachusetts, and Miss Muriel Bradbrook, whose extraordinary knowledge of the Elizabethans has been of great importance. Keith Thomas and Anne Whiteman have communicated material from Oxford, and given me valuable advice.

Like every other writer with a case I have learnt a lot from those with whom I wish to disagree, at least to some extent; here Eric Hobsbawm and Christopher Hill are two names to mention, whilst Brough Macpherson has been a most friendly and useful collaborator and critic. E. H. Carr has encouraged me a great deal too and I should like to record my gratitude to him. Sir Charles Snow, Sir

Anthony Wagner and Asa Briggs have been amongst the patrons of social structural research, and I can only hope that they may like this first instalment of its results.

Even this may seem an inordinate list of debts for so short a book, but I have still to reach my more personal acknowledgements. There is Anna Kallin, late and for so long acknowledged as the reigning princess of the Third Programme. There is Maurice Ashley, editor of *The Listener*, a long-standing, faithful friend to studies of this kind. There are those who took the trouble to write to me after hearing broadcast talks. There is Trevor Dannatt, the architect, whose friendship is so valuable to me and his opinion so important. He introduced me to Douglas Merritt, who designed this book, and has shown an extraordinary insight and sympathy with the work reported upon. There is George Kitson Clark, of the Great Court, himself the history of England, as much as one man can be. Michael Young has taught me many, many things, and Garry Runciman has been a source of help and inspiration ever since 1958 : it would be difficult to convey my sense of indebtedness to them and to Tony Wrigley. Paul Mellon's interest and encouragement have been more important than perhaps he can have realized ; I only hope that he may recognize here something of the England which he can see for himself in his pictures.

I should like to mention the stimulation I have received from research associates at Cambridge, Quentin Skinner and John Dunn especially, and Gordon Schochet too. Mrs Gabrielle Marchbanks has done a great deal for the tables, and John Harrison has helped in innumerable ways. My long-suffering wife, after all those rejected drafts, set to and made out the index in two weeks, amidst everything else.

Trinity College, Cambridge – *August 1965*

The World we have lost

English Society Before and After the Coming of Industry
Chapter 1

In the year 1619 the bakers of London applied to the authorities for an increase in the price of bread. They sent in support of their claim a complete description of a bakery and an account of its weekly costs.[1] There were thirteen or fourteen people in such an establishment: the baker and his wife, four paid employees who were called journeymen, two apprentices, two maidservants and the three or four children of the master baker himself. Six pounds ten shillings a week was reckoned to be the outgoings of this establishment of which only eleven shillings and eightpence went for wages: half a crown a week for each of the journeymen and tenpence for each of the maids. Far and away the greatest cost was for food: two pounds nine shillings out of the six pounds ten shillings, at five shillings a head for the baker and his wife, four shillings a head for their helpers and two shillings for their children. It cost much more in food to keep a journeyman than it cost in money; four times as much to keep a maid. Clothing was charged up too, not only for the man, wife and children, but for the apprentices as well. Even school fees were claimed as a justifiable charge on the price of bread for sale, and it cost sixpence a week for the teaching and clothing of a baker's child.

A London bakery was undoubtedly what we should call a commercial or even an industrial undertaking, turning out loaves by the thousand. Yet the business was carried on in the house of the baker himself. There was probably a *shop* as part of the house, *shop* as in *workshop* and not as meaning a retail establishment. Loaves were not ordinarily sold over the counter: they had to be carried to the open-air market and displayed on stalls.[2] There was a garner behind the house, for which the baker paid two shillings a week in rent, and where he kept his wheat, his *sea-coal* for the fire and his store of salt. The house itself was one of those high, half-timbered over-hanging structures on the narrow London street which we

[1] *See page 241.* [2] *See page 241.*

always think of when we remember the scene in which Shakespeare, Pepys or even Christopher Wren lived. Most of it was taken up with the living-quarters of the dozen people who worked there.

It is obvious that all these people ate in the house since the cost of their food helped to determine the production cost of the bread. Except for the journeymen they were all obliged to sleep in the house at night and live together as a family.

The only word used at that time to describe such a group of people was 'family'. The man at the head of the group, the entrepreneur, the employer, or the manager, was then known as the master or head of the family. He was father to some of its members and in place of father to the rest. There was no sharp distinction between his domestic and his economic functions. His wife was both his partner and his subordinate, a partner because she ran the family, took charge of the food and managed the women-servants, a subordinate because she was woman and wife, mother and in place of mother to the rest.[3]

The paid servants of both sexes had their specified and familiar position in the family, as much part of it as the children but not quite in the same position. At that time the family was not one society only but three societies fused together; the society of man and wife, of parents and children and of master and servant. But when they were young, and servants were, for the most part, young, unmarried people, they were very close to children in their status and their function. Here is the agreement made between the parents of a boy about to become an apprentice and his future master. The boy covenants to dwell as an apprentice with his master for seven years, to keep his secrets and to obey his commandments.[4]

Taverns and alehouses he shall not haunt, dice, cards or any other unlawful games he shall not use, fornication with any woman he shall not commit, matrimony with any woman he shall not contract. He shall not absent himself by night or by day without his master's leave but be a true and faithful servant.

On his side, the master undertakes to teach his apprentice his 'art, science or occupation with moderate correction'.

[3] *See page 241.*　　　　　　　　[4] *See page 241.*

Finding and allowing unto his said servant meat, drink, apparel, washing, lodging and all other things during the said term of seven years, and to give unto his said apprentice at the end of the said term double apparel, to wit, one suit for holydays and one suit for worken days.

Apprentices, therefore, were workers who were also children, extra sons or extra daughters (for girls could be apprenticed too), clothed and educated as well as fed, obliged to obedience and forbidden to marry, unpaid and absolutely dependent until the age of twenty-one. If apprentices were workers in the position of sons and daughters, the sons and daughters of the house were workers too. John Locke laid it down in 1697 that the children of the poor must work for some part of the day when they reached the age of three.[5] The sons and daughters of a London baker were not free to go to school for many years of their young lives, or even to play as they wished when they came back home. Soon they would find themselves doing what they could in *bolting*, that is sieving flour, or in helping the maidservant with her panniers of loaves on the way to the market stall, or in playing their small parts in preparing the never-ending succession of meals for the whole household.

We may see at once, therefore, that the world we have lost, as I have chosen to call it, was no paradise or golden age of equality, tolerance or loving kindness. It is so important that I should not be misunderstood on this point that I will say at once that the coming of industry cannot be shown to have brought economic oppression and exploitation along with it. It was there already. The patriarchal arrangements which we have begun to explore were not new in the England of Shakespeare and Elizabeth. They were as old as the Greeks, as old as European history, and not confined to Europe. And it may well be that they abused and enslaved people quite as remorselessly as the economic arrangements which had replaced them in the England of Blake and Victoria. When people could expect to live for only thirty years in all,[6] how must a man have felt when he realized that so much of his adult life, perhaps all, must go in working for his keep and very little more in someone else's family?

But people do not recognize facts of this sort, and no one is content to expect to live as long as the majority in fact will

[5] *See page 242.*   [6] *See page 242.*

live. Every servant in the old social world was probably quite confident that he or she would some day get married and be at the head of a new family, keeping others in subordination. If it is legitimate to use the words exploitation and oppression in thinking of the economic arrangements of the pre-industrial world, there were nevertheless differences in the manner of oppressing and exploiting. The ancient order of society was felt to be eternal and unchangeable by those who supported, enjoyed and endured it. There was no expectation of reform. How could there be when economic organization was domestic organization, and relationships were rigidly regulated by the social system, by the content of Christianity itself?

Here is a vivid contrast with social expectation in Victorian England, or in industrial countries everywhere today. Every relationship in our world which can be seen to affect our economic life is open to change, is expected indeed to change of itself, or if it does not, to *be* changed, made better, by an omnicompetent authority. This makes for a less stable social world, though it is only one of the features of our society which impels us all in that direction. All industrial societies, we may suppose, are far less stable than their predecessors. They lack the extraordinarily cohesive influence which familial relationships carry with them, that power of reconciling the frustrated and the discontented by emotional means. Social revolution, meaning an irreversible changing of the pattern of social relationships, never happened in traditional, patriarchal, pre-industrial human society. It was almost impossible to contemplate.

Almost, but not quite. Sir Thomas More, in the reign of Henry VIII, could follow Plato in imagining a life without privacy and money, even if he stopped short of imagining a life where children would not know their parents and where promiscuity could be a political institution. Sir William Petty, 150 years later, one of the very first of the political sociologists, could speculate about polygamy; and the England of the Tudors and the Stuarts already knew of social structures and sexual arrangements, existing in the newly discovered world, which were alarmingly different from their own. But it must have been an impossible effort of the imagination to suppose that they were anything like as satisfactory.[7]

It will be noticed that the roles we have allotted to all the

[7] *See page 242.*

members of the capacious family of the master-baker of
London in the year 1619 are, emotionally, all highly symbolic
and highly satisfactory. We may feel that in a whole society
organized like this, in spite of all the subordination, the
exploitation and the obliteration of those who were young, or
feminine, or in service, everyone belonged in a group, a family
group. Everyone had his circle of affection: every relationship
could be seen as a love-relationship.

Not so with us. Who could love the name of a limited company or of a government department as an apprentice could
love his superbly satisfactory father-figure master, even if he
were a bully and a beater, a usurer and a hypocrite? But if a
family is a circle of affection, it can also be the scene of hatred.
The worst tyrants among human beings, the murderers and
the villains, are jealous husbands and resentful wives, possessive parents and deprived children. In the traditional, patriarchal society of Europe, where practically everyone lived out
his whole life within the family, often within one family only,
tension like this must have been incessant and unrelieved,
incapable of release except in crisis. Men, women and children
have to be very close together for a very long time to generate
the emotional power which can give rise to a tragedy of
Sophocles, or Shakespeare, or Racine. Conflict in such a society
was between individual people, on the personal scale. Except
when the Christians fought with the infidels, or Protestants
fought with Catholics, clashes between masses of persons did
not often arise. There could never be a situation such as that
which makes our own time, as some men say, the scene of
perpetual revolution.

All this is true to history only if the little knot of people
making bread in Stuart London was indeed the typical social
unit of the old world in its size, composition and scale. There
are reasons why a baker's household might have been a little
out of the ordinary, for baking was a highly traditional occupation in a society increasingly subject to economic change.
We shall see, in due course, that a family of thirteen people,
which was also a unit of production of thirteen, less the children quite incapable of work, was quite large for English
society at that time. Only the families of the really important,
the nobility and the gentry, the aldermen and the successful
merchants, were ordinarily as large as this. In fact, we can
take the bakery to represent the upper limit in size and scale

of the group in which ordinary people lived and worked. Among the great mass of society which cultivated the land, and which will be the major preoccupation of this essay, the family group was smaller than a London craftsman's entourage. There are other things we should notice about the industrial and commercial scene.

It is worth noticing to begin with, how prominently the town and the craft appear in the folk-memory we still retain from the world we have lost. Agriculture and the countryside do not dominate our recollections to anything like the extent that they dominated that vanished world. We still talk to our children about the apprentice who married his master's daughter: these are the heroes. Or about the outsider who marries the widow left behind by the father/master when he comes to die: these unwelcome strangers to the family are the villains. We refer to bakers as if they really baked in their homes; of spinsters who really sit by the fire and spin. A useful, if a rather arbitrary and romantic guide to the subject in hand, is the famous collection of Fairy Tales compiled by the brothers Grimm in Germany nearly 150 years ago, where the tales we tell to our children mostly have their source.[8] Even in the form given to them by Mr Walt Disney and the other makers of films and picture-books for the youngest members of our rich, leisurely, powerful, puzzled world of successful industrialization, stories like Cinderella are a sharp reminder of what life was once like for the apprentice, the journeyman, the master and all his family in the craftsman's household. Which means, in a sense, that we all know it all already.

We know, or half-remember, that a journeyman really did sometimes spend a year or two on his journeys, serving out that difficult period after he was trained and capable of his craft, but before he had made, or inherited, or had the prospect of marrying, enough money to set up as master by himself. It takes a little reflection to recognize in this practice the reason why so many heroes of the nursery rhymes and stories are on the road, literally seeking their fortunes. We have to go even further to search here for the origin of the picaresque in literature, perhaps for the very germ of the novel. And conscious analysis, directed historical research of a kind only recently supposed to be possible and necessary, has had to be

[8] *See page 242.*

done before even a few fragmentary facts about the tendency of young people to move about could be recovered. It has been found that most young people in service, except, of course, the apprentices, seem to have looked upon a change of job bringing them into a new family as the normal thing every few years.[9]

This feeling that it is all obvious is a curious and exasperating feature of the whole issue, for it means that the historian has not hitherto felt a clear call to examine it as a subject. He has supposed that he knows it already by rote if not by understanding. This means that the force of the contrast between our world and the world which the historian undertakes to describe has hitherto been very indistinct. Without contrast there cannot be full understanding. One reason for feeling puzzled by our own industrial society is that the historian has never set out to tell us what society was like before industry came and seems to assume that everyone knows.

We shall have much more to say about the movement of servants from farmhouse to farmhouse in the old world, and shall return to the problem of understanding ourselves in time, in contrast with our ancestors. Let us emphasize again the scale of life in the working family of the London baker. Few persons in the old world ever found themselves in groups larger than family groups, and there were few families of more than a dozen members. The largest household so far known to us, apart from the royal court and the establishments of the nobility, lay and spiritual, is that of Sir Richard Newdigate, Baronet, in his house of Arbury within his parish of Chilvers Coton in Warwickshire, in the year 1684. There were thirty-seven people in Sir Richard's family: himself; Lady Mary Newdigate his wife; seven daughters, all under the age of sixteen; and twenty-eight servants, seventeen men and boys and eleven women and girls.[10] This was still a family, not an institution, a staff, an office or a firm.

Everything physical was on the human scale, for the commercial worker in London, and the miner who lived and toiled in Newdigate's village of Chilvers Coton. No object in England was larger than London Bridge or St Paul's Cathedral, no structure in the Western World to stand comparison with the Colosseum in Rome. Everything temporal was tied to the human life-span too. The death of the master baker, head of

[9] *See page 242.*   [10] *See page 242.*

the family, ordinarily meant the end of the bakery. Of course there might be a son to succeed, but the master's surviving children would be young if he himself had lived only as long as most men. Or an apprentice might fulfil the final function of apprenticehood, substitute sonship, that is to say, and marry his master's daughter, or even his widow. Surprisingly often, the widow, if she could, would herself carry on the trade.

This, therefore, was not simply a world without factories, without firms, and for the most part without economic continuity. Some partnerships between rich masters existed, especially in London, but since nearly every activity was limited to what could be organized within a family, and the lifetime of its head, there was an unending struggle to manufacture continuity and to provide an expectation of the future. 'One hundred and twenty family uprising and downlying, whereof you may take out six or seven and all the rest were servants and retainers': this was the household of the Herberts, Earls of Pembroke in the years before the Civil War, as it was remembered a generation later by the sentimental antiquarian of the West Country where the Herberts were seated, John Aubrey of the *Lives*.[11] It is wise to be careful of what men liked to report about the size and splendour of the great families in days gone by: £16,000 a year was the Herbert revenue, so John Aubrey claimed, though 'with his offices, and all' the Earl 'had £30,000 per annum. And, as the revenue was great, so the greatness of his retinue and hospitality were answerable'. These are impossible figures, but we know that Lord William Howard kept between forty and fifty servants at Naworth Castle in Cumberland in the 1620's on a much smaller revenue.[12] All this illustrates the symbolic function of the aristocratic family in a society of families, which were generally surprisingly small as we shall see. They were there to defy the limitation on size, and to raise up a line which should remain for ever.

We may pause here to point out that our argument is not complete. There was an organization in the social structure of Europe before the coming of industry which enormously exceeded the family in size and endurance. This was the Christian Church. It is true to say that the ordinary person, especially the female, never went to a gathering larger than could assemble in an ordinary house except when going to

[11] *See page 243.* [12] *See page 243.*

church. When we look at the aristocracy and the church from the point of view of the scale of life and the impermanence of all man-made institutions, we can see that their functions were such as make very little sense in an industrial society like our own. Complicated arrangements then existed, and still exist in England now, which were intended to make it easier for the noble family to give the impression that it had indeed always persisted. Such, for example, were those intricate rules of succession which permitted a cousin, however distant, to succeed to the title and to the headship, provided only he was in the male line. Such was the final remedy in the power of the Crown, the fountain of honour, to declare that an anomalous succession should take place. Nobility was for ever.

But the symbolic provision of permanence is only the beginning of the social functions of the church. At a time when the ability to read with understanding and to write much more than a personal letter was confined for the most part to the ruling minority, in a society which was otherwise oral in its communications, the preaching parson was the great link between the illiterate mass and the political, technical and educated world. Sitting in the 10,000 parish churches of England every Sunday morning, in groups of 20, 50, 100 or 200, the illiterate mass of the people were not only taking part in the single group activity which they ordinarily shared with others outside their own families. They were informing themselves in the only way open to them of what went on in England, Europe, and the world as a whole. The priesthood was indispensable to the religious activity of the old world, at a time when religion was still of primary interest and importance. But the priesthood was also indispensable because of its functions in social communication. This, perhaps, was one reason why the Puritan layman insisted so strongly upon a preaching clergy.

When we insist on the tiny scale of life in the pre-industrial world, especially on the small size of the group in which nearly everybody spent all their lives, there are, of course, certain occasions and institutions which we must not overlook. There were the military practices, the annual muster of the able-bodied men from every county, which took place after harvest in Tudor times.[13] There were regular soldiers too, though not very many of them; variegated bands of the least promising

[13] *See page 243.*

of men straggling behind the banner of some noble adventurer. Much more familiar to Englishmen, at least in the maritime areas, must have been the sailors; twenty, thirty, even fifty men at sea, sometimes for days, or even weeks on end.

Lilliputian, we must feel, when we compare such details with the military and naval organizations of our own day; the whole of the Parliamentary Army which fought at Marston Moor could be accommodated on the *Queen Elizabeth* and the *Queen Mary*.[14] Other organizations and purposes which brought groups of people together were the Assizes in the County Towns; the Quarter Sessions of the County Justices; the meetings of the manorial courts in the villages, of the town councils in the towns, of the companies or craftsmen there, each one to a trade or occupation; the assemblies which sometimes took place of clergy or of nonconformist ministers. Most regular of all, and probably largest in scale and most familiar to ordinary men and women were the weekly market days and the annual fairs in each locality. Then there were the 2,000 schools in England, one for every fifth parish but very few large enough to have more than a single teacher, and the two universities, with less than 10,000 men between them.[15] Then there was Parliament itself. All these occasions and institutions assembled men in some numbers for purposes which could not be called familial. Women too assembled though, save to the markets, they came as spectators rather than as participants.

The fact that it is possible to name most of the large-scale institutions and occasions in a sentence or two makes the contrast with our own world more telling than ever. We have only to think of the hundreds of children sitting every day, all over the country, in their classrooms, the hundreds and thousands together in the factories, the offices, the shops, to recognize the difference. The detailed study of the pre-industrial social world makes this question of scale more critical still. Wherever the facts of economic life and technology required a working group different in size and constitution from the working family, there was discontinuity. Hence the crew of a ship, the team of workers on a building, the fifty or sixty grown men who might be required to work a mine or an armaments manufactory, were all looked upon as exceptional. As indeed they were, so much so that the building trade had had

[14] *See page 243.*   [15] *See page 243.*

its own society from medieval times, and the miners were a community apart wherever they were found.[16]

Not only did the scale of their work and the size of the group which was engaged make them exceptional, the constitution of the group did too. In the baking household we have chosen as our standard, sex and age were mingled together. Fortunate children might go out to school, but adults did not usually go out to work. There was nothing to correspond to the thousands of young men on the assembly line, the hundreds of young women in the offices, the lonely lives of housekeeping wives which we now know only too well. We shall see that those who survived to old age in the much less favourable conditions for survival which then were prevalent, were surprisingly often left to live and die alone, in their tiny cottages or sometimes in the almshouses which were being built so widely in the England of the Tudors and the Stuarts.[17] Poor-law establishments, parochial in purpose and in size, had begun their melancholy chapter in the history of the English people. But institutional life was otherwise almost unknown. There were no hotels, hostels, or blocks of flats for single persons, very few hospitals and none of the kind we are familiar with, almost no young men and women living on their own. The family group where so great a majority lived was what we should undoubtedly call a 'balanced' and 'healthy' group.

When we turn from the hand-made city of London to the hand-moulded immensity of rural England, we may carry the same sentimental prejudice along with us. To every farm there was a family, which spread itself over its portion of the village lands as the family of the master-craftsman filled out his manufactory. When a holding was small, and most were small as are the tiny holdings of European peasants today, a man tilled it with the help of his wife and his children. No single man, we must remember, would usually take charge of the land, any more than a single man would often be found at the head of a workshop in the city. The master of a family was expected to be a householder, whether he was a butcher, a baker, a candlestick maker or simply a husbandman, which was the universal name for one whose skill was in working the land. Marriage we must insist, and it is one of the rules which gave its character to the society of our ancestors, was the entry

[16] *See page 243.*   [17] *See page 243.*

to full membership, in the enfolding countryside, as well as in the scattered urban centres.

But there was a difference in scale and organization of work on the land and in the town. The necessities of rural life did require recurrent groupings of households for common economic purposes, occasionally something like a crowd of men, women and children working together for days on end. Where the ground was still being tilled as open fields, and each household had a number of strips scattered all over the whole open area and not a compact collection of enclosures, ploughing was co-operative, as were many other operations, above all harvesting, and this continued even after enclosure. We do not yet know how important this element of enforced common activity was in the life of the English rural community on the eve of industrialization, or how much difference enclosure made in this respect. But whatever the situation was, the economic transformation of the eighteenth and nineteenth centuries destroyed communality altogether in English rural life. The group of men from several farmsteads working the heavy plough in springtime, the bevy of harvesters from every house in the village wading into the high standing grass to begin the cutting of the hay, had no successors in large-scale economic activity. For the arrangement of these groups was entirely different in principle from the arrangement of a factory, or a firm, or even of a collective farm.

Both before and after enclosure, some peasants did well: their crops were heavier and they had more land to till. To provide the extra labour needed then, the farming householder, like the successful craftsman, would extend his working family by taking on young men and women as servants to live with him and work the fields. This he would have to do, even if the land which he was farming was not his own but rented from the great family in the manor house. Sometimes, we have found, he would prefer to send out his own children as servants and bring in other children and young men to do the work. This is one of the few glimpses we can get into the quality of the emotional life of the family at this time, for it shows that parents may have been unwilling to submit children of their own to the discipline of work at home. It meant, too, that servants were not simply the perquisites of wealth and position. A quarter, or a third, of all the families in the country contained servants in Stuart times, and this meant that very humble people had them as well as the titled and the wealthy. Most of the servants, moreover, male or female, in the great house and in the small, were engaged in working the land.[18]

The boys and the men would do the ploughing, hedging, carting and the heavy, skilled work of the harvest. The women and the girls would keep the house, prepare the meals, make the butter and the cheese, the bread and the beer, and would also look after the cattle and take the fruit to market. At harvest-time, from June to October, every hand was occupied and every back was bent. These were the decisive months for the whole population in our damp northern climate, with its one harvest in a season and reliance on one or two standard crops. So critical was the winning of the grain for bread that the first rule of gentility (a gentleman never worked with his hands for his living) might be abrogated.

We have hinted that a fundamental characteristic of the world we have lost was the scene of labour, which was universally supposed to be the home. It has been implied in the case of industry and in towns, that the hired man who came in to work during the day and went home to his meals and at night was looked on as exceptional. Apart from the provisions about journeymen, who were, in fact, the focus of whatever difficulty in 'labour relations' was experienced at this time in the towns, no standard arrangement has been found which contemplated any permanent division of place of living and place of employment. That such divisions existed, and may even have been commonplace in town and in country, cannot be in doubt. There is evidence that a clothmaker in a big way, in the city of Beauvais in France at any rate, would have machinery in his house for more men than could possibly have lived there. It is thought that men walked in from the villages to Beauvais to do their day's work, just as men used to walk from the villages to the towns to work on the building sites in Victorian England. In those areas of England which first became industrial, there are signs that, like those in Beauvais, they too must have contained economic units which had to be supplied by daily wage labour. It came also, maybe, from the surrounding country, but certainly from the grown sons of families living in the town as well, young men, perhaps, even older men and married men, who cannot have been working where they lived.[19] But when all this is said, the

[18] *See page 244.*   [19] *See page 244.*

division of dwelling place and working place was no recognized feature of the social structure of the towns which our ancestors inhabited. The journey to work, the lonely lodger paying his rent out of a factory wage, are the distinguishing marks of our society, not of theirs. We are forced to suppose that in industrial and commercial matters the working family was assumed to be self-sufficient in its labour, in spite of the vicissitudes of the market.

But the level of activity in agriculture is fundamentally rhythmic, and its labour demands inevitably vary with the time of the year, the weather in the week, as well as with the prices of its products on the market. To work the land at all, especially as we have already hinted with the climate and geology of England, provision had to be made for a pool of labour, which the farming family could use or not as the farmer himself should decide. The manner in which this economic necessity was provided for shows how well the traditional, patriarchal structure of society could be adapted to meet the needs of a particular economy. It has to be traced in the life stories of the men and the women who lived in the villages and in the lists of occupations which were settled in the countryside, as much a part of its life as what went on in the stables and the barns. Let us begin with the life cycle of a poor inhabitant of an English village.

A boy, or a girl, born in a cottage, often, even usually, left home for service at the age of ten, eleven or twelve, though we have found 'servants' only eight or nine years old. He, or she, would then join another family. A servant-in-husbandry, as he would be called, if he were a boy, would stay in the position of servant, though by no means necessarily in the same household, until he got married. So would the girls and the women: marriage when and if it came, would quite often take place with another servant. All this while, and it might be twelve, fifteen or even twenty years, the servant would be kept by the employer, and in no danger of poverty or hunger, even if the modest husbandman with whom he lived was worse housed than his landlord's horses, and worse clothed than his landlord's servants. 'His landlord's horses,' wrote a contemporary of the lowly husbandman, 'lie in finer houses, than he, and his meanest servant wears a cloth beyond him.' But the husbandman had his own servant, nevertheless, for when he said family prayers after a day's exhausting toil 'the wife is sleeping in one corner, the child in another, the servant in a third.'[20]

But poverty awaited the husbandman's servant when he got married, and went himself to live in just such a labourer's cottage as the one in which he had been born. Whoever had been his former master, the labourer, late servant in husbandry, would be liable to fall into want directly his wife began to have children and he lost the earnings of his companion. Once he found himself outside the farming household his living had to come from his wages, and he, with every member of his family, was subject for his labour to the local vagaries in the market. Day-labourer was now his full desscription, for he earned what money came his way by contracting for work a day at a time with the husbandmen of his village. Here was one great source of the extra labour which was needed to keep agriculture going, and the poor cottager could expect only seasonal employment at a wage fixed, as indeed his wage as a servant had been fixed, by the justices of the peace. Two forms of wage were laid out in the published tables, with and without meat and drink. The day-labourer visiting a farm for his work could claim his place at the table along with the servants living-in; it might be said that he was made a member of the working family for that day by breaking bread with the permanent members. It was almost a sacramental matter.

But his own casual earnings were not the only fund on which the labourer had to live. There was the produce of the little plot of land lying round his cottage to begin with. Elizabeth's government had decreed that it should be four acres in size though this cannot have been anything like a general rule. Then there were the pennies thrown to his children for bird scaring, or catching vermin, or minding sheep – the little boy blue who burst into tears in the nursery rhyme might easily have been of nursery age. But above all, there were the earnings of his wife and the whole of his little family at 'industrial' occupations. A little family because every grown child would have to leave, and because death came quickly. It was the cottagers of England who carried on the great woollen industry of England, spinning the yarn which the capitalist clothiers brought to their doors. Industry, in fact, kept the poor alive in the England of our ancestors, and the problem of poverty

[20] *See page 244.*

in their own opinion could only have been solved by the spread
of industrial activity. Though men did not seem to have seen
it in quite this way, the existence of industry also made it
possible for enough people to live on the land to meet the
seasonal demands of agriculture.

Industry at this time was carried on not only by individual
productive units, like the bakery in London, but by the
putting-out system, in which several households were set on
work by one middleman, the clothier-capitalist we have
referred to. Much of it was done in the spare time of the farming population, not simply by the labourers, but by the
farmers and their families as well, the simpler operations, that
is to say, the sorting and carding and spinning of the wool.
But the weaving, the dyeing and dressing of the cloth was
usually the work of families of weavers, shearmen or dyers
which did nothing else for nine months of the year. They
worked on the land of the villages where they lived only in
harvest-time, from late June, when the haymaking began, till
late September when the last of the wheat or the barley would
be brought home.

Hence it came about that the English village contained not
simply the husbandmen, the labourers and their families, with
the smith, the ploughwright, the miller and the men who plied
the agricultural trade, but textile workers too. In the Midlands
there were nailers and miners, and everywhere everyone was
also a worker on the land, during the crisis of harvest-time.
Such are the rough outlines of the system whereby the independent household was preserved, yet made to collaborate
with other independent households in the working of the land,
and in the production of cloth. Capitalism, we must notice, was
a feature of the system, that store of wealth and raw materials
in the hands of the clothier which made it possible for him to
give work to the villagers and yet not move them from the
village. In the world we have lost, then, industry and agriculture lived together in some sort of symmetry, and the unity of
the family was in no way in jeopardy.

*The bourgeoisie, wherever it has got the upper hand, has put an
end to all feudal, patriarchal, idyllic relations. It has pitilessly
torn asunder the motley feudal ties that bound man to his* natural
superiors, *and has left remaining no other nexus between man
and man than naked self-interest, than callous* cash-payment. *It*

has drowned the most heavenly ecstasies of religious fervour, of chivalrous enthusiasm, of philistine sentimentalism, in the icy water of egotistical calculation. It has resolved personal worth into exchange value, and in place of the numberless indefeasible chartered freedoms, has set up that single, unconscionable freedom – Free Trade. In one word, for exploitation veiled by religious and political illusions, it has substituted naked, shameless, direct, brutal exploitation.

The bourgeoisie has stripped of its halo every occupation hitherto honoured and looked up to with reverent awe. It has converted the physician, the lawyer, the priest, the poet, the man of science, into its paid wage-labourers.

The bourgeoisie has torn away from the family its sentimental veil, and has reduced the family relation to a mere money-relation.

These were the fervent words used by the most penetrating of all observers of the world we have lost when they came to pronounce on its passing. The idyllic patriarchalism and the exploitation which Marx and Engels had in mind in this passage from the *Communist Manifesto*[21] written in 1848 is recognizable in the arrangements we have been discussing in this introductory chapter. The ending of the system which ensured that however he was paid, however little he owned, or close he was to the point of starvation, a man usually lived and worked within the family, the circle of affection, released enough dissatisfaction to account for all the restlessness which has marked the progress of the industrial world.

The factory won its victory by outproducing the working family, taking away the market for the products of hand-labour and cutting prices to the point where the craftsman had either to starve or take a job under factory discipline himself. It was no sudden, complete and final triumph, for the seamstresses were working in the garrets right up to the twentieth century, and the horrors of sweated labour which so alarmed our grandfathers took place amongst the out-workers, not on the factory floor. It was not a transformation which affected only commerce, industry and the towns, for the hand-work of the cottages disappeared entirely, till, by the year 1920, rural England was an agrarian remnant, an almost life-less shell. The process was not English alone, at any point in its development, and its effects on the Continent of Europe

[21] *See page 244.*

were in some ways more obviously devastating than ever they were amongst our people. But ours was the society which first ventured into the industrial era, and English men and women were the first who had to try to find a home for themselves in a world where family and household seemed to have no place.

But Marx and the historians who have followed him were surely wrong to call this process by the simple name of the triumph of capitalism, the rise and victory of the bourgeoisie. The presence of capital, we have seen, was the very circumstance which made it possible in earlier times for the working family to preserve its independence both on the land and in the cities, linking together the scattered households of the workers in such a way that no one had to make the daily double journey from home to workshop, from suburb to office and factory. Capitalism, however defined, did not begin at the time when the working household was endangered by the beginnings of the factory system, and economic inequality was not the product of the social transformation which so quickly followed after. Though the enormous, insolent wealth of the new commercial and industrial fortunes emphasized the iniquity of the division between rich and poor, it is doubtful whether Victorian England was any worse in this respect than the England of the Tudors and the Stuarts. It was not the fact of capitalism alone, not simply the concentration of the means of production in the hands of the few and the reduction of the rest to a position of dependence, which opened wide the social gulf, though the writers of the eighteenth and nineteenth centuries give us ample evidence that this was observed and was resented – by the dispossessed peasantry in England especially. More important, it is suggested, far more likely a source for the feeling that there is a world which once we all possessed, a world now passed away, is the fact of the transformation of the family life of everyone which industrialism brought with it.[22]

In the vague and difficult verbiage of our own generation, we can say that the removal of the economic functions from the patriarchal family at the point of industrialization created a mass society. It turned the people who worked into a mass of undifferentiated equals, working in a factory or scattered between the factories and mines, bereft for ever of the feeling

[22] *See page 244.*

that work, a family affair, carried with it. The Marxist historical sociology presents this as the growth of class consciousness amongst the proletariat, and this is an important historical truth. But because it belongs with the large-scale class model for all social change it can also be misleading, as we shall hope to show. Moreover it has tended to divert attention from the structural function of the family in the pre-industrial world, and made impossible up till now a proper, informed contrast between our world and the lost world we have to analyse.

But this is not the only consequence of the failure to look realistically at the familial texture of society at the time of our ancestors, and Marxist historical convention is not the only source of the distortions. Historians have to talk all the time about nations, countries, the units of historical narrative, the arena of historical change. The logical difficulties of defining change in such a way that nations can change autonomously, like chemical elements or compounds, are formidable by themselves. But the historian does not seem to have got even as far as this before he loses his realism. What does the word *England* mean, for the year 1640, shall we say?

Not every single person alive in the country in that year: no historian, however simple-minded, could possibly suppose such a thing. But only the recognition that people came not as individuals, but as families, makes it possible to begin to come closer to the facts. England was an association between the heads of such families, but an association largely confined to those who were literate, who had wealth and status, those, in fact, who belonged, with their families as part of them, to what we have already called the ruling minority. Almost no woman ever belonged to England as an individual, except it be a queen regnant – scarcely a woman in the ordinary sense – or a noble widow and heiress or two, a scattering of widows of successful merchants and yeomen. No individual under the age of thirty was likely to be a member, except in the very highest reaches of society, and very few men who had never been married.

It is problematical how far the mature male heads of families amongst the mass can be counted as part of England for historical purposes: in so far as they had a role at all, it was a negative rather than a positive one, a limitation on what the ruling minority could do rather than an independent source of action and of attitude. We shall return to the relationship between the gentry and the rest, and attempt to make a rough sketch of what the whole was like, though much will have to be left uncertain. It goes without saying, of course, that no one in a position of 'service' was an independent member of society, national or local, and individuals in this position themselves made up 10 per cent or even 15 per cent of the population. Such men and women, boys and girls, were caught up, so to speak, 'subsumed' is the ugly word we shall use, into the personalities of their fathers and masters. 'Subsumption' of this sort might be extended to cover the relationship between the great household in a village community and the ring of smaller households ranged around it, sited on the landlord's estate, engaged for the most part in working his land. That same contemporary whose words we have quoted on the husbandman and his servants had this to say about the husbandman and his lordly neighbour:

A just fear and respect he must have for his landlord, or the gentleman his neighbour, because God hath placed them above him and he hath learnt that by the father he ought to honour [the reference here is to the Fifth Commandment, Honour thy Father . . .] is meant all his superiors.[23]

Anyone who uses the word *England*, therefore, without recognizing these facts about subsumption, is scarcely using it with understanding. A very considerable number of existent individuals must moreover be looked upon as null, as having no function, not even as subsumed into units which did have a function. These were the paupers, anyone who was in receipt of charity for his upkeep, or who had ever been in such a position. This body was surely as much a proletariat as ever there has been in the age of industrialism.

Capitalism, then, is an incomplete description and historians' language is marked by many other incomplete descriptions too, of which their use of the names of countries is but one example. The historical distortions which come about from the use of *capitalism, the rise of the bourgeoisie,* and so on, have arisen from a faulty sense of proportion which we can only now begin to correct. With the 'capitalism changed the world' way of thinking goes a division of history into the ancient, feudal and bourgeois eras or stages. But the facts of

[23] *See page 244.*

the contrast which has to be drawn between the world we have lost and the world we now inhabit tends to make all such divisions as these into subdivisions.

European society is of the patriarchal type, and with some variations, of which the feudal went the furthest, it remained patriarchal in its institutions right up to the coming of the factories, the offices and the rest. European patriarchalism, we may notice, was of a rather surprising kind, for it was marked by the independence of the nuclear family, man, wife and children, not by the extended family of relatives living together in a group of several generations under the same patriarchal head. Yet society was patriarchal, nevertheless, right up to the time of industrial transformation: it can now no longer be said to be patriarchal at all, except vestigially and in its emotional predisposition. The time has now come to divide our European past in a simpler way with industrialization as the point of critical change.

The word alienation is part of the cant of the mid-twentieth century and it began as an attempt to describe the separation of the worker from his world of work. We need not accept all that this expression has come to convey in order to recognize that it does point to something vital to us all in relation to our past. Time was when the whole of life went forward in the family, in a circle of loved, familiar faces, known and fondled objects, all to human size. That time has gone for ever. It makes us very different from our ancestors.

A One-Class Society
Chapter 2

A one-class society may appear at first sight to mean one where there is no inequality, because everyone belonged to the same class. But it has already been laid down that this cannot have been so in the pre-industrial world, at least in Europe. The *ancien régime*, as the historians call it, was marked by a very sharply delineated system of status, which drew firm distinctions between persons and made some superior, most inferior. There were various gradations, all authoritatively established and generally recognized. If class were simply a matter of social status, of the various degrees of respect in which men are held by their fellows, then it could not be said that the world we have lost was a one-class society. On the contrary, it would have to be described as a society with a considerable number of classes, as many as there were distinct steps in the graduated system of status.

But when the word class is used, in conversation and by historians, it does not merely refer to status or to respect. The distribution of wealth and power is also at issue. This is obvious when the phrase class-conflict appears. For it nearly always seems to imply the clash of groups of persons defending and enhancing not simply a common status but also interest and power. The emphasis is on the solidarity of classes as groups of persons which act in championship of their conflicting aims. Such classes have a further characteristic in ordinary usage: they are nation-wide.

It is in this sense that we shall claim that there was, in England at least, only one class in pre-industrial society. A distinction will be drawn between a status group, which is the number of people enjoying or enduring the same social status, and a class, which is a number of people banded together in the exercise of collective power, political and economic. The argument will be that there were a large number of status groups but only one body of persons capable of concerted action over the whole area of society, only one class in fact.

It is unfortunate that an introductory study of this character should have to be concerned with anything as difficult, contentious and technical as the question of class. It is unfortunate also that the only vocabulary which is open to us to discuss it should be that designed for nineteenth- and twentieth-century society. 'Status groups' and 'class' do not fit at all well as descriptions of sets of people belonging to Stuart England, and most of the rest of the terminology used by sociologists is inappropriate too. These expressions have implications belonging to rather different social structures. But literary critics, even novelists have talked about traditional England in these terms, as well as historians and sociologists. We cannot direct our attention to the everyday life of our ancestors and the scale on which they lived it out without any notion of the overall shape of their society, its macro-structure as it might be called, in contrast to its micro-structure where, as we have seen, the family was the key. The macro-structure of Stuart society moreover has become a subject of world-wide discussion because a good part of the contemporary world has to believe in a particular version of what is called The English Revolution for political reasons. Class conflict in the age of Charles I and Cromwell is not simply a matter of social antiquarianism.

There is a sense, of course, in which the phrase 'class-conflict' might be appropriate to pre-industrial society, even if it did contain only one class. For the conflict could be between those who were included within it and everyone else. Perhaps if the expression were always used in this very restricted sense, it would be acceptable as a rough description of what went on. It is certainly no part of our purpose to deny that conflict existed at this time. But historians have not in fact used the phrase in such a restricted way, or in any very closely defined fashion at all. When they have discussed rising and falling classes they have obviously had in mind interaction of a very different kind. Sometimes, perhaps not very often because their language has been so vague, they have made the precise error of confusing a status group with a class and have proceeded as if status groups could rise, fall, conflict, be self-conscious, have a policy. Let us leave these generalities for a moment and look more closely at status symbols and systems in our industrial society as well as in that of our ancestors.

We now inhabit a world of immeasurable wealth and many of us are possessed of a power and a consequence never before known on such a scale. Our society is therefore marked by an intense search after status and after symbols to express it. The most important of those symbols is a personal title, an addition to a man's name, proclaiming who he is, how much success he has had and how much he ought to be respected. There is a whole study of the part which titles and other less satisfactory and specific symbols of status have to play in our contemporary world and on its social, economic, even its political stage. The difficult problem for us in our day is to find out how status and its symbols are to do their necessary psychological work unless they belong to a recognizably coherent system. This used to exist in pre-industrial times but change since then has been so rapid and profound that it survives today only in a form so attenuated that it can hardly fulfil its functions any longer.

The reasons for this are complex, but the most obvious is that we want contradictory things – a system of status and universal social equality. It is easy to illustrate the difficulties. Some issues of relative social importance can still be settled fairly simply; we can put a managing director, for example, on a level with a lieutenant-colonel, though it begins to be a little puzzling when we consider whether the executive secretary of a professional society, say of electrical engineers, is in the same category of status. When it comes to extremes, our status system breaks down altogether. We have no intelligible method for relating a Hollywood *prima donna* and a cardinal-archbishop. We know that they are both influential people, and must be treated with due deference, but we cannot relate them satisfactorily one to another.

We cannot weigh them up against each other, but even if we could we have no set of symbols universally recognized which could give even a rough expression of their relative importance. The film-star can, and will, collect as many signs of superiority as possible, of an enormously variegated sort, but none of them help very much when we compare them to the traditional titles of the senior and successful cleric. For the symbolic superiority of a cardinal-archbishop belongs to a world which the film and television actress cannot share. It is an inheritance from the world we have lost.

'Lost' may not be quite the proper word here, and for two reasons. One is that in some contemporary societies and for certain purposes, the status system of the traditional, pre-industrial work is still in use with all its necessary symbols:

near imaginary use perhaps we ought to say, since the effectiveness both of the traditional status and its trappings are so much reduced. Just as the English still seem to want to live in the structures of the pre-industrial world, prizing the thatched cottage and the half-timbered house as the proper place for the proper Englishman to dwell in, so also do the English go on awarding the symbolic titles which belong to the status system of the world we have lost. We go on creating knights and barons, setting up industrial peerages, and calling cricketers and jockeys 'Sir', though we no longer understand the system which informed these honorifics and are uneasily aware that their distribution may not correspond to the true distribution of consequence in our society. This is typical of the way in which the world we have lost is in some sense still present with us, or at least of the difficulty we have in becoming conscious of its ghostly persistence, and so addressing ourselves to the problem of putting something else in its place.

But the second reason why the word 'lost' is somewhat paradoxical when we talk of the system of status and its symbols in the pre-industrial world is that elsewhere it was not a case of losing but of rejecting. Titles of honour were deliberately obliterated, first in the United States, then in France and so successively in other European countries, at their 'revolutions'. Great Britain is one of a handful of countries which has not yet found it proper to abolish them by law. The subject of status and its symbols is, therefore, of particular interest to English historians. Here is something in our present which we know to affect the lives of everybody, since the hierarchy of status we preserve so meticulously is by no means confined to titles of nobility and marks of gentility, yet which can only be explained by reference to a past we have nearly forgotten. This is one of the ways in which our country, which was the first to be industrialized and to lose most of the economic institutions of the traditional Europe, has nevertheless clung for longest and with most affection to little, unrelated fragments of the world we have lost.

We live, in England, among the material remains of a patriarchal society of peasants and craftsmen: those stately churches, spacious manor houses, farmsteads, cottages, millhouses, bridges, all built for itself by the familial social order which is the subject of this essay. We find them interesting, often quaint and picturesque, and always, if we are honest, a little puzzling too. We are puzzled in exactly the same way when we try to decide whether to put 'Esq.' or 'Mr' on a letter. If we ask ourselves why we use these abbreviations at all, we find that we do not quite know. Yet these are the most common of all status symbols and we use them every day.

We call each other *gentlemen* as well, although we have some difficulty in deciding what the word means. Defining *gentleman* indeed, and disputing about the qualities which go to make one, is a favourite pastime of those who write impressionists' accounts of social history. The rest of us, if ever it occurs to us to decide, dismiss the expression as having by now no meaning at all. It can no longer be defined by contrast since everybody expects to be called a gentleman, and to be addressed in writing as *esquire*. So it is not difficult to guess that the descriptions 'Mister' and 'Esquire' must once have implied that the person addressed was in fact a gentleman. But further than that we usually cannot go.

There could be no more vivid illustration of our dim and partial understanding of the pre-industrial world. In that society of peasants, craftsmen, labourers, husbandmen, and a very few gentry and nobility, the word *gentleman* meant something tangible, substantial enough, if uncertain in precise definition. It was a grade amongst other grades in a carefully graduated system of social status and had a critically important use.

The term gentleman marked the exact point at which the traditional social system divided up the population into two extremely unequal sections. About a twenty-fifth, at most a twentieth, of all the people alive in the England of the Tudors and the Stuarts, the last generations before the coming of industry, belonged to the gentry and to those above them in the social hierarchy. This tiny minority owned most of the wealth, wielded the power and made all the decisions, political, economic and social for the national whole. If you were not a gentleman, if you were not ordinarily called '*Master*' by the commoner folk, or '*Your Worship*'; if you, like nearly all the rest, had a Christian and a surname and nothing more; then you counted for little in the world outside your own household, and for almost nothing outside your small village community and its neighbourhood.

'Nothing' is too strong a word perhaps, and in every society, however constituted, even the smallest unit, the weakest influence, is of some account, has to be allowed for in the general social process. The plain Richard Hodgsons, Robert Boswells, Humphrey Eltons and John Burtons of the English villages, the labourers and husbandmen, the tailors, millers, drovers, watermen, masons, could become constables, parish clerks, churchwardens, ale-conners, even overseers of the poor. They had something of a public life, within the tiny boundaries of the village, and this might give them a minor consequence in the surrounding villages. If they happened to be technically qualified, they might even cast a vote at an election. But in none of these capacities did their opinion matter very much, even in the last. They brought no personal weight to the modest offices which they could hold. As individuals they had no instituted, recognized power over other individuals, always excepting once again those subsumed within their families. Directly they acquired such power, whether by the making or the inheriting of wealth, or by the painful acquisition of a little learning, then they became *worshipful* by that very fact. Then and then only could they know anything substantial of the world, which meant everything which went on outside their own localities, everything rather which was inter-local, affecting more communities and localities than one.

To exercise power, then, to be free of the society of England, to count at all as an active agent in the record we call historical, you had to be a gentleman. When you came to die you had to hold one of those exceptional names in a parish register which bore a prefix or a suffix, about one name in fifteen or twenty seems to have been the average. The commonest addition to a name to be read in a register is *Mr*, for the word 'Master', and *Mrs*, for the word 'Mistress', applied to the maidens as well as the wives and widows. *Gent.* and *Esq.* are rare amongst the additions, as is the word *Dame*, the designation of their wives, and *Knight* and *Baronet* are, of course, much rarer still. The reader with the whole population in his mind, as distinct from the reader with an eye only for the interesting and attractive, will, of course, occasionally come across the titles *Lord* or *Lady*, and the ceremonious phrase 'The right Honourable the . . .' which was often used to introduce them. But the higher titles of nobility are absent for all practical purposes when the whole population is under review. They are rather

like the four-leaved clover to the collector of flowers, or perhaps the winning ticket numbers in a national lottery; one
knows they must exist because the system demands it, but one
never sees them. Nevertheless, page after page, year after
year, decade after decade in the books recording, conscien-
tiously, the burials in an ordinary English parish church will
show some title or other for 3 per cent, 5 per cent or at most
10 per cent of the names, never very much more unless the
parish had extraordinarily aristocratic or even Royal connections. All the rest of the entries are for simple names and
surnames.[24]

Yet the history books we read are studded with much
grander titles, and no one seems to appear in them who was
without any title at all, except perhaps in the cursory chapter
heading 'social'. Which is one way to show again that England
in the pre-industrial era meant a small minority of the English,
small, select and special. Not everyone who belonged to the
majority of those who were nobodies felt this exclusion; contemporaries comment often enough on the rich yeoman, for a
yeoman was the rank or status immediately below the critical
divide, who refused to 'bear the port or mien of a gentleman'.
But if the yeoman himself did not wish it, his son or grandson
would find it difficult to resist the temptation and the pressure
to assume the title and responsibility of gentry. Most of those
on the way up in the world needed little persuasion, for when
a man was successful the reward was tangible and important,
and the higher a family went the more remarkable the difference was from the situation in which its rise began. The great
nobles of the traditional world lived a life of superiority which
we can no longer imagine, because we no longer possess so
clear and overt a system of status.

However lofty the traditional social structure was, the point
of transformation was the change which came with the transition from the commonalty to the gentry. Here was a society
which had no devices for the saving of labour, none that is
when we compare it with our own. The simplest operation in
everyday life needed effort; drawing the water from the well,
striking steel on flint to catch the tinder alight, cutting goose-
feather quills to make a pen, they all took time, trouble and
energy. The working of the land, the labour in the craftsmen's
shop, were infinitely taxing. The surviving peasantry in

[24] *See page 245.*

Western Europe still shock us with their worn hands and faces, their immeasurable fatigue. Yet the primary characteristic of the gentleman was that he never worked with his hands on necessary, as opposed to leisurely, activities.

The simple fact of leisure dividing off this little society of the privileged – it had to be little at a time when the general resources were so small – is the first step in comprehending the attitude of our forefathers to rank and status. The law of the land laid it down how long common men should work and how little they should rest:

And be it further enacted by the authority aforesaid, That all artificers and labourers being hired for wages by the day or week shall, betwixt the midst of the months of March and September, be and continue at their work, at or before five of the clock in the morning, and continue at work, and not depart, until between seven and eight of the clock at night (except it be in the time of breakfast, dinner or drinking, the which times at most shall not exceed two and a half in a day, that is to say, at every drinking one half-hour, for his dinner, one hour, and for his sleep, when he is allowed to sleep, the which is from the midst of May, to the midst of August, half an hour at the most, and at every breakfast one half-hour). And all the said artificers and labourers, between the midst of September, and the midst of March, shall be and continue at their work from the spring of the day in the morning, until the night of the same day, except it be in time afore appointed to breakfast and dinner.

This was laid down in 1563 in the famous Elizabethan Statute of Artificers,[25] as it is usually called, which made compulsory by law the common practice of the time. At the County Assizes, the judges had to inquire whether there were workers who 'do not continue from Five of the Clock in the Morning till Seven at Night in the Summer and from Seven till five in the Winter'.[26] No mention of sleeping-time here, even in the heat of the harvest. Still Breughel's sleeping harvester was an ordinary working man acting on his rights; he was no visionary, no drowsy peasant drunkard.

Although those in work for wages lived a life of rough, incessant toil – no Saturday afternoons, none even of the safeguards of the early Factory Acts – not all the common people were caught up in productive work. This is outstandingly

[25] *See page 245.*   [26] *See page 245.*

evident from Gregory King's famous table of the structure of
English society, reproduced on pages 32–33. It was drawn
up in the 1690's and applied to the year 1688. It divides up
the population of the country in such a way as to show that
more than half the people then alive were dependent – 'Decreasing the Wealth of the Kingdom' is the expression appearing in King's *General Account.*[27]

King's calculation was made on extensive and probably
fairly reliable evidence, and was the only one ever worked out
by a contemporary for a European society in wholly pre-
industrial times. It is now supposed that the reason why so
large a proportion of the population could not wholly support
itself was because there was not enough productive work to
do.[28] The more impressionistic writers in Gregory King's time
and before it did not hesitate to call everyone below a certain
level by insulting names: the *rascals*, or *rascality*, the *proletarii*.
In the 1560's Sir Thomas Smith, a respected lawyer, spoke his
mind in this way, and his is an instructive comment on the
common people of England in their relation with their social
superiors.

For this observer, English society had a fourfold division:

1. '*The first part of the Gentlemen of England called* Nobilitas
   Major.' *This is the nobility, or aristocracy proper.*
2. '*The second sort of Gentlemen called* Nobilitas Minor.' *This is
   the gentry and Smith further divides it into Knights, Esquires
   and gentlemen.*
3. '*Citizens, Burgesses and Yeomen.*'
4. '*The fourth sort of men which do not rule.*'

We shall concern ourselves in due course with the relationship
between these four divisions. Our present interest is in Smith's
detailed description of the lowest of them. These are his words:

*The fourth sort or class amongst us is of those which the old
Romans called* capite sensu proletarii *or* operarii, *day labourers,
poor husbandmen, yea merchants or retailers which have no free
land, copyholders, and all artificers, as tailors, shoemakers, carpenters, brick-makers, brick-layers, etc. These have no voice nor
authority in our commonwealth and no account is made of them,
but only to be ruled and not to rule other, and yet they be not
altogether neglected. For in cities and corporate towns, for default*

[27] *See page 245.*   [28] *See page 246.*

of yeomen, inquests and juries are impanelled of such manner of
people. And in villages they are commonly made churchwardens,
aleconners, and many times constables, which office toucheth more
the commonwealth. [29]

Even though Smith was prepared to use the word *proletarii* of
these people, the old Roman expression meaning those able
to produce nothing but offspring, *proles*, as their contribution
to society, it does not appear that this description includes
the humblest of all. These 'low and base persons' as Smith goes
on to call them may not have made up the complete whole of
the majority of the population which was 'decreasing the
wealth of the kingdom' and some of them may have been
increasers. The really large groups of lowly persons are not
mentioned by Smith. Though King's 'labouring people' appear,
his 'cottagers and paupers' are not mentioned at all. The
truly poor, the begging poor, had no craft and could never
have become constables or ale-conners, as could the proletariat
of Sir Thomas Smith.

Begging was universal, as it is today in some of the countries
of Asia; beggars at the door, outside the churches, in the
market-places and wandering along the roads. Men sometimes
took fright at their numbers, especially in Tudor times, and
the savage laws against sturdy vagabonds became notorious
in the textbooks. Everyone knows that Elizabeth made each
parish responsible for its own poor, and that when a pauper
could be identified as from another community, he or she was
sent along the highway from place to place until the place of
settlement was reached. These outcasts have left their sad
traces in the registers of deaths in our churches: 'a poor walking
woman buried', 'a wandering beggar lad', 'a poore woman
name unknown who had crept into Mr Miller's barn'.

Yet crowds of destitute people were not typical of poverty
in the old world in quite the way that queues of unemployed
are typical of industrial poverty. The trouble then, as we have
hinted, was not so much unemployment, as under-employment,
as it is now called, and once more the comparison is with the
countries of Asia in our own century. Too many members of a
family were half-busied about an inadequate plot of infertile
land; not enough work could be found for the women and
children to do round the cottage fire, in some districts none at

[29] *See page 246.*

Number of Families	Ranks, Degrees, Titles, and Qualifications	Heads per Family	Number of Persons
160	Temporal Lords	40	6,400
26	Spiritual Lords	20	520
800	Baronets	16	12,800
600	Knights	13	7,800
3,000	Esquires	10	30,000
12,000	Gentlemen	8	96,000
5,000	Persons in greater Offices and Places	8	40,000
5,000	Persons in lesser Offices and Places	6	30,000
2,000	Eminent Merchants and Traders by Sea	8	16,000
8,000	Lesser Merchants and Traders by Sea	6	48,000
10,000	Persons in the Law	7	70,000
2,000	Eminent Clergy-men	6	12,000
8,000	Lesser Clergy-men	5	40,000
40,000	Freeholders of the better sort	7	280,000
120,000	Freeholders of the lesser sort	$5\frac{1}{2}$	660,000
150,000	Farmers	5	750,000
15,000	Persons in Liberal Arts and Sciences	5	75,000
50,000	Shopkeepers and Tradesmen	$4\frac{1}{2}$	225,000
60,000	Artizans and Handicrafts	4	240,000
5,000	Naval Officers	4	20,000
4,000	Military Officers	4	16,000
500,586		$5\frac{1}{3}$	2,675,520
50,000	Common Seamen	3	150,000
364,000	Labouring People and Out Servants	$3\frac{1}{2}$	1,275,000
400,000	Cottagers and Paupers	$3\frac{1}{4}$	1,300,000
35,000	Common Soldiers	2	70,000
849,000		$3\frac{1}{4}$	2,795,000
	Vagrants; as Gipsies, Thieves, Beggars, &c.		30,000
			So the
500,586	Increasing the Wealth of the Kingdom	$5\frac{1}{3}$	2,675,520
849,000	Decreasing the Wealth of the Kingdom	$3\frac{1}{4}$	2,825,000
1,349,586	Neat Totals	$4\frac{1}{13}$	5,500,520

Several Families of England Calculated for the Year 1688*

Yearly Income per Family		Yearly Income in general	Yearly Income per Head			Yearly Expence per Head			Yearly Increase per Head			Yearly Increase in general
£	s.	£	£	s.	d.	£	s.	d.	£	s.	d.	£
3,200		512,000	80	0	0	70	0	0	10	0	0	64,000
1,300		33,800	65	0	0	45	0	0	20	0	0	10,400
880		704,000	55	0	0	49	0	0	6	0	0	76,800
650		390,000	50	0	0	45	0	0	5	0	0	39,000
450		1,200,000	45	0	0	41	0	0	4	0	0	120,000
280		2,880,000	35	0	0	32	0	0	3	0	0	288,000
240		1,200,000	30	0	0	26	0	0	4	0	0	160,000
120		600,000	20	0	0	17	0	0	3	0	0	90,000
400		800,000	50	0	0	37	0	0	13	0	0	208,000
198		1,600,000	33	0	0	27	0	0	6	0	0	288,000
154		1,540,000	22	0	0	18	0	0	4	0	0	280,000
72		144,000	12	0	0	10	0	0	2	0	0	24,000
50		400,000	10	0	0	9	4	0	0	16	0	32,000
91		3,640,000	13	0	0	11	15	0	1	5	0	350,000
55		6,600,000	10	0	0	9	10	0	0	10	0	330,000
42	10	6,375,000	8	10	0	8	5	0	0	5	0	187,500
60		900,000	12	0	0	11	0	0	1	0	0	75,000
45		2,250,000	10	0	0	9	0	0	1	0	0	225,000
38		2,280,000	9	10	0	9	0	0	0	10	0	120,000
80		400,000	20	0	0	18	0	0	2	0	0	40,000
60		240,000	15	0	0	14	0	0	1	0	0	16,000
68	18	34,488,800	12	18	0	11	15	4	1	2	8	3,023,700
									Decrease			Decrease
20		1,000,000	7	0	0	7	10	0	0	10	0	75,000
15		5,460,000	4	10	0	4	12	0	0	2	0	127,500
6	10	2,000,000	2	0	0	2	5	0	0	5	0	325,000
14		490,000	7	0	0	7	10	0	0	10	0	35,000
10	10	8,950,000	3	5	0	3	9	0	0	4	0	562,500
		60,000	2	0	0	4	0	0	2	0	0	60,000
general Account is												
68	18	34,488,800	12	18	0	11	15	4	1	2	8	3,023,700
10	10	9,010,000	3	3	0	3	7	6	0	4	6	622,500
32	5	43,491,800	7	18	0	7	9	3	0	8	9	2,401,200

* See note 27, page 245.

all, for there was no rural industry in them. Everywhere work of all kinds varied alarmingly with the state of the weather and of trade, so that hunger was not very far away, as we shall see. Starvation, we perhaps ought to add at once, cannot yet be shown to have been a present menace to the poor in Stuart times.

No one could call a life of this sort a life of leisure, even if it was not a life of ceaseless toil for everybody, and leisure as has been said was a mark of the gentleman. The most celebrated Elizabethan definition of a gentleman comes from Harrison's *Description of Britain*, published in 1577. Besides the sons of gentlemen already recognized, he says:

Whosoever studieth the laws of this realm, who so abideth in the university giving his mind to his books, or professeth physic [that is medicine of course] and the liberal sciences, or beside his service in the room of captain in the wars, or good counsell at home, whereby his common-wealth is benefitted, can live without manual labour, and thereto is able and will bear the port, charge and countenance of a gentleman, he shall for money have a coat and arms [coat of arms, etc.] bestowed upon him by the heralds (who in the charter of the same do of custom pretend antiquity, service and many gay things) and thereunto being made so good cheap shall be called master, which is the title that men give to esquires and gentlemen, and reputed for a gentleman ever after.[30]

Any professional man, any university graduate, any officer in the royal forces, therefore, was a gentleman in England by that very fact, and the business of coats of arms, ancestry and public service could all be assumed; the heralds who were responsible would make it all up if required. Harrison is a little obscure when it comes to the matter of the money necessary to attain gentility, but popular opinion was much more straightforward: 'In England gentry is but ancient riches.' The historian is always coming across families which obey this simple rule. If a family had the money for long enough, just over one succession was generally sufficient, it graduated to the gentry. By money here is meant means sufficient to enable a family to live without doing manual work.

Gentility and its ranks were objective realities as well as honorifics: they counted for example when taxation systems were devised. The Poll Tax, imposed in 1660 for the first time

[30] *See page 246.*

was graduated according to rank: a really ordinary person paid only 6*d.* a year, but a gentleman paid £5, an esquire paid £10, a knight £20, a baronet £30, a baron paid £40 and his heir £30, a viscount £50 (£35), an earl £60 (£40) and a duke £100 (£60).[31] The time when you could be legally compelled to dress according to your rank was passing, though private correspondence is full of resentment at common people wearing the clothes reserved to the socially superior. But the distinction between those who were and those who were not within the gentry was still of overriding importance. It could be said without much distortion of the very elusive facts that this distinction in the eyes of our ancestors was only less significant than the sharpest of all distinctions, that between the Christian and a heathen. Indeed the very phrase 'A Christian and a gentleman', a typical survival of the values of that vanished world, suggests such a comparison. It also leaves open the possibility that a man could in some sense be a gentleman without being a Christian.

The system of status does not seem to have prevented social mobility. Movement into the select minority was straightforward enough in Harrison's view; a man simply had to have the necessary qualifications and be acceptable to those already there. But this is not the end of the matter. A great deal more will have to be found out about the family background and economic resources of men who were able to get entrance to a university, or to a profitable profession, or to commissioned rank in the army and so on, before it will be clear exactly how often gentlemen were recruited in this fashion. All that can be said with much confidence is that it did happen and that it was noticed and accepted by contemporaries.

When we come to consider social mobility rather more closely, we shall find ourselves having to assume that it must have been going on all the while in pre-industrial England, if only because of vital statistics. The scale of this movement may have been small and it undoubtedly varied from time to time, but it went on in both directions, downwards as well as upwards. In fact rather more people must have descended than ascended in society. Social mobility is always most pronounced at the frontiers, so to speak, and in traditional society this meant at the crucial divide between the minority which ruled and the mass which did not rule. The fact that this movement

[31] *See page 246.*

was constantly happening was one of the circumstances which made it possible for the single ruling group to maintain its supremacy and to adapt its membership to changing conditions.

In such a situation it seems hardly likely that simple upward motion in society can have been the final effective cause of political strife and civil commotion. There were other reasons for social mobility than vital statistics; obviously an incompetent family above the line of division which mismanaged its affairs and dissipated its fortune was likely to go down, and a family of capable people below the line which was making money was likely to go up. In spite of the elaborate arrangements to maintain the community of the privileged in their position, which was far easier to ensure in that agrarian society than it is in our own industrial society, interchange due to such influences could not be entirely prevented, and presumably happened most often at times of pronounced economic change. It is possible therefore that periods of particularly intense economic change might have been marked by unusually pronounced social mobility, and this might conceivably have led to unrest and conflict, particularly if there was any blockage, so to speak, any threat of resistance from those unwilling to be replaced. This possibility will be considered when we come to talk of change and revolution in the world we have lost.*

But we shall conclude that friction of this kind cannot have been of any great importance in the classic conflicts of Stuart times, in the English Revolution. Moreover a process of this sort is very different from a conflict of classes as that term has ordinarily been used. It leaves little room for the rise of a class, the capitalist or middle class as a group of persons. Even some of those who wish to retain a modified version of the rise-of-a-capitalist-class view of social development in pre-industrial times have begun to recognize that the capitalists as a group of persons capable of coming into conflict with other groups of persons are unlikely ever to be identified in England under pre-industrial conditions.[32] Rather it is now supposed that the whole of the English gentry, in our own terminology the whole of the ruling segment, was imbued with bourgeois values by the middle years of the seventeenth century. According to this view the world of gentleman, parson, peasant, craftsman and

*See chapter seven   [32] See page 246.

pauper was already a 'fully possessive market society', where conflict must presumably have been due to the internal contradictions of capitalism rather than to the clash of bourgeoisie and aristocrats. If this was so, the rivalries and clashes between Englishmen in Stuart and even Tudor times, intellectual, political and military, can hardly have been of an inter-class character. They must have gone on within the one class.

Social change and development in the pre-industrial world need not, therefore, be thought of in terms of classes which rise, conflict and fall. It perhaps ought to be emphasized once again that this does not mean that opposition of economic interest was absent from that society. No sharper clash of interest, material, economic or even biological, can be easily imagined than that between those with and those without access to the land. In an agrarian economy at times not far removed from the subsistence level in some areas, this might have meant that when harvests were bad some men could count on surviving, whilst others, the landless, could not be so sure. But this confrontation of class interest in the sense that whole unorganized masses of persons were on the one side and a few, concerted persons were on the other, is very different from an overt or covert collision between the rising bourgeoisie on the one hand and the falling feudality on the other. Rather it was an opposition between all those within and all those without the possessing minority which we have already referred to.[33]

Historical thinking about social structure has seldom been as critical as this. The cruder notion of the middle class as a concerted group of persons which defeated other groups of persons and so transformed society is the one which has got itself embedded in our attitude towards our English past. Let us look at the shape of society and at the system of status once again, this time in conjunction with what has been hinted about the localism of all social arrangements below the level of the ruling segment. A more detailed acquaintance with the system of status from this point of view may perhaps further convince us of the inappropriateness of the habitual way of thinking.

The graduated ladder from top to bottom of the social scale has already been referred to as the status system. Status

[33] *See page 246.*

Chart of Rank and Status   Stuart England

		Grade	Title	Forms of Address	Status Name	Occupational Name
GENTRY	NOBILITAS MAJOR	Duke Marquess Earl Viscount Baron	Lord, Lady [See general note]	Honourable, Right Honourable My Lord, My Lady, Your Lordship etc.	Nobleman etc.	None
		Baronet Knight	Sir, Dame*			
	NOBILITAS MINOR	Esquire Gentleman	Mr Mr	Worshipful	Gentleman	[Professions Merchant, Doctor of Medicine, etc. Army Officer, etc.]
		Yeoman	None	Name and Surname only†*	Yeoman	Husbandman
		Husbandman	,,	Name and Surname only‡*	None	Husbandman
		Craftsman (Tradesman, Artificer)	,,	,,	,,	Name of Craft (Carpenter, etc.)
		Labourer	,,	,,	,,	Labourer
		Cottager	,,	,,	,,	None
		Pauper	,,	,,	,,	None

† Sometimes called *Goodman*, *Goodwife* (abbreviated *Goody*).
* Often called *Lady* also – see *General Note*.
‡ * *Worthy* sometimes used.

General note to scheme of Ranks

The common tendency for a person to be called by a rather higher title than the one to which he was strictly entitled was already present. For example the wives of Knights and Baronets were called *Lady* rather than *Dame*. Usage was stricter amongst the nobility and also somewhat complicated. Any nobleman might be called *Lord* (Lord Norfolk, Lord Shaftesbury), but in the higher ranks the actual grade was almost always specified on each occasion (the Duke of Norfolk, the Earl of Shaftesbury). Most noblemen had titles of honour different from their family names (Anthony Ashley Cooper, Earl of Shaftesbury) and some courtesy titles were in use for their heirs. More usually, the heirs to noble titles would be called *Lord* followed by the family name, but the brothers and sisters of heirs to noble titles were often called plain *Mr* or *Mrs*. They were all entitled of course to the general designation *Honourable* as an additional form of address. The grandsons of holders of titles were quite usually called *Mr* without the *Honourable* and so came to be recognized as plain gentry. Usage below the line of gentry, as is emphasized in the text, was very much more uncertain because what status there was was associated with occupation.

depended for the most part on the position a man occupied on that ladder, though there was some admixture of status which arose from his actual function in society and his personal achievement. Status, that is to say, did not come exclusively from the title a man had inherited or had conferred on him. Nearly all the height of the social ladder was to be found within the ruling minority, within that part of the whole society which contained the nobility and the gentry, though the men below that line did share to some extent in the status system. I have tried to represent the facts in the chart opposite, drawing the dividing line below Gentleman.

At the very top of the society came the monarchy, but it was related to the whole in many other ways than that of status and its very special position is not our present concern. Under the Throne came the nobility, two hundred families, a thousand people or so, in a population of some five and a half million – by 1690 in Gregory King's reckoning (see Table page 32).[34] Yet most of the gradations in the system of honour were contained within this little gilded network; his Grace the Duke (or the Archbishop), the Marquess, the Earl, the Viscount, and lowest of all, His Lordship the Baron (or the Bishop). These were the *nobilitas major* of Sir Thomas Smith, but described by him as belonging to the gentlemen of England all the same. Every step in the honorific grading was meticulously marked and every noble family strove to mount the next one upwards of the glittering steps. Differences in wealth sometimes made the distinctions unrealistic, for even in Stuart times a viscount on the coal measures might outweigh a marquess on the Northern moors, but it could not obliterate them.

It cannot be said that the whole society of the nobility ever acted as a group; their identification with the gentry as a whole was reality, not a piece of legal fancy. We now know for certain that a majority of all marriages made by the English nobility from the sixteenth century until the twentieth were made with commoners, mainly with the gentry.[35] This may mark off our English titled families from their continental counterparts, and hierarchy was notoriously less rigid in England than elsewhere in Western Europe. But they had a remarkable privilege of their own nevertheless which gave them a defined, active institution and consolidated political

[34] *See page 247.*   [35] *See page 247.*

power; they had the House of Lords. It may seem extraordinary to assert that in spite of this the peerage in England
was for all purposes except the details of their status at one
with the rest of the ruling segment, the gentry as a whole, yet
this was undoubtedly the case. To look on the peerage as a
class apart, to see it simply as an element surviving from
the feudal age, resenting, and in rivalry with, the humbler
members of the privileged order, is only a partial understanding of the system of status.

Every system of this type must have its rewards, its goals,
its upper reaches, otherwise it will not work. This, then, was
the important function of the English peerage, to provide the
topmost placements in a society of privileged persons all of
whom were gentry and all of whom were members of a different
order than the whole mass of the people. The language of 'The
Estates of the Realm', which made of the Lords Spiritual, the
Lords Temporal and the Commons the constituent parts of
Parliament, might seem to imply that the function of nobility
was much more extensive than this. It is true that in the highly
conventional activity of politics, both at the centre of society
round the throne, and in the localities, titles of nobility had
considerable political potential and did not operate simply as
the final goal of political success. It is true also that the traditional division of Parliament was of structural importance to
its workings and did give the nobles an additional purchase
over political decisions because they had their own House.

But the Estates of the Realm never had corresponded at all
closely to divisions in English society as a whole and the
general history of Parliaments might make a fascinating study
in the complicated relationships between social structures and
the political systems which they generate. In seventeenth-
century England the whole arrangement was recognized as
archaic and there was even some confusion about what the
Estates were, for the Crown rather than the Lords Spiritual
was already being referred to as one of them. What might seem
to us the most critical division of all, that between members
for the boroughs and members for the counties, was passed
over and all members of the Lower House referred to as the
Commons. It is wholly confusing to think of class systems of
subsequent societies, including our own, as descended in any
simple way from the medieval Estates of the Realm.

The nobility could at times form palpable blocks of political power, and this was so in the political system of the eighteenth century in England. But relatively temporary arrangements such as these never did much to threaten the solidarity of the ruling minority. It always seems to have been true that the gap between those who were within and those who were outside the ruling group was greater than the gap between any two orders within the ruling group itself. The differences between say a baronet and an ordinary baron (the lowest type of Lord), who stood above the baronet in the status system, were always smaller in number and degree than the differences between the man who was and he who was not, a gentleman. Perhaps this rule was not quite invariable. It would certainly be difficult to argue it in the case of an exceptionally rich and successful yeoman who refused to take on the status of gentleman though his neighbours expected him to do so, and his son was destined to do so directly the father died. But such cases were few, in spite of what some men of the time said about prosperous yeomen. It is also possible that the centuries from the close of the Middle Ages to the end of Stuart times were marked by an exceptional emphasis on the gentleman as a type of person and on the differences between anyone who could call himself a gentleman and everyone else. The establishment of the Herald's Office and its activities in making Visitations of the counties and recording those who were entitled to gentry could be used to substantiate this claim. When the Visitations ceased at the end of this period, it might perhaps be supposed that the sharp emphasis on gentry was beginning to fade.[36] These considerations might take us a long way from our chosen and rather limited subject, but it can be said that the greater political eminence of noblemen in the eighteenth century as compared with the gentry did not imply any overall change in the relationship between the ruling minority as a whole and the rest of society. In the Middle Ages when the nobility was of such enormous importance the ruling segment as a whole must have been much smaller in size and perhaps smaller in relation to the whole. But it would be surprising if it turned out that it consisted of the nobility alone with no intervening area of privileged persons marked off from the whole.

Baronet, knight, esquire, gentleman – these were the grades below the peerage in Tudor and Stuart times, Smith's *Nobilitas*

[36] *See page 247.*

Minor. All these titles, like the titles of nobility, were honorifics only, not descriptions of function. But we have seen that Harrison does talk of a man's function as qualifying him for gentle status, since a physician, a don, a military officer were gentlemen, he thought, simply by doing the things they did. Another fiscal measure of the Stuart parliaments, an Act passed in 1694[37] which goes into status to a degree of minuteness which has to be read to be believed, is even more straightforward about who and who was not a gentleman. It imposed a tax to be collected 'upon burial of every Gentleman or reputed Gentleman, or owning or writing himself such'. Phrases of this sort are quite common in legal discussion of the crucial difference between those who belonged to the privileged and ruling minority. In fact a man's reputation as a gentleman depended to a considerable degree on what he did, when it was not obvious to all who knew him that he had been born to that status. The Poll Tax quoted earlier lists a whole range of holders of legal, ecclesiastical and even commercial office-holders as liable to taxation at levels corresponding to grades of the nobility and gentry. The equivalent grades were usually rather modest ones, except, it may be noticed, for certain lucrative legal offices.[38]

Such provisions as these amount to an overt, legal recognition of movement into the gentry, even deliberate provision for ensuring that anyone making money or attaining any form of social consequence should succeed to the status. Let us pursue the hierarchy of status below the critical divide, and into the largely undifferentiated mass of ordinary people. Before we do so we may notice that the lowest grades of gentry enormously outnumbered the titled grades. With less than two hundred noble families in his table (page 32), it was reckoned by Gregory King that there were in 1688 eight hundred families of baronets and six hundred of knights, but three thousand of esquires and twelve thousand of ordinary gentlemen. This only makes up a third or more of the full number of those who must be reckoned to have composed the ruling segment at that time, a third of the one in twenty we referred to earlier. The other two-thirds must have been those with the title 'master' (Mr on our letters), self-reputed or locally recognized gentlemen rather than those living on estates in land. This was what might be called the penumbra

[37] *See page 247.*   [38] *See page 248.*

of the privileged group and this again will concern us when we come to social mobility.

Status amongst the common people, the vast majority, went with occupation in so far as it was marked at all; it was a matter of function, not description. The only status name as such which men recognized below the line, so to speak, was the name 'yeoman' (see the *Chart* on page 38). Even this was to some extent a functional term, since a yeoman had to be a fairly substantial owner (not renter) of land which he had to work himself, for he emphatically did not come under the idleness rule which defined gentlemanliness. Alternatively, and here the much greater vagueness of terms for these lower statuses is already to be seen, such a man might be called a freeholder, a greater freeholder (much more likely to have the alternative title yeoman) or a lesser freeholder (probably a freeholder without the vote, that is with less than 40s. a year from his own land). Sometimes, during the final generations of the old order, he might be called a farmer, and this is a functional name altogether. It has survived as the only term we now use for those occupied in agriculture.

Yeoman then, was the status name of the most successful of those who worked the land. This was a name which became sentimentalized very early, whilst the men who had held it under the old order became farmers under the new. It is interesting that there was a *yeoman* status even in the companies of craftsmen in the cities and that it should have come below the status of *master* in those associations. The word yeoman has survived in our vocabulary, whilst the functional name based upon what we call farmer, working the land, the word *husbandman* has disappeared. All yeomen were husbandmen, because they worked the land, but not all husbandmen were yeomen by any means, because most of them had neither the qualifications nor the status. Since a yeoman's sons worked the land without owning it, they were often called husbandmen too, and most husbandmen were workers of land they did not own but rented.

Husbandman was an extremely common description of men in the old world, because it was the description of what so many of them were engaged in, tilling the soil. Alongside of husbandmen came all the other callings, the craftsmen. We may perhaps notice that though husbandmen and craftsmen are given no titles in our table and were addressed always by simple name and surname, followed where necessary by their occupational name, the word *worthy* would sometimes be used as a sort of prefix to their names, though never in quite the way in which *worshipful* was associated with gentry. Yeomen could be called worthy, and the occasional use of this word emphasized the very considerable variation which men called husbandmen or craftsmen might show in their prosperity and importance. There was an enormous difference between a draper in the City of London engaged in large-scale cloth dealings and a tailor or a blacksmith in a village, even if the draper was not substantial enough to be regarded as worshipful and gentle.

'Mechanick' was the title often given to the meaner occupations: John Bunyan, the tinker, was thought of as a 'mechanick preacher'.[39] The craftsmen in the towns must nearly always have worked on a larger scale than those in the countryside, but in town and in country the overriding impression of the grade of craftsman was of its multifarious variety. Miller, tailor, ploughwright, weaver, plumber, dyer, bricklayer, carpenter, mason, tanner, innkeeper, all these are still familiar words and many of them common surnames. Some of the occupations of craftsmen which the historian finds have disappeared so completely from our memory that the ordinary reader does not usually recognize them: there were the fletchers (arrow-makers), badgers (corn-dealers), cordwainers (leather-workers), whittawers (sadlers). Occasionally even the expert is defeated: what did the *plasher* do, who is listed as living at Clayworth in Nottinghamshire in 1688?

All these men, and the yeomen too, were described simply by their Christian and surnames whenever they were mentioned: plain John Hart, husbandman, or James Buckland, carpenter. It is easy to see how it came about that so many of our surnames have derived from their occupations. Not so long before the reign of Elizabeth most Englishmen were without even surnames, and it can easily be seen how natural it was when surnames came in to call Peter the Smith, Peter Smith. On the Continent of Europe the older naming custom survived longer; in Holland for example the common folk did not acquire second names until the time of Napoleon.

There were three further names of common people, though only one of them was in any sense either a description of status

[39] *See page 248.*

or of function: *labourer*, *cottager* and *pauper*. A *labourer* could be either of the other two, and a man who called himself that could not call himself a husbandman, because he did not work land on his own account. He could have no other calling-name, because he had no specific calling; he just worked for other people. *Cottager* was a description, not of a calling but of a means of livelihood which was not specific. Getting a living where you, you and your whole family, could make one, and wringing all that was possible out of the land which might be attached to the hovel you lived in. This is an unwieldy description, but it is as short a way as I have found of placing a cottager in the old order. The final term, *pauper*, speaks for itself.

According to Gregory King (see page 32), the largest group of families in England was in fact the last two; 'Cottagers and Paupers', 400,000 out of 1,300,000. If we regard these as the lowest in the social scale, in spite of the recognition that 'scale' does not strictly apply below the line, the enormous inequality of life in the world we have lost immediately becomes apparent. Not all of these wretched families must be counted as permanently below the level of subsistence, as the early sociologists used to say, or in what was once called primary poverty. But they were for varying periods in poverty of some sort, in need of relief. In fact that whole half and more of the population which Gregory King described as decreasing the wealth of the kingdom may well be supposed to have been living in intermittent poverty in the England of 1688. Indeed it is probably best to assume that at all times before the beginnings of industrialization a good half of all those living were judged by their contemporaries to be poor, and their standards must have been extremely harsh, even in comparison with those laid down by Victorian poor law authorities.[40]

There is another important characteristic in King's figures which we must not overlook, because it demonstrates a general principle which was a striking feature of social arrangements as they were in his day. The total number of people he gives as five and a half million, of which we have seen a little over half (2,825,000) were 'decreasing the wealth of the kingdom' and a little under half (2,675,000) were increasing it. But the difference in the number of families between these two halves was very much greater; only 501,000 families were in the

[40] *See page 248.*

richer section as against 849,000 families in the poorer section. Poor people, therefore, lived in small families, and rich people in big ones, though some members of rich families, the servants, came from poor homes and might themselves die in poverty. The general principle, then, runs as follows: the higher the status of the household or family, the larger it was, and the humbler people were, the smaller were the families they lived in. The majority of families were the small, poorer ones, and the minority the large, richer ones, even though more people in total lived in them than in the smaller ones. Humble families in fact lost some of their members, as servants to richer families. We shall return to the size of the family and household in due course; all we are registering here is its connection with the hierarchy of status.

If the phrase middle class seems to have so many misleading associations when it is used of any part of Stuart society, there was of course a middle range of income and status rather in the numerical sense as there always must be. Indeed the middling sort of people began to enter into social descriptions as early as the eighteenth century and it is interesting to find that it was mostly used of the towns. We must look a little closer at the townsfolk and the bourgeoisie in order to decide the extent to which they can be said to have lived apart from the rest of the population, even though like everybody else they found themselves under the domination of the ruling minority. Can it be said that the two thousand families of 'Merchants and Traders by the Sea' which Gregory King estimated as existing in 1688, or ten thousand of them in all if the lesser ones are included, really formed the bourgeoisie in pre-industrial England? Or would it be realistic and useful to call Sir Thomas Smith's third sort of men, 'Citizens, Burgesses and Yeomen' by the title middle class?

Though yeomen and merchants must often have come from the same stock, and though there might be seen to be some rough sort of equivalents in the position of the more modest burgesses with the substantial peasantry, Sir Thomas Smith is exceptional in linking them in this way. In the provincial towns – how insignificant they were will become obvious in the next chapter – the local grazier who was also a butcher had already appeared in the sixteenth century and his is a figure which persisted until the twentieth century. Nevertheless the towns had a life of their own, small as they were, and any acquaintance with municipal records will show how intense a community feeling could be. It was at the top that the linkage with society as a whole is to be seen and it was a link between the gentry and the merchants which preoccupied the men of the time.

This is what Harrison says about merchants: 'They often change estates with gentlemen as gentlemen do with them; by mutual conversion of one into the other.'[41] William Lambarde, the first historian of an English county, says very much the same thing of Kent in Elizabethan times: 'The gentlemen be not here (throughout) of so ancient stocks as elsewhere, especially in the parts nearest to London, from which city (as it were from a certain rich and wealthy seedplot) courtiers, lawyers and merchants be continuously translated and do become new plants among them.'[42] This interchange was by no means confined to Kent, and as Harrison said it was not simply a flow of merchant families into the gentry: the gentry became merchants too. Westcote, the first to write about the broad seafaring county of Devon, with its flourishing ports, says of the merchants: 'Divers of them are esquires and gentlemen's younger sons, who by means of their travel and transmigration are very well qualified, apt and fit to manage great and high offices.'[43]

Some contemporaries, it is true, do give an impression that the merchants were a community of their own: 'These, by reason of the great privileges they enjoy, every city being as it were a Common Wealth by themselves,'[44] wrote one of them in 1600, somewhat obscurely and ungrammatically it must be confessed. There was an interesting and anxious controversy in the seventeenth century about whether a gentleman's son could become an apprentice and still preserve his gentle status since it meant, as we have seen, serving in someone else's house and actually undertaking menial tasks for a person ordinarily of lower lineage than his own.[45] But whatever prejudice there might have been, however much snobbery affected our ancestors, there can be no doubt that gentlemen did become apprentices in very considerable numbers to the more profitable trades. There can be no doubt either that the sons of the manor house married the daughters of the city merchants, for as much money in the way of a dowry as they could possibly

[41] *See page 249.*   [42] *See page 249.*   [43] *See page 249.*
[44] *See page 249.*   [45] *See page 249.*

get, or that the son of a successful goldsmith, merchant, haberdasher or draper, might marry the daughter of a country gentleman.

Here we return at once to the authoritarian, patriarchal family which bound people together with tough, durable bands of kinship. The gentleman's son who went into the City as an apprentice, and married City money, remained part of the family in the countryside. When the gentry of the county underwent a Visitation from the Heralds, which happened once in a couple of generations, they registered their sons or grandsons, daughters, nephews, living in the City along with all the others married off to other county gentry. So many gentry got into London in this way that the City of London had its Visitations too. It is interesting that the families there very seldom went back more than two or three generations, for the English merchant family retired to the countryside as soon as opportunity presented itself. There were English families which maintained a dual allegiance over many generations, dynasties of prosperous London merchants which were also gentry in the countryside, seated naturally in the Home Counties. But these were few.[46] Londoners who happened to inherit country houses nearly always seem to have taken up their residence there and left the City.

It was often the death of an uncle, a great-uncle or a cousin rather than a father, brother or grandfather which required that the younger, City Branch should move to the family seat. We still talk of the City Branch, just as we still talk of county families, which is one more indication of how our language of status belongs to an older world. When we come to talk of social mobility and vital statistics (see below, Chapter 8) we shall see that even more conspicuous transformations were possible. A man might be merely the eldest in the female line of a minor gentle family, yet end his life as a titled magnate or even a peer. The point of present importance is the web of kinship, to use a phrase of the anthropologists, which enfolded every family in the ruling segment. It was not simply a community of interest, a political or economic grouping, it was a lineage, a clan. Entry into it was by marriage.

Given that there was no bar to intermarriage, therefore, it is extremely difficult to see how any enclave could remain isolated from the rest. The City of London was undoubtedly

[46] *See page 249.*

a community of its own; so extraordinarily rich and powerful did it become in the final generations of the old order that it is understandable that men sometimes described it as a state within a state. But we shall shortly see how it was pretty well alone as an urban community, the only area of the country where rural ways did not penetrate, in the whole of England. Life in London was different from life elsewhere and life in the richest London families very different, perhaps, from life in the country houses whose masters were so much less wealthy than the Aldermen. But however striking the texture of social life in the *haute bourgeoisie* might turn out to be when it is properly studied, this does not justify us in calling the city dweller the member of a different class, forming a conscious, permanent community, capable of seeing itself as separate from the ruling segment.

The difference in outlook must presumably have been at its greatest when some city father had risen from truly humble origins, from well beneath the rank of gentleman. Like the rest of those who prospered in the towns, of course, he was called *master*, he was *worshipful*, by virtue of his personal wealth and power over others. We do not yet know how often such a thing came to pass, or how essential it may have been to have come from some gentle or at least yeoman family before such a career of success as a bourgeois became possible in the pre-industrial world. It is clear, however, that social differences of this sort did not outlast more than a generation. A wealthy clothier, or tanner, or victualler, or perhaps barber surgeon might, if he lived to see them, feel very different from his grandchildren in the countryside whom he shared with the gentleman whose son had married his daughter. But the grandchildren themselves would not experience any uncertainty of status. Moreover, they might succeed very rapidly to the family fortune because of the short expectation of life. This point is usually put in the form of an admission that families can and do sometimes ascend in the traditional societies, but that it took a generation and more. At that time however several generations might well elapse within the ordinary span of life in our time.

We have been able in this outline of an argument to refer only very little to other members of the *middle class*, as we understand it today. We now think of professional people such as doctors and lawyers, technicians of every description, teachers, architects, civil servants as the important people of this type. It is men like these which the nations of Africa and Asia are so sadly lacking in our century, and not so much the businessmen, which correspond (not very exactly) to the merchants of say, Elizabethan England. All that can now be said of *professional* people of this sort in the world we have lost is that, just as in Africa now, there were very, very few of them. Those who did exist, belonged to the ruling minority by definition. We have seen William Harrison admitting it and they have been placed accordingly in our chart on page 38.

Conditions on the Continent were often somewhat different from those in England. In Holland, for example, or in Italy, there seems to have been a greater continuity of succession in urban, patrician families, who perhaps did not marry into the gentle families of the countryside so easily and presumably, therefore, did not attain gentle status so often. The status system differed too, for in some countries the nobility does seem to have been more separate from the rest of the privileged community, and provisions for social descent such as existed in England seem to have been lacking. This is a capital point, which might well have been developed, for the rule of status which laid it down that in England the younger son of a baron was plain *master*, *Mr*, just like a successful merchant, certainly led to an acceptance of social mobility not so apparent elsewhere. In all these directions it may turn out that England was exceptional.

Perhaps the phrase a 'one-class society' would fit no other European country as well as it seems to fit pre-industrial England even with all the complicated exceptions and reservations which have had to be made in the course of this chapter. This title gives rise to no expectation that the workers of the pre-industrial world can be thought of as a community apart from the rest, which is a further advantage over the usual phraseology. Detailed analysis of the working force, or the labour force as the economists say, cannot be undertaken here and it is one more of the subjects which will have to be pursued elsewhere for itself alone. There was a considerable number of wage-earners even before large-scale industry made the wage packet the almost universal form of payment and support. Indeed there is evidence that even in Tudor times well over a half or even two-thirds of all households received some part at least of their income from wages. Nevertheless the paupers, when they were fortunate enough to receive wages, the labourers, the artificers, even the husbandmen and the yeomen who pocketed such payments from their employers were in a very different situation indeed from the worker in the factory, the shop or the office. They did not all share a common work situation by any means, as does the working class in the contemporary industrial world.

A considerable part of the labour force, moreover, cannot have been householders at all. These were the servants living in the households of their masters and the grown and growing children still at home and at work at the bench or in the fields. Most of them were young of course, though since the age of marriage was so late, they were only comparatively young in relation to the age of the population as a whole. They were separated into the myriad familial cells which went to make up the society. Here we return once again to the minute scale of life, the small size of human groups before the coming of industry. Working persons were held apart from each other by the social system. Many or most of them were subsumed, as we have said, within the personalities of their fathers and masters. If it had not been for the terminology which was invented for a society like our own, it would never have occurred to us even to wonder whether they could be thought of as a community, a class of their own.

The working families were poor, and we have seen men of the time openly talking of them as the proletariat. 'Miserable men,' Westcote calls them, 'in regard of their labour and poverty.'[47] Everyone was quite well aware throughout the life of that social order that the poorer peasantry might at any time break out into violence. Talking about the 'pulling and contest' after money at a time of deflation, John Locke said in 1696 that this struggle usually went on between 'the landed men and the merchant'.

For the labourer's share, being seldom more than a bare subsistence, never allows that body of man time or opportunity to raise their thoughts above that, or struggle with the richer for theirs (as one common interest), unless when some common or great distress, uniting them in one universal ferment, makes them forget respect, and emboldens them to carve to their wants with armed force, and then sometimes they break in upon the rich and sweep all like

[47] *See page 249.*

a deluge. But this rarely happens but in the mal-administration of a neglected or mismanaged government.[48]

Journeymen out of their time, but unable to set up for themselves; small masters miserably dependent on the capital of rich masters; husbandmen pinched for their rent by avaricious landlords; these were likewise looked upon as dangerous men who might sometimes become desperate.

But the head of the poorest family was at least the head of something. The workers did not form a million *outs* facing a handful of *ins*. They were not in what we should call a mass situation. They could not be what we should call a class. For this, it has been claimed, if the expression can be used at all, was a one-class society. It must be clear that the question of how the *élite*, the ruling segment, was related to the rest is not an easy one to answer. A great deal of patient, intricate work of discovery and analysis will have to be undertaken by the historians before they can begin to decide such issues as these. They will have to show an imaginative sensitivity to all those subtle influences which enable a minority to live for all the rest. When they come to do this, it is the symbolic life of our ancestors which will be the most difficult to handle, and especially their symbols of status.

[48] *See page 249.*

The Village Community
Chapter 3

Nothing seems more poignant and appropriate to us than that Falstaff should have died babbling of green fields. Indeed we still think of our English surroundings in this way; lush little meadows and, more commonplace still, the group of thatched cottages, standing in irregular relationship with manor-house, inn and church. A picture of England which the Englishman goes to make sure about when his holidays come round, and which foreigners see when they look on us from outside, especially from the North American Continent.

It is now an entirely false picture, of course, and by this time most of us surely know quite well that it is false. Nevertheless, its persisting attractiveness, the effect it still has on our national image of ourselves and what we should hope for our future, is one further example of the influence upon us of the lost world which vanished with the coming of industrial, urban life. In our day, at least four Englishmen out of every ten live in cities, or conurbations as we strangely name them. Over half of us live in towns of 50,000 inhabitants and more,[49] which are so vast that none of our rural ancestors would recognize his surroundings as human, should he find his way on to one of the streets through some impossible chronological vagary. He might suppose that he had been spirited to London by one of the fairies, Queen Mab perhaps, or some hobgoblin or other which everyone still half-believed in in Shakespeare's time.

London even then was a city on an industrial scale, though industry, as we use the word, did not exist there. The inn in Eastcheap where Falstaff lay plucking at the sheets, his nose sharp as a pen, was quite a long way from green fields, perhaps a mile and a half or two miles, probably as far as it was possible to get in the stupendous assemblage of buildings which went to make up the City of London. By the end of the pre-industrial era London was undoubtedly the biggest city in Europe and, if men had but known it, probably already the biggest in the world, though still much smaller than the Rome of the ancients, which was the largest city men then knew about.

[49] See page 250.

One Englishman in every ten lived in London, which actually topped the half-million mark by the end of the seventeenth century.[50] But urban, mass living in an environment entirely man-made, if no way machine-made, ended at that point in England. If three-quarters and more people live in cities in our day, then in Tudor and Stuart times the position was exactly the reverse. When Elizabeth reigned, Charles and Cromwell fought the Civil War, and William and Mary came to the throne after the Glorious Revolution, some three-quarters of the whole people lived in villages.

These villages were, moreover, small even on the standards of Europe at that time. It is difficult to be certain what was the scale of each settlement, and a great deal of work has still to be done on the elementary facts about the human geography of our country in its historical dimension. It is quite certain that there was no average size in the sense that most villages could be expected to contain roughly the same number of people. There were large villages and little villages, just as there were great and small towns and cities: the composition and organization of settlements varied enormously, from region to region and even to some degree within the same limited area. But the numerical mean or average, that is the number of places divided into the total population in England and Wales in late Stuart times, was somewhere between 250 and 450. The only example which can yet be quoted of an appreciable number of places in the same area, yields even smaller figures. This is the Wingham division of the county of Kent in 1705 where there were forty separately named places in the collection of lists of inhabitants, with a total of 6,411 people: the average, or mean, size of a settlement was thus 160 people. Much of the Stuart population lived out their lives in settlements so small that in the twentieth century we should regard them as miniatures, curiosities.

But even in the Wingham area, there was one community of 1,172 people, and 42 per cent of the people lived in settlements larger than 400 people. Like all figures, those we have presented for the whole country, and for this particular area, are deceptive to some degree. Though the figure for the actual national average in the seventeenth century was almost certainly in the 300s, yet the median or middle-sized village was probably well over 400 and, just as in Kent, a considerable

[50] *See page 250.*

minority presumably lived in larger places, with perhaps 500 or more inhabitants.[51] It is possible then, to give a rather different impression for the country as a whole, when it is remembered that a quarter of the people were living in London and the towns. Something like two-thirds of the whole population of the country can be supposed to have dwelt in settlements of 500 or more, and a tenth of them in a real city on the twentieth century scale. But when we make the gross comparison with our own day which is the general object of this superficial survey, these different angles of view change the prospect very little. Life in a community of 500 or 600 souls can have been very little different from life in a community of 300 or 400, in contrast to life in a modern industrial centre of 50,000 or more.

The facts of the minuscule scale of living in the world we have lost, therefore, are almost as conspicuous for the size of the communities in which men dwelt as they are for the size of the group in which they lived and worked. England, apart from the phenomenon of London, may have been exceptionally laid out, more blanketed by its fields than many other areas of Europe. But though the details of the distribution of persons between villages, hamlets might be a better word, have still to be worked out, there can be little doubt about the gross facts. Gregory King reckoned that there were 530,000 people living in London in 1688, nearly 10 per cent of the population of the country; 870,000 living in 'The other Cities and Market Towns', that is nearly 16 per cent, and 4,100,000 living in 'The Villages and Hamlets', over 74 per cent. Since we already have some idea of the scale of life in London we must look at these last two categories separately as the difference in order of magnitude between London and the rest is truly impressive.

Gregory King does not specify the number of 'Cities and Market Towns' in his table, but Professor Glass has discovered in King's workings a table of some 800 places which he seemed to have had in mind as accounting for the 870,000 people in his second category.[52] This would make the mean size of an English city, or local town-centre, only a little over 1,000, not much more than one five-hundredth of the size of London. The height of the step between London and the next level of size is, perhaps, even more surprising, from half a million, to about 25,000 to 30,000. This was reached only by four places, probably Bristol, Norwich, York and Southampton. These four giants among the provincial cities contained no more than 11¼ per cent of the population which lived in places which could be called in any sense urban. Below them came 10 cities of about 18,000 people, 30 cities (or 'great towns' as King is careful to say) of about 2,200 and then 100 of about 1,300 inhabitants. The majority of the town-dwelling population outside London, if the adjective town-dwelling is permissible at all, lived in 250 places of some 900 people and 400 further places of something over 650. Between them these two classes of 'town' contained well over a half of all those outside the capital not dwelling in villages or hamlets.

England, therefore, was decidedly not an urban country before the arrival of industry. If King and the other men of his day who discussed the matter are to be trusted, and such evidence as has yet been surveyed all points in the same direction, England was a large rural hinterland attached to a vast metropolis through a network of insignificant local centres. There was little to correspond with the great provincial towns of France. After the really big cities of Paris, Lyons and Marseilles, came Rouen, Orleans, Amiens, Bordeaux, Rheims, Angers, all six of which had between 35,000 and 50,000 people and more.[53] Even Beauvais, a medium-sized clothing city, had some 15,000 or 20,000, and the relatively minor provincial capital of Aix-en-Provence numbered 27,500 people in 1695 when a fairly accurate count was made.[54] We may compare this with an almost contemporary census of similar reliability, carried out with the knowledge, and perhaps the co-operation, of King himself, in his own birthplace, Lichfield in Staffordshire.[55] A cathedral city and a county centre, it contained 2,861 people in the same year, 1695.

Our country had no city-states, like Italy: no Florence, no Venice, not even a Frankfurt-am-Main, or a Salzburg. Even London, for all its fantastic size, could not be called a civic site: it was then, as it has sadly continued to be, except in select areas and for a brief period under the Georges, a disorderly sprawl, as much of a haphazard muddle as any English rural village. We are right to think of the world we have lost as a bucolic world, in our country, at least, even if we are wrong to go on believing that we ought all to be living in the countryside still.

[53] *See page 251.*   [54] *See page 251.*   [55] *See page 251.*

This is the justification for our talking almost exclusively about rural life and village institutions in the pre-industrial world in England. The scale and quality of the experience of our ancestors must have been determined by them: urban living cannot have been anything like as important to them as it seems to have become in our folk memory of the past and in most historians' accounts of it. There is another and quite accidental reason why village life will have to occupy us so largely. Our evidence comes from rural villages, and even purely demographic study may, for technical reasons, have to be confined to village life for some time to come. We shall find ourselves from time to time, however, remarking here on rural/urban differences particularly between London and the rest of the country.

Sometimes it is surprising that these differences were as small as they seem to have been, but Gregory King's own writing is proof that the men of the time were well aware that society did vary between town and country. The whole of King's *Observations* is marked by attempts to distinguish rural from urban figures, and he provides tables showing that in London and the towns there were more married couples, more servants, more widows and fewer children than in the country. Our preliminary evidence in some cases contradicts even Gregory King but we shall not be able to claim that we know enough to pronounce in general on the contrast between town and country.

When we talk of England as being almost entirely a landscape of green meadows and wide-open fields with village communities scattered amongst them, it is a network rather than a scattering that we have in mind. The very large numbers of small settlements in which so much of the population lived were in fact all connected by the local rural centres. They were independent as communities, but their independence implied the existence of communities larger than themselves. Though these larger villages and towns turn out to be so small as compared with the provincial cities of the rest of Western Europe, they were nevertheless differently constituted from the others because they were centres of exchange as well as of communication. The whole pattern must therefore be thought of as a reticulation rather than as a particulation, a web spread over the whole geography is the metaphor which will come most easily to the mind. We shall use the same expression for

the society of the gentry which did so much to maintain unity
and consciousness over the complete area. But the bondages
which come from roads, rivers, markets, fairs and neighbourhood were always present too.

The word settlement is right for the villages and hamlets of
our country. They were in fact the knots of households originally set down by the first colonizers of the island, still being
inhabited and run by their successors after a thousand years
and more. Each group of farmsteads was surrounded by the
land which had been laid out for it, presumably enough to
support the inhabitants. In some areas, therefore, where the
land was rich and even and easy to till, and where the rivers
flowed together, settlements came thick and fast. Norfolk has
no less than 660 ancient parishes, and in that most prosperous
of the shires in earlier times, there were 969 medieval churches;
you can sometimes see ten spires or towers from one vantage
point.[56] Yet even in Norfolk, on the Breckland, there are miles
and miles of desolate landscape where few dwelt and
where the settlements are well out of sight of each other. In
the highlands of England, the whole area north and west of
the famous line drawn from Bristol to the Wash, church was
separated from church by five, seven or even ten miles. Yorkshire, which is more than twice as big as Norfolk, had but 459
parishes in Stuart times, Cornwall only 61, Westmorland
only 26, and Lancashire, the county where industrial transformation was to be at its most sudden and intense, not more
than 36.

Parishes are not settlements. There are often several distinct
hamlets in one parish, or more than one parish in a village.
About three settlements to two parishes is, perhaps, about
right. These parish figures, therefore, are only very rough indications of the variation found in size, density and structure
of settlements between various parts of the country, especially
between the highland and lowland zones. In the highlands,
chapelries had grown up to accommodate the growing population which had often already appeared in response to early
industrial activity, especially the making of wool and cloth.
Yet, even in these regions parish and settlement were sometimes congruent, or rather the parish covered an area com-
prising only one hamlet, or two, as in the lowlands. This was
so at Widecombe-in-the-Moor, in Devonshire, from whose

[56] *See page 252.*

boundaries Dartmoor still stretches away as far as the eye can
see. Life amongst inhabitants of that parish, or of Greystoke in
Cumberland, locked in the mountains of the Lake District,
was one thing. Life in the large and prosperous village of
Colyton on the Devon seaboard, or in the single little bunch
of housesteads which went to make up Cogenhoe in Northamp-
tonshire, two hundred people on only 800 acres, yet with their
own church and rector, was another thing again.

The villages of Greystoke, Colyton and Cogenhoe[57] come
into the story many times, for they are amongst the ten or a
dozen village communities which have been examined in some
detail for the purpose of this essay. But the subtler elements
which went to make up the differences between community
and community have not yet been reached. It is not yet known
how much effect the final origin of the inhabitants might have
had on the way they arranged their community life, laid out
their fields and worked them, or conducted their religious
worship. For the highlanders in Britain, as everyone remem-
bers, are Celtic by descent, and the lowlanders are Saxon.[58]
Another difference in the texture of local life which certainly
had a part to play was the extent to which it was *industrialized*,
in the old meaning of the phrase, how many of the households
were wholly or partly working for the clothier, or the nailer or
how many of the menfolk worked the mines. So powerful was
this force becoming that in many places it may have been
decisive, overriding differences in origin, or tradition, even the
influence of geographical position.

There were differences between village communities which
came from recent agricultural history as well, and these have
taken pride of place in the story which historians have had to
tell. Most important of all have been questions of enclosure.
Did this settlement once work its land as open fields, co-
operatively, until some grasping or enterprising Tudor landlord managed to bring about enclosure? To enclose a village
meant that the inhabitants had to abandon their co-operative
customs, and break up their great open fields into little,
hedged plots, one single piece to each landholder and, of
course, the largest by far for the landlord himself. Or was the
open field, co-operative system then still in force there? Or
had the land, perhaps, as in Kent or in East Anglia, always
been enclosed? These are clearly fundamental questions to ask

[57] *See page 252.*   [58] *See page 252.*

of any village community in the traditional world, since working the land was the fundamental activity of all its members,
and co-operating for the purpose a powerful link between the
constituent households. But no very large proportion of the
cultivated land had been enclosed by the years 1700–10,[59]
which is the final decade of the old world for our purposes.
Where enclosure had taken place, moreover, even recently,
the differences it had made from the point of view of the life
of the community were perhaps less than might be expected.

Enclosure could not destroy the distances between the community and its neighbours. Though the detailed arrangements
for the working of the land were no longer undertaken at the
manor court, and though that court might be dying as an
institution, nevertheless, the community still had its affairs
to run co-operatively. The church had to be administered, or
perhaps two churches in the same village. The poor law had
to be carried out; the roads had to be kept up; the constable
appointed to maintain the peace. The more important the
common responsibilities of any community, presumably, the
stronger the association between its members, because each
one's interest is engaged. But living together in one township,
isolated, spatially, from others of comparable size, of very
much the same structure, inevitably means a communal sense
and communal activity, even if that activity is trivial and
symbolic, as it is in the *social club* which we treasure so much
in our day.

The strength of this sense of community in the English
villager can be seen when he removed himself beyond the ocean,
and settled again, surrounded by the alien, virgin land, which
required new household groupings. In the final years of the
traditional order in England, when the English were establishing their townships on the eastern seaboard of the North
American continent, the village community at home was of
course the model. The men from the ancient enclosed villages
of East Anglia and the newly enclosed communities of the
Midlands showed no less communal sense, no greater unwillingness to serve the new community, than the men from
villages where the immemorial open fields still lay undisturbed
under the wide, grey English sky. Open-field villagers would
sometimes insist on the open-field system for a new township
in Massachusetts. But it is not recorded that those from else-

[59] *See page 252.*

where would welcome this return to the ancient co-operative system.[60]

There is very little reason to believe, therefore, that the husbandry, the working landholders, of the English village community who went out to join the Puritan commonwealth which grew up on the rocky soil of New England were seeking refuge from the enclosing landlord. Nevertheless they were certainly disinclined, in their surroundings, to allow a gentry to grow up amongst them, and quite determined to have no truck with ecclesiastical dignitaries. However, gentle folk were never entirely absent from any part of the American colonies, even from quintessentially Puritan Massachusetts; in the southern areas, as everyone knows, the gentry were much more prominent and even the Anglican hierarchy took root. The plantation-owners of Virginia looked upon themselves from the very beginning as the overseas branches of English county families, and there is evidence that the gentry did indeed take the initiative in opening up the leafy green plain between the Atlantic and the Appalachians though they had great difficulty in settling it.[61] Indeed, the role of the gentry in the creation of America must have been an important one, if the analysis of English society presented here is at all accurate. Still, at the American Revolution, as we have seen, all this disappeared from the official life, political and social, of the new United States, and has had to be pieced together by subsequent historians. The pattern of Puritan society in Massachusetts became the pattern of American society generally, in this as in so much else. It was a pattern which no doubt came to some extent from the life of the English towns, but whose major origin can be clearly seen in those villages of Stuart England where no gentlemanly household was to be found and where the yeomen and the husbandmen ran everything themselves.

It would be easy in our own century to exaggerate the extent to which the new Englishmen of the American continent deliberately rejected the system of status established amongst the old Englishmen of Europe, for we are so interested in social differentiation, and so apt to seize upon every sign of social resentment or of disaffection. But there can be no doubt that the social hierarchy deeply affected the lives of ordinary people in the Old World. The presence, or absence, of the gentry in an English village made a vital difference. Without

[60] *See page 252.*   [61] *See page 253.*

the gentry, or any member of the ruling minority in their midst, the members of an English village community were indeed free to run their own affairs, almost as free, it might seem, as the members of the townships set up in New England. Galby, in Leicestershire, never had a resident squire, and the free villagers have been traced for centuries, running their community as they would.[62] Many communities like this must have been present, scattered amongst the villages where the manor-house was the largest building, apart from the church, and deference to its occupants the first principle of village life. Perhaps a fifth of all the village communities of England may have been in this position.

The surprising thing about this figure, on reflection, is how small it is. The gentry were, at most, a twentieth of the population, yet they managed to spread themselves over two-thirds of the countryside. This is a rough estimate and it would, perhaps, be best if the source of it were given here. In 1680, a survey was published with the following title:

Index Villaris; or, An Exact Register of all the Cities, Market-Towns, Parishes, Villages, Private Seats of the King, Nobility and Gentry.

The author of this large and on the whole remarkably reliable work, compiled among other sources from the records of the Hearth Tax, was John Adams, an eminent early maker of maps of our country and acquainted with Gregory King.[63] He gave each entry in his index a marking to indicate noblemen's seats: those with one, two, three or more than three, gentlemen's seats: those which had gentry in numbers unknown to the compiler; and those which had no gentry at all. Rough calculation from the evidence painstakingly recorded in this book shows that titled families, aristocratic or merely genteel, were indeed widespread.

If the English settlers in America felt that you could not move in the old country without coming up against the honourables and the worshipfuls, this survey shows that they had some justification.

It must be used with caution, of course, even if the original information was reliable. Noblemen had more seats than one: the same work names no less than twelve houses for Henry Somerset, Duke of Beaufort, Marquess and Earl of Worcester,

[62] *See page 253.*   [63] *See page 253.*

Number of Named Places	%	Description of Titled Residents		
13	2·3	Noblemen		
360	64·0	Gentlemen	33 (5·9%)	Baronets
			5 (0·9%)	Knights
			85 (15·1%)	Two Gentlemen or more
			174 (30·9%)	One Gentleman
			63 (11·2%)	Gentlemen, number unspecified
106	19·0	No titled residents recorded		
83	14·7	Not clear		
562	100·0			

Lord Herbert of Chepstow, Raglan and Gower. He had Worcester House in the Strand, in London; Badminton and Wollaston Grange in Gloucestershire; Monmouth Castle, Chepstow Castle, Raglan Castle, Chepstow Grange and Tintern Abbey in Monmouthshire; Crickhowel Castle and Tretower Castle in Brecknockshire and Swansea Castle in Glamorgan. The Duke of Norfolk had ten seats, including one in the very centre of the city of Norwich, castles in four English counties and Norfolk House in London. One Earl had nine seats, and one baron had eight. No family could possibly occupy so many houses at any one time, but in the villages where they stood, these baronial mansions spoke eloquently of the power of their owners. If you grew up under the shadow of a castle, or outside the walls of a lordly park, you knew who ruled England, even if the place was in the hands of tenants.[64]

Though by such means as this, the nobility managed to be present in something like every fortieth village, the baronets, knights, esquires and gentlemen were literally everywhere. Some counties had more in proportion than others; in some they were richer, in some they were more aristocratic; but they were to be found over the whole countryside, and in the towns and cities too.[65] Even in those villages we have mentioned where the yeomen held sway, dominating manor and church and deciding everything for themselves, there might well be some land held by an absent gentleman. And if there were none in the settlement, there would be some in the next hamlet, or village, and not far away a gentlemanly seat. The families of the ruling segment pressed, like the atmosphere,

[64] *See page 253.*   [65] *See page 253.*

evenly, over the whole face of England. It is time to look at the actual constitution of a village community to see how it felt.

On April 7th, 1676, the curate of the parish of Goodnestone-next-Wingham, in Kent, made his reply to the Archbishop of Canterbury, who wanted to know how many people lived under his care, and how many came to communion.[66] He chose to answer in unexpected detail, and presented his list under the following five heads; families of gentlemen, families of yeomen, families of tradesmen, families of labourers and families of poor men. There were 62 households at Goodnestone in that year, and they contained 277 people; the average size of household, therefore, was 4·47, rather higher than Gregory King's figure for the whole country. But the average is deceptive. This is how the households went:

Goodnestone-next-Wingham, Kent, April, 1676

Status of Households	No.	Range of sizes	Numbers of Persons	Numbers of Children	Numbers of Servants	Mean Size
Gentry	3	23, 2, 3	28	7	16	9·3
Yeomen	26	12–2	151	64	34	5·8
Tradesmen	9	8–1	35	16	2	3·9
Labourers	12	6–2	38	15	0	3·2
Poor Men	12	6–1	25	11	0	2·1
Totals	62	23–1	277	113	52	4·47

Approaching two-thirds of the people, 179 out of the 277, were living in the households of the gentry and the yeomen. Though the tradesmen, the labourers and the poor people made up 33 of the families, a clear majority, they contained less than one-third of the inhabitants. In this village community of Stuart times, the average size of family was small, on Victorian standards, but most people were, nevertheless, living in large households.

As we have already said, this was a universal law of society in the traditional world before the coming of industry. It did not mean that most people were born of rich parents who were of consequence and whose families or households were accordingly large, in a society where, as we have seen, social conse-

[66] *See page 254.*

quence went with size of household. Quite the reverse, for, in the village community of Goodnestone, no less than 52 persons, men, women and children, were servants, born in a humbler family, and yet living in another, more substantial one. This is 18·8 per cent of the whole population,[67] an offering, so to speak, of the children of the poor to those above them. But not always an offering to the ruling minority, to the gentry. In Goodnestone, the three gentle families had 16 servants between them, certainly a large number but the yeomanry had more; 23 of the yeomen households had servants, 34 in number, and even the tradesmen had two, a girl in one household and a youth in another. More than half of the 33 men and boys and the 19 women and girls who were servants in this community were serving the yeomenry, and they were serving them in husbandry, on the land and in the land-working households, not as personal menials, not as housemaids or cooks or kitchen helpers. Back at home, they left their parents with their younger brothers and sisters, or even alone in the cottages. Five of the 12 labourers' families consisted of man and wife alone, their children gone, or yet to be born: if they had gone, we now know where they were.

Gentlemen, yeomen, tradesmen, labourers and paupers, these were the social orders in the community according to the curate of Goodnestone. But they do not quite conform to the titles we have laid down in our last chapter; husbandmen are missing here, included, no doubt, among the yeomen by their curate. Once more, the vagaries of titles might mislead us, if it were not possible to prompt our reading of this revealing document from scores of others like it.[68] This peculiarity might obscure from us just how the inhabitant of Goodnestone would think of his community as a shape, as a society ranged in an order which was used by the priest in charge when he wrote out all the names.

Looking at the community under his spiritual care, he saw first and foremost the huge family of 23 people living at the manor-house. The head of the household was Edward Hales, Esq., who seems to have been a tenant of the London merchant family of Pennington, owners of the manor of Goodnestone, and, no doubt, of most of the land in the village.[69] In the squire's household there was his wife, six children and fifteen servants, nine boys and men and six women and girls.

[67] *See page 254.*　　[68] *See page 254.*　　[69] *See page 254.*

Also in Goodnestone were two other small households of gentry, whom we may imagine as satellites to the Hales. These brought up the total of people born of gentle blood in this community to 12. Only these individuals out of the 281 in his parish belonged, like the parson himself, to the fully literate minority, the people with some knowledge of the world beyond the parish of Goodnestone and this particular area of the county of Kent. But the land in the parish was not worked by the family of Hales, though the nine men and boys in the manor house must have tilled a good-sized manor farm, with the daily help, when it was required, of some of the twelve labourers living in the village. Most of the land was actually run by a dozen substantial families of yeomen and husbandmen whether or not it belonged to the squire. There were two families called Neame, one with 14 and the other with 7 in the household; three called Wanstall, 8, 8 and 3; William Tucker with 10, Richard Fuller and Stephen Church with 9 apiece, and John Pet with 8. These dozen families contained over a hundred people, a quarter of whom were servants, mostly young men. Squire and the larger yeomanry almost constituted the village community of Goodnestone-next-Wingham in 1676.

Not completely, of course, for over half its members have yet to be considered. There were 14 more families of the smaller yeomen or husbandmen, the nine tradesmen, and a dozen each of labourers and of paupers. There was, in addition, an institution which we have not yet mentioned, a hospital for the destitute, with one man and three women in it, bringing total population up to 281. It is not true to say that nobody apart from gentry and yeomanry counted for anything in the village community, though the pauper families and the hospitallers can be dismissed as of no positive account whatsoever. Each of the husbandmen, the tradesmen and even the labourers might have had some public life, as we have already seen. The male head of such a household could occupy office in the village community, and it is possible that by more than the usual back-breaking, unremitting toil, some cunning and intelligence, and above all considerable good fortune in the wives he married, in the relatives who died, a man of the grade of husbandman or labourer might, in his lifetime, become a substantial yeoman. We know that this happened, and we know that over the generations there was an astonishing interchange between the names of those peasant households which were prospering and those which were languishing. In the one community where we can actually trace the fortunes of each homestead at six separate points in one decade, the period between 1618 and 1628, we witness a considerable change in the size of some of them from year to year.[70]

But at any one time, and for any important purpose which could have a political effect beyond the little area of the village, these smaller households can be disregarded. The tradesmen, it is true, added a little variety to village society; there were two families of carpenters at Goodnestone, and one of these had a servant; two of brickmakers; one each headed by a weaver; a shoemaker; a hempster (probably a tailor), and a solitary woman calling herself a grocer. She is a little exceptional, but otherwise it is a normal list of occupations for a rural community, in the old world, if a little short: no smith of any sort is surprising, and it is to be supposed that the specialized agricultural callings like shepherd, or thatcher, or drover, are included here under the *Labourers*, perhaps even some under *Yeomen*.

There was, evidently, no inn at Goodnestone, and the priest, a curate, seems to have lived outside the village. This, again, was quite an ordinary thing, but a resident married parson, with his wife, children and servants, would have had a substantial effect on the little society there, and so might a prosperous hostelry on a highroad.[71] The most important possible difference would have been the absence of the family of Hales: a decision to live temporarily, or permanently, elsewhere would have considerably altered the social balance as would the death of the head of the family whilst his son was still a minor. But while the estate continued to be a whole, some tenant would occupy the great house, and the man in authority there, along with those at the head of the table in the twelve substantial yeomen households, ran the village. Nearly three hundred people went to make up the body of the community, but by far the most important member was its head, the squire, and a dozen or fifteen other mature, male heads of household provided all the other working parts.

A different opinion is possible on this point. The walls round the squire's park, the keepers who kept the villagers from his game, the separate pews, high box-pews in the

[70] *See page 254.*   [71] *See page 255.*

eighteenth century, which he and his household occupied in church, also operated to cut him off from the village community. An absentee, or a minor, a politician on the county or the national level, perpetually preoccupied with business more important than the fixing of the parish poor-rate or the upkeep of the river-bridge, could not be looked upon as the leader, the metaphorical father of village society. The literature of the Tudor and Stuart age is so full of laments about the decay of housekeeping, which meant, amongst so many other things, holding open-house for the tenantry. There are endless exhortations to the gentry to keep away from the city and the court. There must have been some grounds for the conviction that the country gentry were leaving their own people unsupported, without means of access to that greater world in which the gentry alone could freely move. But no choice between two such different opinions can be made for Edward Hales, Esquire, and the village of Goodnestone; the evidence will not yield it.

Social description, in fact, is a difficult and intricate task, often tedious to the reader. It is necessary to talk in terms of one community, for generalized statements lack the stuff of life, yet no community is entirely typical. We may have spent too much time already on our chosen village, and there are communities now open to examination whose working can be reconstructed in far greater detail. But the shape of society at Goodnestone is particularly well-marked, and it is a convenient model for all the rest. Each of the 40 villages in Kent in 1705 whose listings we have referred to before, seems to have been constructed, with variations, very much on this classic model.[72]

Shepherdswell, for example, though it had fewer people than Goodnestone, 160 instead of 281, contained more large families: one of 15, one of 13 and one of 10. There was a group of 6 working families, as we have called them, which each had 6 or 7 people, and the average overall was 5 to a household. At Hugham, the average was even higher, at 5·7, and out of 187 people there was one family of 20, one of 17 and two of 11. Lest it should be thought that these large households containing so many working servants, land-working servants, were typical of Kent only, and of the early eighteenth century, they may be compared with the situation at Ealing in 1599.[73] In

[72] *See page 255.*   [73] *See page 255.*

this still rural village the Goodnestone pattern was quite evident: 404 people in 85 families, an average of 4·75: a gentleman's family of 21, dominating all the rest, and 20 working families of between 7 and 11 apiece. In the village which we have got to know best of all, Clayworth in Nottinghamshire, the landed gentry had smaller establishments, between 7 and 10 apiece.[74] There were four of them in this village of about 400 people, and some of the yeomen (called 'Freeholders' and 'Farmers' here by the parson who described them) had families of a similar size. But the working families at Clayworth can easily be separated from those whose masters lived without manual exertion, and this distinction is generally obvious from the first glance at a list of members of a village community in pre-industrial England.

This sufficiently illustrates the difference in scale in these communities. In every one we have examined there was a substantial number of servants, though the actual proportion of the population in service seems to have varied considerably, for reasons we can only begin to guess at. The percentage could be as low as 4 and as high as 25, or even more, which begins to rival the rich London parishes of the 1690's where nearly a third of all the people could be servants.[75] In every one of the village communities too, the families of craftsmen, labourers and paupers tended to be smaller than the families of yeomen, and those of the gentry to be largest. The traffic in children from the humbler to the more successful families shows up in the relative numbers in the various groups. Poverty, in our day, or, at least, in the very recent past, was associated with large numbers of children, but the table for Goodnestone, on page 64, shows that in the seventeenth century exactly the reverse was true. The richer you were, the more children you had in your household. In this village in 1676, the gentry with children had an average of 3·5 in their families, the yeomen 2·9, the tradesmen 2·3, the labourers 2·1 and the paupers 1·8.

These figures from Goodnestone are too good to be true and it is common enough to find humble families with many children at home, too many for the meagre resources of the wage-earner and a promise of destitution for his widow if he should die too soon. Nevertheless, the association of few children with modest position and resources is almost as

[74] *See page 255.*   [75] *See page 255.*

marked a feature of social structure in the traditional world as the association of smaller families generally with the poor. It was not simply a matter of the poor offering up their children to the rich as servants; they probably also had fewer children born to them, and of those which were born, fewer survived. It is likely that works on the expectation of life and size of the biological family will confirm what early impressions seem to show, which is that poor men and their wives could not expect to live together long enough to have as many offspring as the rich. This loss of potential labour-power was a matter of consequence, for it always must be remembered that the actual work on most of the plots of land was done by the working family, the man, his wife and children.

At harvest-time, of course, there was a difference: the individual farming family could no longer cope with the work. From the making of the hay in June until the winning of the corn and pease in late September, every able-bodied person in the village community was at work on everyone's land. How much co-operation there was is difficult to say, but when the crisis of the agricultural year came round, right up to the time of mechanized farming, the village acted as a community. When all was in, there was harvest home.

It is usual, in most places, after they get all the pease pulled or the last grain down, to invite all the workfolks and their wives (that helped them that harvest) to supper, and then they have puddings, bacon, or boiled beef, flesh or apple pies, and then cream brought in platters, and every one a spoon; then after all they have hot cakes and ale; for they bake cakes and send for ale against that time: some will cut their cake and put it into the cream, and this feast is called cream-pot, or cream-kit; for on the morning that they get all done the workfolks will ask their dames if they have good store of cream and say they must have the cream-kit anon.[76]

This was the Yorkshire custom in the 1640's when it was necessary, at harvest-time, to go even beyond the carpenters, the wheelwrights and the millers, in order to bring in the sheaves off the fields. The richer men had to make a home in the barns during harvest for folk, pastoral in their ways, who came down from the wild moorland. Migration of labour at harvest was common enough in the eighteenth century,

[76] *See page 255.*

but eating and drinking together was a universal characteristic of rural life at all times. Whatever the churchwardens
or the overseers of the poor did, when the church-bell was
rung in celebration, or the churchyard mowed, there was an
entry in the ill-written accounts for ale drunk on the occasion.[77] The meticulous, unpopular Rector of Clayworth in
the last quarter of the seventeenth century, entertained the
husbandry of the two settlements in his parish separately to
dinner every year.

When the curate of Goodnestone returned the names of all
his parishioners in April, 1676, 'according to their families,
according to their quality and according to their religion', he
did as he was bid and told his lordship, the bishop, how many
of them had been to holy communion that Eastertide. Apart
from sixteen exceptions every person in the community known
by their priest to be qualified for the sacrament had actually
taken it at some time during the festival, which fell in that
year between March 19th and 26th: 128 people communicated
that is to say, out of a population of 281. Even the defaulters
had promised to make amends at Whitsuntide, all but the one
family in the village which was nonconformist. But William
Wanstall, senior, one of the absentees, was given no such grace;
he had been 'excluded the Holy Sacrament for his notorious
drunkenness, but since hath promised reformation'. Francis
Nicholson, the priest-in-charge, was evidently a devoted pas-
tor, for he could give an account of every one of the absentees.
Mrs Elizabeth Richards, the widowed head of one of the households of gentry, was excused as 'melancholy', and Barbara
Pain since she was 'under a dismal calamity, the unnatural
death of her husband', who had left her at the head of a
yeoman family, three children and two servants.[78]

This very remarkable record of communicants draws attention to a feature of the village community and of the whole
of the world we have now half-forgotten which has scarcely
been mentioned so far. All our ancestors were literal Christian
believers, all of the time. Not only zealous priests, such as
Francis Nicholson, not only serious-minded laymen, but also
the intellectuals and the publicly responsible looked on the
Christian religion as the explanation of life, and on religious
service as its proper end. Not everyone was equally devout, of
course, and it would be simple-minded to suppose that none of

[77] *See page 255.*   [78] *See page 255.*

these villagers ever had their doubts. Much of their devotion
must have been formal, and some of it mere conformity. But
their world was a Christian world and their religious activity
was spontaneous, not forced on them from above. When
Francis Nicholson refused the cup to William Wanstall, in
March, 1676, the scores of other people in the church that
morning no doubt approved of what he did, as no doubt
Wanstall deserved this very public rebuke. When William
Sampson, the formidable Rector of Clayworth, did exactly the
same thing in April, 1679, to Ralph Meers and Anne Fenton
'upon a common fame that they lived and lodged together, not
being married', he also had the community behind him. He
knew what he was doing too, for Anne Fenton's first baby was
christened two months' later, only a week or two, presumably,
after she had married Ralph Meers.[79]

It has been shown only very recently how it came about that
the mass of the English people lost their Christian belief, and
how religion came to be a middle-class matter. When the
arrival of industry created huge societies of persons in the
towns with an entirely different outlook from these Stuart
villagers, practically no one went to church, not if he was
working class and was left untouched by religious emotion.[80]
Christianity was no longer in the social air which everyone
breathed together, rich and poor, gentleman, husbandman,
artificer, labourer and pauper. So much has been written
about the abuses of the clergy in earlier times, so much about
the controversies and doubts, about the revivals, especially
the Wesleyan revival, that the religious attitude of common
folk has been lost sight of. Perhaps the twelve labourers who
lived at Goodnestone in 1676 did not know very clearly what
Our Lord's Supper meant, and perhaps they felt that it would
displease Squire Hales if they stayed away, but every single
one of them took communion. Their descendants in the slums
of London in the 1830's, '40's and '50's did not do so: they
already looked on Christianity as belonging to the rural
world which they had lost. It was something for their employers, something for the respectable, which, perhaps, they
might go in for if ever they attained respectability and com-
fort. This was not true of the hard-working, needy, half-
starved labourers of pre-industrial times.

At Clayworth, at that same Eastertide of 1676, an even

[79] *See page 255.*   [80] *See page 256.*

greater proportion of the villagers took the sacrament than at Goodnestone, 200 out of 401. How powerful the effect of even formal Christianity could be is shown by an anecdote which Sampson records of a servant-boy there whose mother died. The meagre wages of servants, some fifty shillings a year for a skilled woman and five pounds for a grown man, were subject to tithe in this village, and the Rector was in combat with masters, maids, and men for the money. This poor lad let his side down by coming and paying 'fully for his wages at one farthing i' the shilling. The occasion of his mother's death brought him to an honest mind'. But later in his ministry, Sampson found that the number of communicants went down to about 125, though the population did not seem to fall. This is about the same proportion as at Cogenhoe, in 1612, when the Rector there recorded 63 'Communicants upon Easter Day', just over half the qualified adults. This may be something like the normal number of the members of English village communities attending the chief festival of the Church in the days before the coming of industry, but there are plenty of indications from other places and in less detailed sources, of a much smaller attendance.[81]

Perhaps it is more than usually dangerous to judge of religious life from the few scattered records of this sort which have so far been found and examined. Perhaps it may turn out in the end that Christianity was ceasing to be the most important activity of all communities of men and women before ever industrialization transformed the social scene. But we shall see in due course how powerful was the control of Christian belief and imperatives over the sexual habits of the peasantry, exercised not so much by the authority of parson and ecclesiastical court as by the force of universally held opinion. Once men began to differ over religion, the life of the community was affected, and the whole history of the seventeenth century, local and national, was perpetually vexed by the quarrel between the Puritan and the traditionalists, just as Tudor England had been disturbed by the Reformation itself. But the separatists were Christians too. The intensity of their convictions and the fierceness of their protest testify to the secure hold which Christianity had over everyone. The failure of the Puritan Commonwealth in England is too easily interpreted as a weakening of Christian beliefs. After all, the

[81] *See page 256.*

Puritan policy succeeded in New England, where far fewer of
the settlers have turned out to be Puritans than was once
supposed.

Every meeting of the village community took place in the
Church, if there was a church or chapel close enough. At Clayworth every Easter Monday, the village community met there
and chose the three churchwardens, two for the *town*, that is
Clayworth itself, and one for Wiseton, the separate hamlet
within the parish; we have seen that many, perhaps most,
parishes were geographically divided like this. Two overseers
of the poor were chosen for Clayworth as well as two 'burrough
men', who might elsewhere be constables, but here they had
agricultural duties too. Only male heads of households were
eligible to serve, but gentlemen, freeholders (or yeomen),
husbandmen and labourers are all found recorded as selected
for each office in the Clayworth Town Book.[82]

This function of the church building as a meeting place for
all the purposes of the community, must be stressed. Here they
were, these farming householders, not all of whom could read,
sitting in the building put up by their fore-runners many
centuries before, and which they, in their turn, annually
repaired and even beautified. In the place where they came so
often to Christian service they chose their neighbours for the
traditional offices, secular and spiritual. When English villagers
found themselves in America, one of the first buildings which
they put up for the new village was the *Meeting House*, for
the town meeting had a great deal to decide in starting all anew.
The *Meeting House* was also, of course, the Christian church of
the village being born.[83]

The only public appearance of women and children, almost
their only expedition outside the circle of the family, was at
service in Church. Wives and maidservants might take and sell
their poultry and their eggs to market, or even their apples and
cherries, but otherwise they stayed at home. It has already
been emphasized that ordinary people did not usually find
themselves in a group inside a building, larger than the household, except in church. For the menfolk, especially for the
substantial ones, there were the occasional meetings of the
manor-courts, which still controlled agriculture over most of
the countryside. In some places, these meetings were perhaps
as important as the Easter Monday gathering in the Saxon-

[82] *See page 256.*   [83] *See page 256.*

towered church of Saint Peter at Clayworth every year. For
the men, too, there were the alehouses, much too famous in
popular history as the poor man's parliament. The single
village inn seems in fact to have been rare; most drinking was
done in the cottages of people having permission from the
magistrates to keep an alehouse, on the strict understanding
that there was to be no tippling and that no liquor was to
change hands during time of divine service.[84] The alewife, for
it was often a widow brewing for sale what most women had
to brew for their own households, did not even have to have a
painted sign, in that age when a sign was all that an illiterate
could recognize. All she had to do was to hang a bush outside
her door.

But the renowned English inn was not the creation of
Samuel Johnson and Charles Dickens. Outside London it was
the hostelry for travellers, placed on the important roads and
common in a country where travel was so painfully slow, but
not intended first and foremost for the local people. It could
be a large and important institution, on the scale of life which
was then the rule, and have an effect on the locality. An alehouse at Harefield in Middlesex in 1699 – it was one of four in
this village and not granted the title of inn by the man who
made the list of the community – was kept by John and
Catharine Baily, and they had in their house the largest
family of grown and growing children we have yet traced in
pre-industrial England. They had twelve children alive, aged
from two to twenty-eight; the two eldest had left home, but
of the ten who were left, six were above the age of twelve,
all old enough to help run the family establishment, with their
aunt, Catharine Baily's sister, who lived there as well. No need
of any servants for John Baily, who was also a smith. Meanwhile his potential rival, the New Inn at Harefield, was marked
'Empty not finisht'.[85]

There was plenty of drinking done in the village community,
and not all of it in celebration of some activity or meeting.
Men like Goodman William Wanstall, the excommunicated
drunkard of Goodnestone, are met with fairly often. (*Goodman*
was used of a substantial householder who was not a *Mr* and
Goodwife, or *Goody* for his partner or his widow.) There is a
famous legend from Malmesbury, in Wiltshire, of Sir Thomas
Hobbes the curate of St Mary's about the time of the Spanish

[84] *See page 256.*   [85] *See page 256.*

Armada and father of Thomas Hobbes, the great philosopher. (*Sir,* as Shakespeare used it, could mean a clergyman as well as a knight.) 'Trafells is Troumps', he is supposed to have bawled out to his congregation one Sunday morning, starting suddenly from his slumber in the pulpit, after all Saturday night playing cards with the citizens of that little market-town. Trafells was a word for clubs. Whether this happened or not,[86] it would be wrong to think of the alehouse at this time as playing the part which it came to play for working men in early industrial towns, where it was to be the only meeting place at their disposal, and almost the only social institution. In Francis Place's world the public house was in place of the church as well as the alehouse in the pre-industrial village.

In 1688 parson Sampson made a second list of all the in-habitants of the village of Clayworth, twelve years after the one which, like the curate of Goodnestone, he had drawn up for the ecclesiastical census of 1676. This time he wrote it out, not alphabetically, *ad evitandam invidiam* – to avoid envy – as he did the first, but in order of social importance like most of the other listings we have found. The gentleman's family had returned into residence after a minority and Sampson could boldly begin: 'Mr Thomas Wawen, Lord of the Soil.' So the young gentleman was, in spite of the fact that nothing like half of the land at Clayworth belonged to him.[87] His overlordship consisted in the traditional position of the lord of the manor, and in the power which he had over the tenants of the land he did own.

Like every other landlord, Thomas Wawen was to some degree bound by manorial custom which had the force of local law, and general custom. This might tie his hands as to the length and conditions of his leases, even the amount of his rents. Custom, what his neighbours, the village generally, thought, as well as universal expectation, would inevitably influence him in making the many other decisions open to him. He had to decide, to begin with, how much of his land he would keep under his own hand, as the saying was, and work from his house with his servants. Then he had to determine how much he would rely on those servants, or how much work he would get done by labourers coming in from the village and working their day's work on his land. Another decision to be

[86] *See page 256.*   [87] *See page 257.*

made was whether he would feed such day-labourers during their working-time or pay them extra so that they could bring their own food. If he had to *table* them, then his housekeeping would have to be on a scale to correspond with his obligations. The only way for him to avoid having his workers in his house altogether would be either to let all his land and buy his provisions, a possible but not very easy prospect, or to make arrangements for one or other of the local husbandmen, workers of the land, to come and undertake all the operations on his home farm.[88]

A landlord who lived away from the community in another of his houses, or one who lived in London in hired accommodation and took no responsibility for running any of his land, would of course tend to let as much of his estate as he could. His bailiff or his tenant would, no doubt, also get as much of the work done as possible by putting it out 'to task'. The economically-minded amongst the owners of land, moreover, might reckon precisely how much more profitable it would be to make one choice or another amongst those we have listed. But the social duty of every 'Lord of the Soil' was made quite plain to him: he was expected to reside in his manor-house or at least in one of those he owned. He, or his resident tenant, was also firmly expected to work as much of the home-farmland as possible, maintain a household-full of servants and keep up a table for the day-labourers. It was not by any means a matter of custom alone. Raising crops and tending stock go on in the night as well as the day, and this gave the household servant system a permanent advantage. Before the coming of the bicycle and the paved highway, there was a fixed distance from the labourer's cottage beyond which a full day's work was out of the question – it took too long to get there and back. These were some of the conditions which made it impossible for the landowner to act as entrepreneur in the modern fashion, to run their land as our farmers do, using daytime labour alone, hired from outside the house, on the model of the business or the factory.

Even in the twentieth century the limits to economic rationalism in farming are still in evidence, in the socialist as well as in the capitalist areas of the world. But three hundred years ago, this issue could scarcely arise. Working the land, managing, nurturing a 'family' were then one and the same thing,

[88] *See page 257.*

and could no more be 'rationalized' than the cherishing of a wife or the bringing up of children. Even the nobleman with several seats in the countryside, and with a strong preference for living in his London house on his rents, recognized this sometimes irksome fact. Hence the feeling about the 'country' in opposition to the 'Town', and hence a great deal of aristocratic guilt and ambivalence. Hence, also, the plots of many of our English dramas, of the Elizabethan age, or of the time of the Restoration: and many of the emotional assumptions and overtones of our literature. 'I wish you were married and living in the country,' said Lord Rochester, the rake, to the cur which had bitten him. Even he could find no worse an imprecation.[89] Smaller men, right down to the humblest husbandman, or the labourer on his cottage patch, had no occasion to see any separation whatsoever between keeping house and working the soil.

The village community was, as we have said, the group of households at the centre of a particular area of cultivated land. It might or might not be a manor, have its own church, or have one owner. If it did have a single owner, he might work it all himself, with one large household,[90] or, at least, as one estate. More probably, he let it out, either in large parcels, or in some large lots and some small (presumably the most usual), or all in small holdings. Apart from the large landowner or landowners, a village might, and usually did, contain a mixture of freeholders and tenants, again some in a big and some in a small way. There would also be a number of families, often a sizeable minority, with only a scrap of land round a cottage, or no land at all. The accepted view seems to be that these were on the increase as the eighteenth century drew near, but the demonstration of this for the whole country would be a very difficult undertaking. These were the families not only of the labourers and the paupers, but of most of the craftsmen as well, the masons and the ploughwrights, the weavers, the tailors, the cobblers, the carpenters and the rest.

But whatever the official description and the distribution of property and the numbers of the callings represented in it, as a community the village consisted of households in association. To the facts of geography, being together in the one place, were added all the bonds which are forged between human beings when they are permanently alongside each other; bonds

[89] *See page 257.*   [90] *See page 257.*

of intermarriage and of kinship, of common ancestry and common experience and of friendship and co-operation in matters of common concern. Consequence within the community went with weight of responsibility and with wealth; its expression was the size of the agrarian household which a man had to keep in operation.

The difficulties of talking about typicality have already been mentioned, and what follows must be read with that in mind. Most of the yeomen, husbandmen, labourers, artificers and paupers, from whom we nearly all descend, lived in the village community which we have attempted to describe. They grew up in a society of 300, 400 or 500 strong, perhaps more often in a hamlet separated from other hamlets which made up the parish, than in a village which was one group of houses side by side. From their earliest years, they must have been conscious of the standing of the family into which they were born, within a group of other familes, sometimes ten, sometimes twenty, more often thirty, forty or fifty altogether. If they came from the lower families, within a dozen years of birth they might find themselves as servants in the larger families. If they grew up in more prosperous and important households, they would always be conscious that there were other people round them who were not their brothers and sisters, servants who were not often blood relatives at all. Only a small number in the middle can have been outside this interchange of persons as servants. This was the motion up and down which gave vertical structure to the whole. It demonstrates how the village community was a patriarchal matter, even if it cannot itself have been a family.

There are complications which go beyond the present purpose and uncertainties which are inevitable in social descriptions in this attempt to analyse the village community. It may be thought surprising that no very clear distinction for sociological purposes can be drawn along the jurisdictional lines which our ancestors themselves laid down and insisted upon. The truth is that for our purpose a group of households did not have to be a parish, or a manor, to be a unit, and the complications of definition do not finally matter when we try to make an imaginative judgement of the social experience of individuals. The fact, to which we shall come in due course,[91] that so much geographical movement went on between village

[91] *See page 257.*

communities, makes very little difference either. To be a social unit conscious of itself, and removed, distinct from others, it was not necessary for the village community to be cut off from interchange with its companions. On the contrary; it was in perpetual negotiation with its neighbours, and this was an essential feature of its individuality. But each village community, we have claimed, played a part in the whole national community of the country only through the gentry. We have also stated that no group inside a village could possibly have threatened the supremacy of its ruling structure. These are questions to which we shall have to return.

Everyday Life in the Old World

Births, Marriages and Deaths
Chapter 4

> *My child is yet a stranger in the world*
> *She hath not seen the change of fourteen years*
> *Let two more summers wither in their pride*
> *Ere we may think her ripe to be a bride.*

Capulet says this in the second scene of Romeo and Juliet.
But whatever he said and whatever he felt, his child Juliet
did take Romeo to husband at about her fourteenth birthday.
Not that this was too young for marriage in her mother's
opinion, but marriage to Romeo, a Montague, would have been
wrong at any age. She says to her daughter

> *Well, think of marriage now; younger than you,*
> *Here in Verona, ladies of esteem,*
> *Are made already mothers. By my count*
> *I was your mother much upon these years*
> *That you are now a maid.*

So she had been married at twelve, or early thirteen, and all
those other ladies of Verona also. Miranda was married in her
fifteenth year in the *Tempest*. It all seems clear and consistent
enough. The women in Shakespeare's plays, and so presumably the Englishwomen of Shakespeare's day, might marry
in their early teens, or even before that, and very often did
so.[92]

Yet this is not true. We have examined every record we can
find to test it and they all declare that, in Elizabethan and
Jacobean England, marriage was rare at these early ages and
not as common in the late teens as it is now. At twelve
marriage as we understand it was virtually unknown.

Some of the evidence for these blank statements will have
to be presented here and we shall have to discuss the possible
differences in what constituted marriage. See Chapter 6 below
which considers the issue of *espousals*, a promise which became
marriage as we understand it if sexual intercourse took place.
People could marry by licence as well as by banns in England

[92] *See page 258.*

then, just as they still can in the Church of England today.
They had to apply for the licence to the bishop of the diocese
they lived in, and very often they were required to give their
ages; the reason was that no one under 21 could be married
by the Church without his parents' permission: it was a grave
sin to do so at an older age without good reason. We have
examined a thousand licences containing the ages of the
applicants, issued by the diocese of Canterbury between 1619
and 1660 to people marrying for the first time.[93] One woman
gave her age as 13, four as 15, twelve as 16: all the rest were
17 and over, and 966 of the women got married for the first
time after the age of 19, that is nearly 85 per cent. The commonest age of first marriage for women in this sample was 22,
and the median age – the age below which as many got married
as got married above it – was about $22\frac{3}{4}$: the average, mean
age was about 24. Bridegrooms were something like three
years older than brides, though some of the unions recorded
show an extraordinary discrepancy in age. Only ten men
married below the age of 20, two of them at 18, and the most
common age was 24; the median age was something like $25\frac{1}{2}$
and the mean age over $27\frac{3}{4}$.

Put in the familiar form we use in conversation, the average
age of these Elizabethan and Jacobean brides was something
like 24 and the average of bridegrooms was nearly 28. Surely
these figures by themselves ought to be sufficient to dispel
belief that our ancestors married much younger than we do.

But the literary references are so straightforward, and
Shakespeare at least so influential that we must go further:
there seems to be some desire in our day to believe in this
particular mistake. Did the gentry marry early? – after all
Romeo and Juliet were not ordinary people.

This is more difficult to test at present, because the numbers
are so small, but the indications are that the privileged did
marry sooner than the rest of the population; there is some
suggestion too that the higher the social status, the younger
age at first marriage. But the gap is not very wide between the
rich and the ordinary people, particularly for bridegrooms. It
decidedly does not confirm the impression made by Shakespeare and the other literary sources. Their evidence must be
called systematically deceptive in this matter. It is best to
look at the facts in a table.

[93] *See page 258.*

Mean Age at First Marriage

	Mean age of Brides	Mean age of Bridegrooms
All applicants for licences, Diocese of Canterbury, 1619–60 (1,082 brides, 1,070 bridegrooms)	23·95	26·87
Gentry only amongst Canterbury applicants (84 brides, 84 bridegrooms)	21·66	26·54
Marriages of nobles,* from about 1600 to about 1625 (325 brides, 313 bridegrooms)	19·39	24·28
Marriages of nobles,* from about 1625 to about 1650 (510 brides, 403 bridegrooms)	20·67	25·99

* Kindly communicated by Mr T. H. Hollingsworth, of the University of Glasgow.[94]

There are substantial differences in this table and the more detailed figures bear them out. Twice as high a proportion of girls from gentle families in the Canterbury licences got married under the age of twenty as did in the sample as a whole. The child bride of thirteen and two of the four fifteen-year-olds we have already cited were gentlewomen. But even for the nobility the contrast with the population at large was not very dramatic, and the figures show that aristocrats tended to marry later as the Stuart age drew on. Better evidence will be available very soon, but when everything now known is added to that presented here the conclusion is inescapable. It is not true to say that in earlier times, in the world we have lost as we have called it, people, either ordinary or privileged, married younger then we marry now. If anything they were older, certainly very much older in relation to their expectation of life.

Juliet's mother's statement is a little extraordinary in quite another way. It is common knowledge now that the age of sexual maturity in women has fallen surprisingly during the last two or three generations in Western countries, and is falling now, perhaps even more rapidly. In Sweden in 1905 girls began to menstruate at 15·7 years, by 1949 the age had fallen to 14·1. In the United States the age of menarche as it is called was already as low as 14·1 years in 1904, but in 1951 it was 12·9. In Norway, which has the longest record yet published, it was 17·1 in 1850 and 13·5 in 1951, and the age in

[94] *See page 258.*

England in the later year was just about the same.[95] If Lady Capulet and her daughter were sexually mature and capable of having children at an earlier age four hundred years ago than women are today in most countries, then they must have been very exceptional indeed. And if the age of sexual maturity for women in Norway in 1850 is any indication of what it was in Elizabethan England, it is impossible that the general age of marriage can have been anything like as low as twelve, thirteen or fourteen. The elementary facts of life were against it.

It should not be long before we have very much better factual foundation for statements of this sort, which may seem a little odd as an approach to the everyday life of our ancestors, but which do concern their habitual behaviour and the whole course of their lives. Before this point is pursued, there is even more to be said about Romeo and Juliet and the facts about sexuality which are at issue in that drama.

First of all there is the possibility that Shakespeare was deliberately writing a play about love and marriage amongst boys and girls. Scholars have discovered that he actually reduced Juliet's age; in the poem containing the plot for the play, Arthur Broke's *Romeus and Juliet*, published in 1562, Juliet was sixteen. Four years later another author who told the story, William Painter in his collection of novels *The Palace of Pleasure*, made Juliet eighteen years old. When Shakespeare came to adapt it thirty years afterwards he may possibly have had to reduce the heroine's age to suit the boy-actor who was to play her part, but some of his other heroines seem to be mature enough, Viola in *Twelfth Night* for example. The insistence on Juliet's being a young girl looks quite deliberate.

Since this is a point of some importance to our whole attitude to the life of our ancestors, their romantic life that is to say as well as their everyday outlook and appearance, we ought perhaps to go a little further into Shakespeare's literary contemporaries and into some of the other evidence bearing on the point. There is a passage in Henry Porter's comedy *Two Angry Women of Abington*, 1599, which suggests that marriage in the middle teens was familiar enough, if not marriage before that. Mall, a very willing young woman, is speaking. Even at fourteen she had thought time was dawdling since she still had no husband, and she continues:

[95] *See page 258.*

> *Good Lord, thought I, fifteen will ne'er be here,*
> *For I have heard my mother say that then*
> *Pretty maids were fit for handsome men.*
> *Fifteen past, sixteen and seventeen too,*
> *What, thought I, will not this husband do?*
> *Will no man marry me?*

Mall certainly seems to have been nubile well before her wedding-day: the hint of uncertainty as to the age when a girl would be physically fit for marriage must be noticed. Another character in the drama of that decade makes a rather different complaint: 'They study twenty years together to make us grow straight as a wand, and then marry us off to men we do not like' (Lyly, *Mother Bombie*, 1594).[96] Shakespeare himself gives us further examples of child-marriage: Marina in *Pericles* is fourteen years old when she is taken to the brothel, rescued and betrothed to Lysimachus, and Perdita in the *Winter's Tale* is sixteen.*

It is true that children did marry in Tudor England, though under exceptional circumstances, and the marriage was of a kind we should scarcely recognize. Life was uncertain and the head of the household at any one time had to be so much concerned with the succession, that the marriage partner to be taken by the heir apparent was always a matter of the first importance where there was an estate and name to be safeguarded. In 1593, Robert Furse, of Moreshead in Devonshire, a substantial yeoman on his way up in the world and engaged like every other yeoman of ability in building up his family, matched his son at the age of nine years and three months to Susan Alford, an orphan and the ward of a kinsman: the marriage was to take place at the age of fifteen.[97] In this instance either death intervened or one or other of the children exercised the undoubted right not to carry out the bargain made for them by their parents and guardians, for no marriage took place. This was obviously a fairly usual arrangement, and the postponement of the actual union must be noted.

The records of the diocesan courts, which deal with disputes over marriage, contain numbers of cases of affianced minors, some of whom did actually live together and were expected to

[96] *See page 259.*   [97] *See page 259.*

* *I am indebted to Dr Muriel Bradbrook, Vice-Mistress of Girton College, Cambridge, for all the literary references to child-marriage quoted above, and the discussion of them is hers.*

have done so. Frederick Furnivall, that marvellous Victorian literary antiquarian, published in 1897 for his Early English Text Society a volume with the title *Child Marriages, Divorces and Ratifications, etc.*, which may itself have done much to foster the tradition that the marriage of children was an ordinary occurrence in Tudor times. In the single Diocese of Chester between the years 1561 and 1566 he found documents concerning some thirty couples married early, some of them at a very early age indeed; there were matches between babes-in-arms, matches between teen-agers, matches between children entirely unwilling to live with each other. One poor lad of eleven or twelve, according to the testimony of his bride of thirteen or fourteen, was brought to bed with her weeping to go home with his father, 'and there lay still till in the morning ... with his back towards her all night'. 'He never touched her bare skin', so he himself affirmed.

We could scarcely expect the exuberant Furnivall to put these intriguing facts into any sort of numerical proportion. If we do it for him we can estimate that well over 10,000 weddings must in fact have taken place in the Diocese of Chester during the six years in question. These wretched children cannot, therefore, have made up one-half of one per cent of all persons marrying in that area in that period. In nearly all the documents which Furnivall prints it is made plain that the settlement of property was at issue. None of the married children mentioned lived together until late in their teens, and it is hinted that some were not fit to do so even then.

Child-marriages of this kind may well have been commoner in the sixteenth century than in the seventeenth. But whatever their nature and purpose they cannot be called representative of the marriages of the great majority who had no land, no houses and no property worth assuring in this peculiar fashion. The possibility still remains that it was part of Shakespeare's dramatic intention to make Romeo and Juliet, and perhaps some of his other heroes and heroines too, younger than was usual in his day. If anything, legal and biographical evidence of the kind presented by Furnivall tends to give substance to the claim that literary evidence may be systematically deceptive in these matters. Certainly some of the witnesses to the Chester cases remarked in surprise and disapproval of the youth of the parties concerned; they knew they were talking of extraordinary people. The Elizabethan writers certainly give no hint that this was what they were doing. But then poets, dramatists and novelists are seldom commenting on ordinary people. Even when the effect they strive for is precisely this, they often succeed in making heroes and heroines completely out of the ordinary.

It is true, and very important to the social historian, that the spontaneous assumptions in the literature of any age, the behaviour of the minor characters, the conventions against which irony and humour must be understood, reveal with great precision facts of considerable interest about the structure of society. We shall find ourselves arguing in something like this way from time to time in this essay. But it is indeed hazardous to infer an institution or a habit characteristic of a whole society or a whole era from the central character of a literary work and its story, from *Pamela*, for example, or from Elizabeth Bennett in *Pride and Prejudice* just as much as from Juliet or Viola. The outcome may be to make people believe that what was the entirely exceptional, was in fact the perfectly normal. This is what seems to have happened with the Capulet ladies and the Elizabethan age of marriage. It is easy to see how a very similar distortion might come about if some future historian used *Lolita* or *West Side Story* as a source book for our own sexual habits, uncorrected by other evidence unliterary and statistical.

This is a cogent argument in favour of statistical awareness, and of the sociological imagination, in studies of this sort. Conventional historical or literary inference is not enough. Statistical awareness provides the point for a further reflection on Lady Capulet and her daughter. It is, in fact, just possible that the 'Old Lady', as one of her speech headings called her, could have been physiologically mature enough to conceive the young one in her thirteenth or her fourteenth year. But it could have happened, so it may turn out, only because of her privileged circumstances and particular physique.

Elizabeth Manners married the second Earl of Exeter in 1589 at thirteen years old, a month or so either way; she had a child at about fourteen years five months.* Lady Capulet and her companions amongst the matrons of Verona could have been just like this young English noblewoman of Shakespeare's own day – though a little more precocious even than

* *I owe this entirely to the researches of Mr Hollingsworth and it is reproduced with his permission.*

she. Moreover none of the figures which have been mentioned must be thought of as precise indications of the one age only at which women reached maturity. They are all *median* ages, the middle point about which *actual* ages range themselves.

The particular physique of individuals, and also probably their general level of health and nutrition, would decide whether the age of maturity fell below or above the median. The fact that the median was 17·1 in Norway in 1850 does not mean that sexual maturity never arrived at 15, 14, or even 13 or 12. It only states that it arrived as many times before 17·1 years in the group examined as it arrived after that age. Juliet then could conceivably have been capable of bearing children even though the median age of the menarche for girls of that age generally was in her day four or five years later than the age she had reached when she met Romeo. But it also means, of course, that a considerable proportion of her contemporaries, particularly the girls in humble families, would have had to wait until the age of 18, 19 or even 20 before the arrival of maturity.

All this may seem to be an unnecessary complication of the task of the sociological historian at this early stage in his studies, and to have very little to do with an introductory essay of this type. But everything we can get to know about differences between the privileged people and the rest in pre-industrial times is of significance, and perhaps especially in this matter, for the following reason. The fall in the age of the menarch in the twentieth century is a puzzle to the physiologists, and is susceptible of more than one explanation, or may be due to a combination of more than one set of circumstances. The better feeding and superior living conditions generally of our own day look as if they must have something to do with the fact that adult height has been increasing by a centimetre a decade all over Western Europe since 1850. Certainly there must be some connection between nurture and physical achievement in order to explain why there was a difference of three and a half inches in height and eleven and a half pounds in weight between the boys from the poorest and the boys from the best-off working-class homes in the city of York in 1899.[98] When these considerations are taken back into pre-industrial society, the implications are clear. Only the privileged few fed as well, or lived as comfortably, in earlier times as we all do

[98] *See page 259.*

now, though the health of even the best provided for was exceedingly precarious even then. It begins to look, therefore, as if only people like Lady Capulet and her daughter could ordinarily hope to be mature enough to marry, or to have children anyway, at thirteen or fourteen.

Now if this was true of all privileged people in the world we have lost, of all members of the ruling stratum as we have called it, in relation to the rest, and of the gentry as a society in relation to those below them in the scale, then it implies a very remarkable contrast between the two sections of the population. The privileged must have been taller, heavier, better developed and earlier to mature than the rest; the males must have had beards and broken voices much sooner, the women must have become full women much more quickly.

Privileged persons married a little earlier than the rest of the population, and it is possible that they also on the average matured somewhat earlier too. We have spelt out syllable by syllable the analysis of this particular element of the effect upon us today of our dim, half-knowledge of the past of our society in order to provide one example of the type of evidence used throughout this study. It must be obvious how little progress has yet been made in exploiting that evidence and how much more can and will be known as time goes on. At present there is a perpetual challenge to the imagination to find illuminating questions to ask of the evidence and ways of answering them properly.

The delusion about marriageable age is, perhaps, the most conspicuous of all the errors we seem to want to make about everyday life in the old world, but is not the only one. More far reaching in its consequences for the view we take of ourselves, and the plans we make for our society and its welfare, is the supposition which has already been extensively discussed, that the family group in the pre-industrial world was large. It is erroneously believed that it was large because it contained whole groups of kinsfolk living together. The impression seems to be that sons and daughters stayed with their parents after marriage and had their children there: therefore the family group must often have been multi-generational. What after all does patriarch mean if not the ancient, bearded head of such a family group? It is assumed that when a woman's husband died she returned to her original family group and was supported by it. A widowed mother might live with her married daughter, or a family would support various in-laws. It is also said that there would also be joint families of another type, because two married couples would often find it more convenient to share one household, just as perhaps they shared one plot of land. In any case, and this seems to be the most deep-seated and important generalization of all, in the familial, patriarchal world the family was the source of welfare. Sickness, unemployment, bereavement were all the responsibility of the family, and so to a large extent was education. To fulfil all these functions the family in the old world would have had to be large. Something like this seems to be the general impression of family life among our ancestors.

But their families were *not* large; at least the average family was relatively small. The facts which we have referred to, showing that a very high proportion of people actually lived in large families although the average size was small, complicate the picture. Furthermore, the general rule which governed the size and the constitution of the family has yet to be laid down.

This rule is as follows: no two married couples or more went to make up a family group; whether parents and children, brothers and sisters, employers and servants or married couples associated only for convenience.[99] When a son got married he left the family of his parents and started a family of his own. If he was not in a position to do this, then he could not get married, nor could his sister unless the man who was to take her for his bride was also in a position to start a new family.

But it has been insisted that marriage was an act of profound importance to the social structure. It meant the creation of a new economic unit as well as a life-long association of persons previously separate and caught-up in existing families. It gave the man full membership of the community, and added a cell to village society. It is understandable, therefore, that marriage could not come about unless a slot was vacant, so to speak, and the aspiring couple was fit to fill it up. It might be a cottage which had fallen empty, so that a manservant and a womanservant could now marry and go to live there as cottagers. For the more fortunate it would be a plot of land which had to be taken up and worked by some yeoman's or some husbandman's son, with his wife to help him. It might be a bakery, or a joinery, or a loom which had to be manned

[99] *See page 259.*

anew. This meant that all young people ordinarily had to wait before they married, unless they were gentlefolk, though they might well have to wait even then for rather different reasons. Therefore the age at marriage would necessarily tend to be high, except at times of great expansion economically or, more surprising, after a great deal of mortality. Once it is realized that our ancestors had the same rule as we have, or would like to have, no two married couples in one family, then size of family and age at marriage are seen to be linked together, and linked with a third extremely important circumstance, expectation of life.

In the village of Cogenhoe in 1628 there were 33 families; 6, nearly one in five, seem to have had resident in-laws. This is the highest proportion we have so far found in an English pre-industrial community. At Clayworth in 1676, 7 out of 98 families had in-laws, not one in twelve, but in 1688 the proportion had fallen to 3 in 91. Only 13 out of the 176 households at Chilvers Coton in 1684 had in-laws, which is about $7\frac{1}{2}$ per cent. By no means all of these in-laws were parents of the husband or wife at the head of the household: in fact only one case of this occurred at Clayworth in the lists of 1676 and 1688, and only 3 at Chilvers Coton in 1684. In all the communities for which evidence has so far been recovered the presence of children living at home after marriage was even rarer than the presence of parents living with married children. There were three such families at Chilvers Coton out of the 176, there were none amongst the 86 families living at Ealing in 1599, none at Clayworth in either 1676 or 1688; there was one at Cogenhoe in 1620, but none in the other five years in the record. Unless all these communities happen to have been very exceptional indeed, living with in-laws can only have been occasional in the world we have lost. It is impossible that it can have been the ordinary, expected thing to do.

We have only to think for a moment of our immediate acquaintance and neighbourhood today to recognize how much more often families contain in-laws now than they did in the communities we have discussed. In Woodford in 1957, 23 per cent of all people of pensionable age who had at least one married child shared their dwellings with a married couple, one of the partners being a son or daughter. In Bethnal Green in 1954 the proportion was 21 per cent.[100] When we compare

[100] *See page 259.*

these seventeenth-century English peasant communities with the peasant communities which have survived into contemporary Western Europe, the result is even more surprising. In the eastern part of the Netherlands, peasant farming still survives. During the early 1950's, no less than 25 per cent of farms there were being worked by married couples living with their in-laws.[101] This compares as we have seen with the quite low percentage in those seventeenth-century English communities we have so far examined. There may be many reasons for this startling change; much more research will have to be done about the family then and now before we can be certain why this has taken place. An obvious cause is the lengthening of life. In Stuart England very few people lived with their in-laws, because they less often had in-laws to live with. A couple seldom had their parents living with them because their parents survived less frequently to an age where this might become necessary.

It might be added that they probably had less difficulty about housing. This is not quite a distinct reason, because we ourselves would find housing easier no doubt if we all lived shorter lives. But it seems nevertheless to be true that the relative cost of housing in pre-industrial times was less, perhaps considerably, than it is now. The humblest dwelling of all, a cottage for the labouring poor, could, it seems, be put up new for less than three years of the annual income of a labourer, and the justices of the peace seem always to be authorizing or ordering such undertakings as if they were a casual matter. Landlords and overseers of the poor would put them up apparently as a matter of course, and one of the persistent, if probably baseless, traditions of the village community was that if a poor man could build a cottage on the waste, the common grazing land, of a manor overnight, he could occupy it undisturbed. This tradition reflects the restrictions which stood in the way of building. It needed the permission of the justices to convert a house into a cottage, to divide a cottage between families or to turn a barn or part of a barn into a dwelling.[102]

Where lists of the houses in a village have survived, however, some seem always to have been vacant, especially in the later seventeenth century. This is a feature of the Hearth Tax returns of the 1660's, '70's and '80's.[103] Not that homelessness was unknown in those years or at any time in that era of

[101] *See page 259.*   [102] *See page 259.*   [103] *See page 260.*

endemic poverty and wretchedness. One, Simon Gibbs, writes the clerk to the Justices of Warwickshire in January 1667, 'is destitute of an habitation for his wife and five small children, having long lain out of doors'. A cottage was ordered to be erected on the common of that village.[104]

But the housing standards and the housing difficulties of our ancestors go beyond the very restricted ground which can be covered here. It will be obvious by now how crucial the expectation of life turns out to be when comparing our own everyday experience with that of our ancestors. Unfortunately we are not yet in a position to contrast the two in any detail. In the following table, life-expectancy in our own country in our own time is compared with that in Egypt thirty years ago, and with what is known with any accuracy of life-expectancy in England in the later seventeenth century. It will be seen that the only figure which can be recovered from the work of Gregory King on the English evidence is for life-expectancy at birth, and that for other ages the well-known table made out for Breslau by his contemporary Edmund Halley, the astronomer, has had to be used. The comparison too is between figures for males in recent times and figures which presumably cover both sexes together in earlier times.

Expectation of Life[105]

At Age	England & Wales, 1690's (Gregory King) Both Sexes	Breslau, 1690's (Edmund Halley) Both Sexes	Egypt, 1936–8 (UN Year Book) Males	U.K., 1951 (UN Year Book) Males
0	32	27·54	42·9	65·8
10		40·25	46·86	58·7
20		33·93	39·77	49·1
30		27·64	32·96	39·7
40		22·05	26·12	30·5
50		17·05	19·42	21·7
60		12·33	13·29	14·3
70		7·74	8·6	7·88

According to King and Halley, expectation of life at birth in the 1690's was a little under half of what it was in Britain for males in the 1950's, and ten years less than what it was for Egyptian males in the 1930's. We cannot yet check their

[104] *See page 260.*   [105] *See page 260.*

estimates, though they fit in fairly well with what is known for the seventeenth century both in France and in England. Halley's figures for Breslau seem a little low for expectation of life at birth and a little high for later ages. They exaggerate perhaps the two outstanding features of the table, which are the relatively long expectation of life at ages later than 0, and the fact that expectation actually went up, not down, between the end of the first year and the tenth year. The second and extraordinary effect is visible in the Egyptian figures too, and reveals a high, in Breslau a very high, infant and child mortality. The other effect is more familiar and should warn us not to exaggerate the brevity of life in earlier times. Even if Halley's Breslau estimates are too optimistic for Englishmen in his day at ages upwards of ten, it is still quite likely that a man of twenty-one could have something like thirty years to live, pretty much the same time as a newborn baby. If he married at thirty – not an unlikely age as we have seen – he could probably expect to live twenty-five years with his wife. This was a substantial period as lifetimes went then, but not long enough to ensure that he would see his own son married. When all this is said, the fact remains that the men and women of Stuart England must have had considerably poorer chances of survival than those living in the twentieth century, even in a country so very badly off as Egypt was in the 1930's.

Perhaps the peasants who persist in Holland today are, in fact, living very much as our own English peasant forefathers, but with the complication that they go on living twice as long. Nevertheless there are stray pieces of evidence which go to show that, even when she did survive her husband, a widowed mother could not always rely on her children to give her a home. At Clayworth in 1676 dwelt the little craftsman's family of Bacon: Francis Bacon the father, Joan Bacon his wife, Nicholas, Anne and Francis their children. His occupation was that of cooper, maker of barrels, which were the only important form of packaging in the old days. In 1688 his son Nicholas had succeeded him as the cooper at Clayworth, since Francis Bacon himself had been buried on April 25th, 1685. The Bacon family now consisted of Nicholas, his wife Elizabeth, and two of her children, Elizabeth and Gervas Welter. Nicholas had married Elizabeth Welter as a widow on June 1st, 1686; their own twin children, very probably conceived before their marriage, had died as babies in 1687. Now Nicholas's mother

Joan and his sister Anne were still alive and in Clayworth in
1688, but not in the family home. They were being supported
in the 'Common-Houses on Alms' — paupers in a charitable
institution in fact. Anne Bacon was a delinquent, far more
blameworthy than the unfortunate women who attract so
much attention in our day: in July, 1687, she had had a bastard child by a married man. Little Naphtaly Loversage (the
father was Nicholas Loversage, a shepherd's son) died a six-
month-old baby.

It is true that Nicholas Loversage made an honest woman
of her directly his first wife died, which was very soon after
the Rector drew up the list of parishioners in May, 1688. But
we have no evidence that Loversage gave house-room to his
new wife's mother, and there is nothing to explain the behaviour of his wife's brother Nicholas in turning mother and
sister out of the family cottage when he himself got married,
leaving them to the mercy of the parish poor-law overseers and
to charitable relief. It may be unfair to condemn Nicholas
Bacon, for the full circumstances never will be known; indeed
it is quite extraordinary that so much has been discovered
about the very private lives of these obscure villagers who
lived so long ago.[106] The Bacons and Loversages look a shift-
less, irresponsible lot, though Gervas Welter, father of Nicholas
Bacon's two step-children, was a blacksmith, and blacksmiths,
shepherds and coopers were respectable enough occupations.
In the twentieth century it is tempting to speculate on the
emotional effect of this break-up of marriages and homes on
the children, on Nicholas's naughty sister Anne, and on his
wife's two orphans. But it may be unwise to go as far as this.
The emotional pattern of that society has vanished for ever,
and people may then have had quite a different attitude to
sudden death, orphanage, widowhood and living with step-
parents.

Nevertheless the step-mother and her evil influence is so
conspicuous a feature of the fairy tales and of the literature as
a whole, that it seems to correspond to something important
in the lives of those who repeated them. The lonely old
widowed woman, witch in possibility and sometimes in fact,
is a familiar figure too. It cannot be without significance that
35·5 per cent of all the children alive in Clayworth in May,
1688, were orphans in the sense that one parent or other had

[106] *See page 260.*

died whilst they were still dependent. It must be significant too that something like a half of the solitaries, or even three-quarters – not many exact figures are yet available of the very small proportion of people in the old world who had to live alone – were widowed women.[107] In the face of facts like these, therefore, it may become difficult for us to go on being so sorry for ourselves because of the vast numbers of broken homes, and solitary, neglected people, which we think of as characteristic of high industrialism in our day. The society of the pre-industrial world was inured to bereavement and the shortness of life. It clearly had to be.

There are other elementary facts about births, marriages and deaths which may seem to be almost as surprising as the ones already cited. It is natural to think, for example, of the traditional marriage arrangement and ceremonial in the terms of Shakespeare's plays. We might contrast those famous accounts with the words of the same contemporary who recorded the details of harvest home in Yorkshire in the 1640's. He must be talking of the gentry, perhaps substantial yeomen too.

Concerning our Fashions at our Country Weddings

Usually the young man's father, or he himself writes to the father of the maid to know if he shall be welcome to the house, if he shall have further-ance if he come in such a way or how he liketh of the notion. Then if he [presumably the woman's father] pretend any excuse, only thanking him for his good will, then it is as good as a denial. If the motion be thought well of, and embraced, then the young man goeth perhaps twice to see how the maid standeth affected. Then if he see that she be tractable, and that her inclination is towards him, then the third time that he visiteth, he perhaps giveth her a ten-shilling piece of gold, or a ring of that price; or perhaps a twenty-shilling piece, or a ring of that price, then the next time, or the next after that, a pair of gloves of 6s. 8d. a pair; and after that, each other time, some conceited toy or novelty of less value. They visit usually every three weeks or a month, and are usually half a year, or very near, from the first going to the conclusion.

So soon as the young folks are agreed and contracted, then the father of the maid carrieth her over to the young man's house to see how they like of all, and there doth the young man's father meet them to treat of a dower, and likewise of a jointure or feoffment [this was what was settled on her] for the woman. And then do they also appoint and set down the day of the marriage, which may perhaps be about a fortnight or three weeks after, and in that time do they get made the wedding clothes, and make provision against the wedding dinner, which is usually at the maid's father's. Their use is [it is usual] to buy gloves to give to each of their friends a pair on that day; the man should be at

[107] *See page 260.*

the cost for them, but sometimes the man gives the gloves to the men and the women to the women, or else he to her friends and she to his. They give them that morning when they are almost ready to go to church to be married.

Then so soon as the bride is tired [attired] and that they are ready to go forth, the bridegroom comes, and takes her by the hand, and saith: 'Mistress, I hope you are willing', or else kisseth her before them, and then followeth her father out of the doors. Then one of the bridegroom his men ushereth the bride, and goes foremost, and the rest of the young men usher each of them a maid to church. The bridegroom and the brides brothers or friends tend at dinner: he perhaps fetcheth her home to his house a month after, and the portion is paid that morning that she goes away. When the young man comes to fetch away his bride some of his best friends, and young men his neighbours, come along with him, and others perhaps meet them in the way, and then there is the same jollity at his house. For they perhaps have love? wine [sic – as in original] ready to give to the company when they light [alight] then a dinner, supper and breakfast next day.[108]

It sounds rather like the marriage rites which anthropologists record of alien societies, and there are clear signs, if only in passing, of things like the bride-price and the betrothal, which, as we shall see, was separated from the later marriage. What may be most surprising is that the married couple did not go away together after the feast in the home of the bride, but weeks later. The point which will have to be considered in due course is whether or not sexual intercourse was permissible or condoned, by the church or the opinion of the village, between the contract and the marriage ceremony, or between the ceremony and the actual departure.

The marriage customs of Stuart Yorkshire may have differed widely from those elsewhere in England and Wales, and a great deal of work would have to be done to discover quite how the mass of the people got married; the really lowly people that is to say, the mere husbandmen, the artificers, the labourers, the paupers. Ralph Meers, the servant in the house of the Wawens at Clayworth in 1676, could surely not have afforded the rings, the sovereigns or half-sovereigns when he married Anne Fenton, his fellow servant, and set up as a labourer. There can have been no portion to speak of for Anne, though she may well have saved her wages, all of them, at 30*s.* or £2 a year against that wonderful day, and no question of a horse for them to alight from at the cottage door.

It would be even more out of the question to think of Nicholas Bacon behaving like the bridegroom in this account

[108] *See page 260.*

when he married Elizabeth Welter, the widow, or to suppose
that they had to take such care to have the permission of their
parents, since both of their fathers were dead, and, in any case,
a widow disposed of herself in marriage. There was no smiling
father to go to the church when Anne Bacon married Nicholas
Loversage the summer after their baby boy died. In fact something like one quarter of all marriages were not first marriages
at all. Not all of them were glad and youthful affairs when the
virgin bride and groom went to the altar in the presence of
their parents. Young people must very often have had to wait
for a parent to die before getting married. In the one great
church of the growing weaving community of Manchester in
the years 1653–7 over half of the girls marrying for the first
time were fatherless.[109] Many of them presumably came from
the houses of their step-fathers, or step-mothers, but these
examples should do something to revise sentimental notions
about marriages in earlier times, and to underline the difference
made by shorter life. You could not with any confidence expect
to see your grandchildren in the world we have lost.

The figures given for the proportion of remarriages and of
fatherless brides are provisional once again, though they too
will very soon be supplemented from more exhaustive work.
The scarcity of grandchildren will be much more difficult to
substantiate for any given individual, because every birth to
a son or daughter away from the parental home would have to
be traced. But some confidence can be placed in a provisional
figure for the proportion of households in any community
which contained grandchildren either of the head, or of anyone
else living there. These were the multigenerational households
which many people have wrongly supposed to have been
characteristic of society in pre-industrial times. This figure
never reaches one in ten: there was no household at all to
be found in Ealing in 1599 which contained a grandchild,
only one in Clayworth in 1688, and none in 1676; only four
out of 176 in Chilvers Coton in 1684. Society as a whole was
forced to rely upon its oral memory for many important
things, since writing was so restricted an accomplishment; only
an old man could tell a young one who took up a holding
whether it ever flooded, perhaps only a man with many, many
years at one job could master the skill to make a mill of a
particular type. Yet old men were not at all common and

[109] *See page 260.*

conversation across the generations must have been relatively rare, much more so than it is today.

An illusion must be guarded against here nevertheless. Though so few people reached the age of seventy, it was regarded as the allotted span of life all the same. Some attained it, and those who did were observed to be in very old age; this is how the phrase must be understood. Some husbands and wives lived long enough to see their great-grandchildren, and even occasionally their great-great-grandchildren too. But the consequence which men attached to being very old at that time, though very understandable in view of its relative rarity and possible usefulness, made them exaggerate their ages. Anyone who has read parish registers is aware of this, for every now and again a particularly venerable age will be recorded at burial, and examination will sometimes show how much the old man had added to it to impress his neighbours.

The heavier mortality of that age made for more frequent remarriage. Records of the number of times people had been married unfortunately only rarely survive, but it so happens that the listing of the people of Clayworth in 1688 was carried out with such care that this information can be worked out from it. There were at that date 72 husbands in the village, and no less than 21 are recorded as having been married more than once: 13 of them had been married twice, 1 a number of times unspecified, 3 three times, 3 four times, and 1 five times. Of the 72 wives, 9 had been previously married; 1 of the 7 widowers and 1 of the 21 widows are known to have been married more than once. This is spectacular confirmation for one single community of a law which seems to obtain for the whole pre-industrial world, that once a man reached the marriage age he would tend to go on getting married whenever he found himself without a wife. At Adel in Yorkshire one old man married his sixth wife in 1698 and his seventh in 1702.[110] The law holds for women too, but is weaker in their case, because widows found it more difficult to get husbands than widowers to get wives. Together with the much marrying majority of the older people there may also have been a small community of persons who did not marry at all.

We have given this celibate community the name of the *nubile unmarried*, and it seems probable that a fair proportion of its members were servants. But discussion of this very

[110] *See page 261.*

interesting issue soon becomes too complex for the present purpose.[111] The relatively low expectation of life combined with the relatively high age at marriage had an effect on the personal experience of men and women of the time which was of more general importance for the structure of their society than is obvious at first sight.

These two circumstances implied a relatively short duration of marriage. Once again care must be taken not to exaggerate its importance and we have seen that expectation of life in the middle years was surprisingly long in relation to expectation of life at birth. Nevertheless when a man married in the old world he cannot have had on average much more than 27 or at most 30 years to live, whereas today the expectation is more like 45. This means that a 'generation' now lasts half as long again as it used to do.

For the breaking up of a marriage by the death of the husband brought the end to an undertaking almost as surely as the beginning of a marriage meant its foundation. When a wife died, this result can rarely have followed, though the importance of a capable woman at the head of a farming or even a craftsman's household is easily overlooked. Replacing her with someone approximately suited to her duties with the children and in household management generally must often have been a difficult matter. But when the husband and the father died, everything on which the family depended was put in jeopardy. The effect would vary, of course, with the point of his career when catastrophe came, with the number, age and capacity of his sons, the vigour and determination of his widow and her attractiveness as a possible wife for someone else. 'Attractiveness' here must be read almost exclusively as an economic advantage, for when the land she now controlled was freehold and enough to live well upon, she would have had very little time to wait for a new husband. Alternatively it might pass to the late man's son or other heir who, perhaps, was already helping to work it, again without making much difference to the undertaking.

But if the land had been leasehold and the lease had been for life; if there was no son left of the right age, or daughter ready to be married to a man who could take over; if the undertaking had been a commercial or industrial one, with the proper successor not immediately to hand; under all these circumstances and many more, the day of the end of the marriage would also

[111] *See page 261.*

be the day of the end of the family enterprise, or at least the end of a particular régime, of a generation. It is obvious how much more *permanent* in this sense agricultural and landed activities were than commercial, industrial and urban ones. Even on the land the passing of a generation meant a crisis in each farming household, of a kind which our economic institutions are now much less likely to undergo. This implied a surprisingly high rate of turnover, so to speak, in institutions as well as in persons. How quickly people succeeded one to another in the same small settlement will be seen in due course.

In the second place, the brevity of the average marriage set a strict limit to the number of children who could be born to it. It might seem at first sight that in the circumstances which then prevailed, when contraception has always been supposed to have been absent, most families would have a birth a year until the wife's menopause. But suckling a baby inhibits conception to a marked degree, and the French historical demographers have shown that in their country fertility of women fell markedly in the late thirties, and ended earlier than it does now.[112] They reckon eight children to a marriage made at the median age for both husband and wife and lasting for the full period of the wife's fertility. Of course, if her marriage was one of those exceptional ones which started before the age of twenty, and if she had one or more sets of twins, or was more than ordinarily fertile in other ways as well, a woman might have very many more deliveries of babies. Even without twins the upper limits for children born is as many as twenty-three, and Louis Henry, the pioneer of historical demography, has actually found one case of twenty-one. This occurred, we may notice, amongst the prosperous bourgeoisie of the city of Geneva in the late seventeenth century.

The same researchers have shown that by the end of that century this society was already in the age of contraception.[113] But whatever happened in the great houses of Geneva, amongst the peasantry of France, in the Norman village of Crulai, for example, which has been studied in final detail, and in the area of Beauvais just north of Paris, not as many as five children would, in fact, be born to an ordinary marriage. The reason for this, let it be said again, was that so few marriages lasted long enough for the full number of eight births to take place. The others were broken by death.

[112] *See page 261.*   [113] *See page 261.*

Five births to two people at a time when expectation of life was so low is a dangerously small number, dangerous in the sense that the population is approaching the point when it will no longer replace itself.[114] It has been reckoned that not much more than half these babies would survive to the age of twenty in the villages of northern France in the seventeenth century. We cannot yet confirm these figures for our own country, and this is not the place to discuss fertility and mortality in any technical way. The historical demographers should be able within the next few years to come to fairly certain conclusions about these fundamentally important characteristics of the life of our ancestors, to compare them with conditions in our day here and in other parts of Europe and the world, and to discover how much they varied from time to time and place to place in pre-industrial England. But certain simple and crude indications can be recovered with very little effort.

If the number of registered baptisms over any given period in an English parish in Stuart times is divided into the number of marriages, the quotient gives some rough notion of how many births each marriage must have led to. It cannot, of course, be thought of as a rate of replacement, because of the high proportion of remarriage. This figure rarely reaches five, and where registration appears to be best it approaches the figure obtained in a similar way by the French. Often, even when registration looks reasonably good, it falls to three and three-quarters or even three and a half.[115] Given the expectation of life which King supposed was prevalent in his time it is obvious that the population of any one community or of the whole country was, in fact, liable to decline when the quotient was as low as this, even allowing for the statistical effect of remarriage. It might decline simply from lack of enough replacement, even though no artificial restriction was at work to keep down births, even though many, perhaps most, fathers and mothers wished to have a large family of active and mature children to help with the family farm or workshop, to add to their social consequence and, above all, to take over the family when they died. Nevertheless the evidence from across the Channel, with a wisp or two from our own country, goes to show that there may have been more dramatic influences at work at that time to keep population down to the level required by the available means of subsistence.

[114] *See page 261.*   [115] *See page 262.*

This fateful issue must be left to our next chapter. Probably the most conspicuous feature of traditional society to be gathered from its vital statistics is its overwhelming youthfulness. Gregory King calculated that above 45 per cent of all the people alive in his day were children, with some variation between town and country; there were, he reckoned, 33 per cent in London, 40 per cent in the other urban areas, and 47 per cent in the villages. It will be a long time before we can confirm or criticize these figures from a wide sample of Stuart population, but the following table shows that King's estimates of age composition were about right for three of the communities we can examine. They fit in to all our other preliminary evidence and place Stuart England alongside such twentieth-century Asian communities as Ceylon.

Comparative Age Table

Age Group	Ealing (Pop. 427) 1599	Lichfield (Pop. 2861) 1695	Stoke-on-Trent (Pop. 1629) 1701	England and Wales (From Gregory King) 1695	England and Wales 1821	Ceylon 1955	England and Wales 1958
0–9	20·6%	24·2%	28·1%	27·6%	27·9%	29·4%	14·8%
10–19	28·8%	21·5%	19·8%	20·2%	21·1%	21·6%	14·2%
20–29	13·4%	13·8%	14·3%	15·5%	15·7%	16·7%	13·8%
30–39	12·7%	15·9%	13·9%	11·7%	11·8%	13·4%	14·1%
40–49	7·0%	10·2%	8·7%	8·4%	9·3%	10·0%	13·9%
50–59	10·5%	6·4%	6·9%	5·8%	6·6%	6·0%	13·2%
60 and above	7·0%	8·0%	8·4%	10·7%	7·3%	3·5%	16·9%

When it comes to the average age, King's figure of $27\frac{1}{2}$ for the whole country in his day seems about right. It was 26·3 years at Ealing, and about 26 at Lichfield and at Stoke. The median age, the age at which the population divided, shows more variation from place to place, as might perhaps be expected. The 1,107 people living at Buckfastleigh in Devon in 1698 had a median age of as high as 25·1 years; at Lichfield it was 23·6, at Ealing 22·2, and at Chilvers Coton in Warwickshire in 1684 (population 780) it was as low as 20·8.[116]

We must imagine our ancestors, therefore, in the perpetual presence of their young offspring. A good 70 per cent of all

[116] *See page 262.*

households contained children – this figure is remarkably constant from place to place and date to date – and there were between two and a half and three children to every household with them. Sometimes the numbers in those groups of five and above could reach a quarter of the whole number of children in a village, though most children always lived in groups smaller than this. In the pre-industrial world there were children everywhere; playing in the village street and fields when they were very small, hanging round the farmyards and getting in the way, until they had grown enough to be given child-sized jobs to do; thronging the churches; for ever clinging to the skirts of women in the house and wherever they went and above all crowding round the cottage fires.

The perpetual distraction of childish noise and talk must have affected everyone almost all the time, except of course the gentleman in his study or the lady in her boudoir; incessant interruptions to answer questions, quieten fears, rescue from danger or make peace between the quarrelling. These crowds and crowds of little children are strangely absent from the written record, even if they are conspicuous enough in the pictures painted at the time, particularly the outside scenes. There is something mysterious about the silence of all these multitudes of babes in arms, toddlers and adolescents in the statements men made at the time about their own experience. Children appear, of course, but so seldom and in such an indefinite way that we know very little indeed about child nurture in pre-industrial times, and no confident promise can be made of knowledge yet to come.

We cannot say whether fathers helped in the tending of infants or whether women and girls, sisters and aunts as well as mothers, did it all as women's peculiar business. We do not know how the instruction of children was divided between the parents, though it is natural to suppose that boys at least would learn how men behaved and how they worked the lathe, the plane, the plough, the loom from watching their fathers all and every day. Such letters as they learnt, and the stories of the past, traditionally came to them at their mothers' knees, and their religious training too. But there is nothing as yet to confirm that this tradition is wholly correct. We are even more ignorant of what happened when the children left the house and went out to play; whether it was in family groups, or whether it was neighbourhood gangs, even village gangs, embracing rich and poor, the privileged along with the rest. We do not know very much about what they played, or even about what they were encouraged to play or to do.

We know a little about what they were taught when they went to school, which was almost all Christianity and a little classics, and about the rigour of their treatment there. But very few of them went to school, and we can only suppose that when they were at home they were as peremptorily treated as they would have been in the classroom. The most important material object in the world of the child may well have been the rod, but these myriads of children have left almost nothing material behind them. A cradle or two in most old houses, a hobby horse, a whipping top and one or two other traditional toys, that is all, and most of these once belonged to little gentlemen and gentlewomen, not to the ordinary children, our own ancestors.

The Stuart gentry seem to have dressed their children like themselves, at least for the purpose of having their pictures painted. The peasants and craftsmen appear to have done the same. But we cannot say how far children were universally thought of as little adults, though the notion of a world of the child distinct from the world of the grown-up seems to be no older than the early Victorians. Nothing can as yet be said on what is called by the psychologists toilet training, and reckoned by them to be of great importance in the formation of personality; there seems no likelihood of our discovering whether indeed it varied from Puritan to Anglican, from gentry to peasantry, from town to country. We do not even know for certain how babies were carried about. It is in fact an effort of the mind to remember all the time that children were always present in such numbers in the traditional world, nearly half the whole community living in a condition of semi-obliteration, many of them never destined to become persons at all. Indeed a number of them can never have handled a penny which they could pocket and call their own, even if they actually survived to the age of twenty-one.

Immaturity implies authority, and those who cannot look after themselves have to be commanded. The authoritarianism of traditional social life and educational practice becomes a little easier to understand when the youthfulness of so much of the community is borne in mind. A very high proportion of dependent bodies, mouths to feed and clothes and fuel to find, energy to summon up for the heavy work or rearing children, weights down the active members of society. This is of crucial significance when it comes to the chances of technical and economic progress, and finally of industrial transformation. It is so in Asia in our day and it must have been so in England and in Europe before 1700. A great deal of time and ingenuity has gone in trying to reconstruct the story of the growth of population over the years of first industrialization, and the time has now come to turn attention to its age-composition before and during that little-understood process.

But a glance at the table will show that no simple result is to be expected from such a study. The England of 1821, when economic transformation was in full cry, was almost exactly the same in its age composition, in the relationship between youth and age considered merely in terms of numbers present, as it had been in Gregory King's time. No easy contrast can be drawn between the world we have lost and the world we now inhabit when it comes to births, marriages and deaths. Nevertheless these neglected numerical facts have a great deal to tell, even in the crude and inchoate form in which they are so far available to us. It is remarkable too how much we can learn from trying to find out whether our Elizabethan forerunners really did marry their wives as young as Romeo married Juliet.

Did the Peasants
Really Starve?
Chapter 5

'The starving peasantry' is a common phrase, especially in popular literature. The words bring to mind a picture in simple black and white of conditions as they were in the bad old days of the reformer and the good old days of the sentimentalist. Perhaps 'starving' should not be taken to mean actually dying of lack of food; rather, badly fed and clothed, wretchedly housed in hovels, miserable in general. Still, in our own day the phrase has reverted to its grimmer meaning, reminding us of the contrast between the rich, industrialized parts of the world where food is plentiful, and the poorer areas, where industry has not yet got a hold and where literal starvation does occur.

It is therefore of considerable importance to decide how far famine was an endemic feature of the world we have lost and how far England as a country was exposed to it in the generations which led up to the industrial revolution. Did the peasants really starve, in Hertfordshire and Hampshire, in Cumberland and Cornwall, just as they sometimes starved in the area called the Beauvaisis in France, which surrounds and includes the ancient cathedral city of Beauvais?

There can be no doubt that the peasants and the craftsmen living in this region were liable to starve at times during the seventeenth and early eighteenth century, and that starvation also occurred in other parts of France. It is not yet quite clear how far these people can be taken as typical of the whole of that country, and of the whole period before the arrival of industry, all over Europe. The Beauvaisis may have been particularly vulnerable because it was a region gathering only one harvest a year and dependent upon a single crop for food. It was also given over to the production of woollen cloth, heavily industrialized in the old sense.[117] We may notice the very close resemblance between these conditions and those which prevailed over much of our own country at that time.

If the state of the evidence about starvation amongst the

[117] See page 262.

French peasantry is somewhat uncertain, it is to be expected that the situation in England should be still more obscure. We do not yet know whether the men and women of the villages and towns of our landscape in the old days lived out their lives in present or distant fear that their food supply might some day run out. Because the subject is of such overriding interest and significance, it seems worth while to present such early evidence as we already have, though most of it is negative. If in fact this fear was present among them it must have had an effect on many of the features of their lives which have been discussed so far.

The fund of food was obviously related to the age at marriage. This was a point fully recognized by Thomas Malthus, the pioneer of studies of this sort. A society conscious that its food resources might be outstripped by the growth of its population will have to control the rate of formation of families if starvation is to be avoided, and this means that marriage will have to be postponed. It also means that the procreation of children outside marriage must be strictly forbidden, and this implies authoritarian sexual morals. These we shall discuss in due course. But the possibility of starvation by no means implies that every marriage must lead to the formation of a new household: rather the reverse. It might be thought that the economies which could come from living in large households, multi-generational groups of kin, would have been an influence against the existence of small families of one married couple and their children. Since we now know that small families were the rule, and that men and women were prepared to postpone marriage to a late age in relation to their life-expectancy in order perhaps to maintain that rule, then we can conclude that this feature of their social structure was of some significance. But its importance is enhanced if it can be shown that there was a danger of starvation.

The characteristics of society in the world we have lost, therefore, play in with each other in a variety of ways, and each part of our subject is also our whole subject. In this superficial survey we can only touch on the principles and open up possibilities. It must be pointed out that the risk of starvation would not necessarily show itself in conspicuous events, the famines of the history books. Perhaps perpetual undernourishment, or undernourishment lasting for several disastrous harvests, might be its usual manifestation.

The influence of climate, good and bad years, mild and severe winters, must be stressed as we think of these things. Where the less fortunate members of a society are at the mercy of the weather and around the margin of subsistence, the tendency will surely be that the fluctuating situation will occasionally become extreme. We should therefore expect catastrophe from time to time, when famine would openly appear. This is what happened in the Beauvaisis and this is why it seems legitimate to suppose that the inhabitants of that area, living in perpetual awareness that the day might come again when they would not be able to get enough food to keep alive, would behave accordingly. We have said that the economic geography of that area of France was very like that of England, in fact of Britain as a whole. It is known that Scotland suffered from famine in Stuart times, though its occurrence has yet to be systematically studied.[118] The question of starvation amongst the English is an intricate, if undecided, problem.

We may begin our presentation of the rather fragmentary evidence by citing a contemporary, a rare example of a peasant speaking for himself, or in this case for herself. The account she gives is enlightening for many reasons. What follows is a passage from the diary of John Locke, dated March 1st, 1681.

This day I saw one Alice George, a woman as she said of 108 years old at Alhallontide last [November 1st 1680]. She lived in St Giles parish in Oxford and hath lived in and about Oxford since she was a young woman. She was born at Saltwyche [? Salwarp] in Worcestershire, her maiden name was Alice Guise. Her father lived to 83, her mother to 96 and her mother's mother to 111. When she was young she was fair haired and neither fat nor lean, but very slender in the waist, for her size she was to be reckoned rather amongst the tall than short women. Her condition was but mean, and her maintenance her labour, and she said she was able to have reaped as much in a day as any man, and had as much wages. She was married at 30, and had 15 children, viz. 10 sons and 5 daughters baptized, besides 3 miscarriages. She has 3 sons still alive, her eldest John living the next door to her, 77 years old the 25th of this month. She goes upright though with a staff in one hand, but yet I saw her stoop twice without resting upon anything, taking up once a pot and another time her glove from the ground.

[118] *See page 262.*

Her hearing is very good and her smelling so quick that as soon as she came near me she said I smelt very sweet, I having a pair of new gloves on that were not strong scented. Her eyes she complains of as failing her, since her last sickness, which was an ague that seized her about 2 years since and held her about a year. And yet she made shift to thread a needle before us, though she seemed not to see the end of the thread very perfectly. She was as comely a face as ever I saw any old woman and age hath neither made her deformed nor decrepit.

The greatest part of her food now is bread and cheese or bread and butter and ale. Sack [sherry] revives her when she can get it. For flesh she cannot now eat, unless it be roasting pig which she loves. She had, she said, in her youth a good stomach [appetite] and ate what came her way, oftener wanting victuals than a stomach. Her memory and understanding perfectly good and quick, and amongst a great deal of discourse we had with her and stories she told she spoke not one idle or impertinent [irrelevant] word. Before this last ague she used to go to church constantly on Sundays, Wednesdays and Saturdays. Since that she walks not beyond her little garden.

She has been ever since her being married troubled with vapours [either flatulence or depression] and is so still, but never took any physic but once about 40 years since, viz. one pennyworth of Jallap [aperient] which the apothecary out of kindness making a large pennyworth wrought more than sufficiently. She said she was 16 in '88 [1588], and went then to Worcester to see Queen Elizabeth, but came an hour too late, which agrees with her account of her age.[119]

Locke was a practising physician, an exact recorder and very reliable witness, so that we can believe that this is what Goody George did tell him, and that this was her true physical condition. We may, nevertheless, have our reservations about the ages she gives, particularly that for her grandmother, in view of the tendency to exaggerate which has been noticed. If she did have eighteen pregnancies after the age of thirty (this is obviously a round figure in the account and she may have been twenty-seven, twenty-eight or twenty-nine at marriage) then she is something of a record for English women of her time, and difficult to parallel even in France where so many more cases have been investigated. But most of her story rings true.[120]

[119] *See page 262.*   [120] *See page 262.*

Women did work with men in the field, especially at harvest. 'The best sort of women-shearers [sickle-wielders]' says the Yorkshire farming-book quoted twice before, should have 'mowers' wages'; 'we should do them an injury if we should take them from their company and not make them equal to those in wages whom they can equalize in work.'[121] Her church attendance is probable enough, as has been seen, though it may come as a surprise to see how often our ancestors held their services. It is not without its interest that she lived alone next door to her son. She was another of the solitary widows we have already referred to, but like so many of the citizens of Bethnal Green today she had managed to get within an easy walk of a member of her family. A superficial survey of a city like Lichfield shows that this was common enough then, though perhaps not in anything like the degree that it has been found in twentieth-century working-class areas: in a street of some sixty-five households, only fifty-two surnames were counted in Lichfield in the survey of 1696.[122]

But her statements about what she ate, what she liked and how often she had to go without are the most interesting. The whole account reads rather like an explanation of how much she had to do to keep her stomach full. Still, she does not mention starvation or anything of that kind. John Graunt, the first man in history to study burial returns, was sceptical about starvation in England in his time. 'Of 229,250 which have died,' he wrote in 1661 referring to burials in London over twenty recent years, 'we find not above fifty-one to have been *starved*, excepting helpless infants at nurse, which being caused rather by carelessness, ignorance, and infirmity of the milch-women, is not properly an effect, or sign of want of food in the country or the means to get it.'[123]

If there was so seldom any lack of food to keep people alive in the huge city of London with its mass of paupers, surely the possibility of starvation can be dismissed out of hand for the years which Graunt had surveyed. But it can still be asked why he went to the trouble of denying that starvation ever happened. In order to be sure of what it is that is being sought after, it would be useful to see quite what is meant by the French historical demographers when they write of crises of subsistence occurring in French villages. They occurred when the price of bread rose so far that peasants and craftsmen could no

[121] *See page 263.*   [122] *See page 263.*   [123] *See page 263.*

longer afford to buy enough to eat, and became liable to starve.[124]

The crises in the villages of the Beauvaisis came at irregular intervals: 1625, 1648–53, 1693–4 were some of the dates. The parish registers of these communities, and of the churches of the city of Beauvais itself, would show a sudden rise in burials; double, or even treble the normal would be entered. Towards the first peak in mortality, marriages would drop and conceptions would go down too; they have to be reckoned by subtracting nine months from the date of birth, and the year used is the harvest year, from August 1st to July 31st. Conceptions in fact tended to disappear, because lack of nourishment inhibits ovulation. By the time the second peak in mortality came, for these crises were often though not always doubleheaded, the poor would be eating grass off the fields and offal from dung-heaps in the streets, dying perhaps more often from the effects of things like this and from the onset of endemic diseases than from starvation as such. The rich, though they might suffer from the infections spread about in this way, would not be affected by starvation.

Professor Goubert, the French historian of these lugubrious events, chooses this story to show what might happen to one family.

There was a family in Beauvais in the parish of Saint-Etienne in the year 1693 named Cocu: Jean Cocu, weaver of serges, and his wife with three daughters, all four spinning wool for him, since the youngest daughter was already nine years old. The family earned 108 sols a week, but they ate 70 pounds of bread between them. With bread up to $\frac{1}{2}$ a sol a pound, their livelihood was secure. With bread at 1 sol a pound, it began to get difficult. With bread at 2 sols, then at 3·2, 3·3 and 3·4 – as it was in 1649, in 1652, in 1662, in 1694, in 1710 – it was misery.

Crisis in agriculture was nearly always intensified by crisis in manufacturing: it certainly was in 1693, so work began to fall off, then income. They went without; perhaps they were able to lay their hands on a coin or two saved up for a rainy day; they pawned their things; they began to eat unwholesome food, bran bread, cooked nettles, mouldy cereals, entrails of animals picked up outside the slaughter-houses. The 'contagion' manifested itself in various ways; after hunger came lassitude, starvation, 'pernicious

[124] *See page 263.*

and mortifying fevers'. The family was registered at the Office of the Poor in December, 1693. In March, 1694, the youngest daughter died; in May the eldest daughter and the father. All that remained of a particularly fortunate family, fortunate because everyone in it worked, was a widow and an orphan. Because of the price of bread.[125]

In order to demonstrate that the crisis of subsistence was a possibility in England at the same time as it was obviously a possibility in France, we should have to show that three conclusions can be certainly drawn from at least one English parish register at a time when the price of food was particularly high. The first is that there was a sudden, sharp increase in mortality; the second is that at the same time there was a corresponding fall in conceptions and perhaps in marriages; the third is that the stated cause of death of some of those buried was in fact starvation or diseases caused by malnutrition. There are other features associated with such crises which have to be looked for also, such as an increase in infantile mortality and in abortions. But any register showing the three listed features at any time of dearth must be taken as providing proof that in that parish the inhabitants were undergoing a crisis of subsistence.

It must be said at once that only one such English instance has so far been found. Although very little concerted work has yet been possible on the subject, Graunt seems to have been right when he claimed that starvation was extremely rare in England as a stated cause of death. But the simplicity of this negative conclusion is obscured by the exasperating rarity of parish registers which give any indication as to why the person buried died. The third, and most conclusive, of the features listed, therefore, is almost universally absent from the English evidence, and the other two are seldom found in as extreme a form as they are to be seen in France. Nearly all of the English registers which have been studied so far yield entirely negative conclusions; they contain no examples of harvest years where a conspicuous rise in burials was accompanied by a corresponding fall in conceptions and in marriages.

We may here be faced with a sociological discovery of the first historical importance, that our country in the seventeenth century was already immune from these periodical disasters,

[125] *See page 263.*

whereas France was not. Perhaps the English peasantry were justified rather later on in despising the French for eating black bread and wearing wooden shoes. We do not yet know, though it should not be long now before we shall find out. Let us take the wool-weaving parish of Ashton-under-Lyne in Lancashire as an example of an incomplete crisis of subsistence, occurring during the harvest year 1623–4. Its incompleteness, its difference, that is to say, from the classical French model, consists first in the fact that the evidence is imperfect, owing to gaps in the register, and second in that not all of the symptoms are present in a very clear or pronounced form.[126]

The harvest year 1623–4 was one of bad crops and high prices all over the country: the weather was very nasty. The textile industry was in the depth of depression, just as it was in Beauvais 1693–4. There had been a sudden rise in burials at Ashton two years before 1620–1, but after this they returned to their average of about seventy-five a year. In the harvest year 1623–4 184 people were buried, that is some $2\frac{1}{2}$ times the normal, and conceptions fell from an average of about 105 to 60. Unfortunately causes of death are not given and the words 'famine', 'starvation', etc. do not appear. These events could provisionally be classed as an English crisis of subsistence though not a severe one. They are confirmed in a general way by what is known to have been happening in a wool manufacturing area in Yorkshire at the same time.

The one parish which undoubtedly did suffer this disaster, experienced it during these same months in the early 1620's when the situation at Ashton-under-Lyne was so gloomy. The register of the church of Greystoke in the Cumberland hills contains 474 baptisms during the decade 1610–19, with extremes of 40 and 58, 368 burials (20 and 61) and 96 marriages (6 and 15). The expected average then must have been about 47 baptisms, 37 burials and 10 marriages every year. Even here alas, there is a chasm in the register from December 1st, 1620, to June 16th, 1622, so that the full story of the crisis cannot be told and we cannot reconstruct the harvest year over the critical months.[127]

In the calendar year 1623 no less than 161 people were buried in the churchyard at Greystoke, which is over four times the expected number. Only 20 babies were baptized, which is almost down to half the average, and marriages fell

[126] *See page 263.*   [127] *See page 264.*

about as much, to 4. We cannot say how conceptions behaved at the height of the crisis, but in the worst period for burials, which was September to November, 1623, there were only 3 conceptions, no marriages and 62 registered deaths. We know that some of these deaths were due to starvation, for the entries actually confess this melancholy fact.

Extracts from the Register of Greystoke 1623
29th January: 'A poor fellow destitute of succour and was brought out of the street in Johnby into the house of Anthony Clemmerson, constable there, where he died.'
27th March: 'A poor hungerstarved beggar child, Dorothy, daughter of Henry Patteson, Miller.'
28th March: 'Thomas Simpson, a poor hungerstarved beggar boy and son of one Richard Simpson of Brough by Mandgyes house in Thorp.'
19th May: 'At night James Irwin, a poor beggar stripling born upon the borders of England. He died in Johnby in great misery.'
12th July: 'Thomas, child of Richard Bell, a poor man, which child died for very want of food and maintenance to live.'
11th September: 'Leonard, son of Anthony Cowlman, of Johnby, late deceased, which child died for want of food and maintenance to live.'
12th September: 'Jaine, wife of Anthony Cowlman, late deceased, which woman died in Edward Dawson's barn of Greystoke for want of maintenance.'
27th September: 'John, son of John Lancaster, late of Greystoke, a waller by trade, which child died for want of food and means.'
[*The register tells us that he was baptized on October 17th, 1619, so he was four years old.*]
4th October: 'Agnes, wife of John Lancaster, late of Greystoke, a waller by his trade, which woman died for want of means to live.'
27th October: 'William child of Lancelot Brown, which Lancelot went forth of the country [the district] for want of means.'

The fells of Cumberland, with their scattered flocks of sheep and their thin crops of cereals, were very different from the sad Beauvais plain, though they may have suffered as badly from too great a press of people dependent upon a textile industry stricken with depression. 'The smallness, barrenness, and the multitude of inhabitants in the habitable places of this country is . . . far incomparable to the other counties of the kingdom,' declared the justices of the neighbouring county of Westmorland in the year 1622, then already attempting to make some headway against the conditions which were to have such a tragic effect at Greystoke.[128] The deaths which took place there were not, as was usual in France, predominantly of children, in spite of the impression which may be created by the extracts we have printed here.

But if these dismal details are to be made the most of, we must notice the fact that there were two cases of a mother and child both dying of famine at almost the same time, and that one of these pathetic families was without a shelter. Wandering beggars, like the miserable James Irwin, were, as we have already said, a feature of the countryside at all times, and most noticeable under the Tudors. They may perhaps have attracted more attention than is numerically justified, for it will be seen that Gregory King's table provides for only 30,000 of them in the whole population. A significant thing for the study of men's attitude to the means of keeping themselves and their families alive is the action of Lancelot Brown, named in the last entry, who appears to have left the starveling hillsides of Cumberland to try to find subsistence in some more fortunate part of England.

His child died nevertheless, and perhaps the loss of the breadwinner, rather than exhaustion of the food supply, must be held to be the immediate, if not the final, cause of death. We cannot yet tell, any more than we can say whether or not the wandering father would have found much more favourable conditions anywhere in the highland zone of England in the dreadful season 1623–4. Other parish registers show a pattern similar to that at Ashton-under-Lyne, and some of those which run unbroken through the troubled years 1640 to 1660 reveal what may turn out to be a terrible climacteric about 1645, just as the war between King and Parliament was reaching its crisis. At Colyton in Devonshire it is reckoned that something like a quarter of the thousand and more inhabitants were buried during the calendar year 1645; but there the words 'great sickness' appear in the register.[129]

The task of isolating deaths due to starvation from those which can be ascribed more confidently to infectious diseases has still to be undertaken for any parish. Perhaps it will not be long before we are able to make use of medical advances in the study of nutritional diseases which demonstrate that their

[128] *See page 264.*   [129] *See page 264.*

casualties show a particular pattern of mortality as to age of victim, sex and time of year at which death is most likely. Certainly pellagra, which is the most conspicuous deficiency disease amongst corn-eating populations such as those of seventeenth-century England, has been shown to have such a pattern. Once we learn to distinguish this from the characteristic mortality pattern of bubonic plague, it may be possible to infer which one of these two was the cause of any particular excess of deaths by the analysis of registers which contain no more information than date of burial, sex and maturity of the corpse.[130]

When entries like those from Greystoke are found, or when the clerk of the rich metropolitan, parliamentary parish of St Margaret's, Westminster, records the causes of death during the summer months of the year 1557 and ascribes 16 out of 181 to 'famine', we can be fairly certain that individuals were dying of lack of food. This must have been true at Wednesbury in Staffordshire in 1674, where the registers read under November 22nd: 'John Russel being famished through want of food (Josiah Freeman being overseer), was buried with the solemnity of many tears.' Food prices were very high in the area at about that time, and the mid-1670's resembled the early 1620's in many respects in this area. But poor John Russel's fate was obviously thought by his indignant neighbours to have been due to the neglect of the overseer of the poor.[131]

In the extreme conditions which wrecked the family of Cocu in Beauvais it seems probable that no system of poor relief could have been effective, and the arrangements in that city were apparently exceptionally good. Transfer payments, as the economists call them, between the prosperous and the dependent could never have prevented crises of subsistence of the kind found by the French historical demographers. There was simply not enough food to go round at such times, and poor people were inevitably in danger from high prices. More efficient means of distribution between country and country, region and region, even village and village might have mitigated the crises, and a really ambitious policy of storage could have gone far towards eliminating them. Everything in the French evidence points to the absence of adequate stocks of corn and of the means of distributing it when it was wanted. It would have been necessary to have had an accurate

[130] *See page 264.*   [131] *See page 264.*

idea of the numbers of people who had to be fed in order to make quite certain that food would never run out, and there are indications that counts of the population were in fact carried out for the purpose in some cities: at Ypres in the 15th century, for example, or perhaps at Coventry in the year 1520. The story of what Joseph did in preparation for the Seven Lean Years in Egypt might well have been written for the administrators of the pre-industrial world.

Once we are alive to the real possibility of famine the perpetual preoccupation of the authorities of that era, governmental and municipal, with the supply of food for the poor takes on a new significance. The insistence on fair prices for all victuals and especially of bread is a reminder that people might starve even where supplies were available, if they had exhausted their savings and lost their employment, or even sometimes if taxation had pressed them too hard. Hence the strict control of all dealings in breadstuffs and all handlers of them, especially buyers and sellers of wheat. The stocks of corn so conspicuous in the records of Tudor and Stuart London were examples of a policy which had to be pursued all the time and in deadly earnest.[132] It was indeed a matter of life and death, and felt to be so by King, Mayor, Justice of the Peace and Overseer of the Poor alike. Right up to the time of the French Revolution and beyond in Europe the threat of high prices for food was the commonest and most potent cause of public disorder. It was dangerous when overseers were as neglectful as Josiah Freeman of Wednesbury, and during the years of scarcity in the early 1620's corn was stored locally. The harvest year 1623-4 was in many places the worst of a succession of bad harvest years, and in this it is typical of the crises detected in France. It is also typical of these black periods that this one should have ended in an outbreak of plague.

At this point arises the most difficult of the many questions which will have to be settled before we can make up our minds about the issue which confronts us. We have to decide whether liability to starvation, extinction owing to an insufficient supply of food, must be taken as a defining characteristic of the world we have lost, and fear of such catastrophe an attribute which all our ancestors shared, but which we no longer experience, at least not in respect of ourselves. Are many of the deaths

[132] *See page 264.*

which are put down by historical writers with such facility to
the plague, pestilence, endemic diseases, in fact to be attri-
buted to lack of food? If not always to a famine, to a sudden-
felt visitation of the sort so far discussed, then more often to
months and months, or even years, of under-nourishment?
Perhaps Alice George might have fallen victim to bubonic
plague, if she had been as unlucky as so many of her contemporaries, either in the early 1590's, the 1620's or in the awful
year 1665–6. She might have died of plague if she had been
more than usually hungry at those times, run down through
undernourishment would be the Victorian way to put it. Not
that she was conscious of the danger. By the time of her old
age all she remembered was her belly often being empty.

Perhaps, however, it was the other way round. Perhaps the
enormous totals of deaths which appear under some years in
the registers of individual villages, often isolated villages surrounded by others where nothing untoward is recorded, were
in fact due to the plague or some other infectious disease,
although the parish clerk did not say so in the register. Though
this is unlikely, it would be unwise at the present stage of
study to leave any possibility out of the question. In the end
it may be possible to separate pestilence and famine in such a
way as to be perfectly clear about the possibility of starvation.

But it is very striking how often these peaks in mortality
do not seem to communicate themselves to neighbouring
parishes. It is so in France and in Devonshire. The great
mortality in Colyton in 1645 did not affect all the surrounding
villages whose registers survive. The village of Hartland, fifty
miles to the west, its magnificent tower rearing above the
lofty cliffs of the north Devon coast, was completely untouched
although the community was of the same size as Colyton and
registration as good. It is very easy to see how a famine and
sickness which accompanied it could be local. The neighbouring
towns and villages might have enough to last but not enough
to help the afflicted settlement, even if the means and measures
were present to make it possible. It is more difficult to see how
the bubonic plague could be so local, considering its desperate
infectiousness, especially in view of the very considerable
movement of persons which we know went on between community and community. It must however be said that even
then quarantine was often enforced on plague-stricken areas.[133]

[133] *See page 265.*

There can be no doubt about the horrors of the plague. In its external form, when the buboes appear at the joints and all over the body, it is a dreadful and very dangerous disease; and in its pneumonic form, when the lungs are affected, it is one of the worst that human beings can contract. Once it got hold in any of the settlements already described, the chances of very heavy mortality were obviously high, because people lived in such close contact with each other, and their houses must all have been infested with rats and lice, the medium of transmission of bubonic plague. It is possible that the pneumonic form had disappeared by the sixteen hundreds. All this has been the subject of much writing since the time of Pepys and Defoe, and is perhaps too well known. The argument about health and welfare in earlier times has always tended to go forward in terms of visitation of the plague and other contagious diseases, and the possibility of failures in subsistence has been somewhat obscured. Not that the eye-witness accounts of the over-publicized Great Plague of London can be called exaggerated. There are heartrending records of what happened in rural villages too. In one small hamlet, a parish register informs us, more or less incidentally, everyone died, and the last full-grown man to get the disease actually dug his own grave in the yard and buried himself in it. He seems to have taken this strange action because he was certain he must die and because he knew that the servant-girl and the boy, who alone would be left alive, would never be able to get his body out of the house. This was at Malpas in Cheshire in September, 1625.[134]

Here again is evidence of an attitude to death which cannot easily be shared in the twentieth century. The same John Locke whose diary was quoted, is said by an eye-witness to have closed his own eyes when he was on the point of dying, not however of the plague.[135] The crisis of subsistence which the French demographers describe is a peculiarly awful phenomenon for us to read about today. But the attitude must have been rather different at the time, when so many people were dying every day, whom we would expect to live for many years. Something like a third or half of all the burials registered in the seventeenth century were of 'sons and daughters', mostly children presumably. Able-bodied, active young persons, nursing mothers, wage-earning fathers died in large num-

[134] *See page 265.*   [135] *See page 265.*

bers also, in addition to the old and the chronically ill. A contemporary realist might have said that very many of those who starved would have died anyway within a few years. He could also have pointed to the undoubted upsurge in marriages and then in births, together with the low level of burials, which succeeded the catastrophe, and did something to make up the losses.

Of course, such an outlook was impossible then, just as it was impossible for the connection between rats, lice and bubonic infection to be understood. No Stuart Englishman, not even Locke or Graunt, would have thought of vital statistics in such a way. It takes a complete transformation of attitude to recognize what a death-rate might be, and why it is important: only a handful of people ever developed anything like that attitude in the world we have lost, and even they did not get very far. It has been recently shown that some authorities could control plague infection to a surprising degree, but by rule-of-thumb methods, never by scientific insight.[136] The ordinary feeling about the black years, amongst the peasantry at least, was to behave as if they had never happened; there are many records of the more serious-minded of their contemporaries remarking on this very natural reaction.

Whatever its nature, and however it was related to diet and the means of subsistence generally, the important fact about the plague in England in the final years before the coming of industry is that it lost its virulence, though it by no means disappeared. The Great Plague of the history books and popular memory, the visitation of London and much of the country in 1665–6, was the last in our country which can be compared in its catastrophic effects with the French demographic crises. It is impossible as yet to conjecture whether this disappearance could be related in any way with the remarkable developments which Professor Goubert goes on to trace out in eighteenth-century France after the 1740's, at least for the area of Beauvais. Crises of subsistence ceased to occur, infantile mortality went down, and the precarious balance between increase and decrease of population gave way to a steady upward trend. This transformation led to the disappearance of the old demographic régime, as he calls it, and the succession of the modern demographic régime, in which all in Western Europe and

[136] *See page 265.*

highly industrialized countries still live. The alteration of the relation between population and the means of subsistence, if it did indeed occur in France generally before the year 1750, happened without benefit of industrialism on the modern scale.[137]

Perhaps these facts from France should persuade us that liability to starvation without warning cannot be counted as a defining characteristic of the world we have lost in the same way as the facts of the scale of life which have been discussed already. The mild, retiring English clergyman, Thomas Malthus, first formulated the population and subsistence law in the form used by all subsequent economists. This was as late as 1797, when large-scale industry was already under way in his own country, for the first time in history anywhere, and he did not admit that this economic transformation made his law obsolete. It was fashionable until quite recently to claim that Malthus was wrong in his persistence, but the awful fate of Ireland in the decade after his death, during the Great Famine as it is called, is surely a sufficient demonstration that the crisis of subsistence was not abolished all over the British Isles by the coming of industry. It may nevertheless be deceptive to read the circumstance of Ireland and Irish society in the 1840's too easily back into the pre-industrial past of our own country. Let us return to the situation of the English village community before the year 1700, for there are further circumstances affecting it which have a bearing on the question of whether the peasants really starved in England in the old days.

The operation of what Malthus called the prudential check may first be noticed once again. This kept population within the resources of food by postponing marriage. In spite of the possibility that women reached sexual maturity rather late, if they had all begun to have children immediately they had become fecund, the number born to each marriage would have been far more than the eight which has been laid down for the average when uninterrupted, and the five for marriages overall. For this reason the age at marriage provides a very sensitive indicator of social conditions. It may record the effects of economic expansiveness, or men's appreciation of it. It may sometimes record the failure of the prudential check to operate on young immigrants to new industrial towns, at a long remove from the traditional, authoritarian atmosphere of the village. Nevertheless, it is by no means clear that earlier marriage for

[137] *See page 265.*

the mass of the people was always the permanent result of the growth of urban centres and of industry, and it is not yet known whether we should seek here for the reason why population so often rose as European countries became industrialized. But it is obvious that a knowledge of the age of marriage and its variations is of the greatest importance to historical analysis; the mistake about the typicality of Juliet is not a trivial mistake at all.

Infantile mortality is a very well-known and much used index of welfare, and certainly varies with adequacy of nourishment. The French crises of subsistence, as has been stated, were marked by very sharp increases of deaths amongst the new born, and in abortions too, though abortions are very difficult to reckon even from French parish registers. It so happens that Ashton-under-Lyne is one of the very few places where burials of abortions are registered in our parish books at the relevant time, and they were higher in the early 1620's than at any other time when the clerk recorded them, reaching nearly 7 per cent of births in 1623.[138] But even at this level they did not much exceed the rate of nearly 6 per cent which can be derived from John Graunt's extracts from the London bills of mortality for the early 1630's, and neither figure is as high as the estimated rate for our own day.[139]

More marked at Ashton during the years of crisis was the peak in the total of 'nuncupative' babies, or 'chrissoms' as they were called, who had to be buried. Chrissoms were those who died before there was time to baptize them; they were put into a grave wrapped in the christening cloth which had been prepared for the ceremony at the font. Our ancestors had other curious and to our generation rather ghoulish customs. In some places when a mother died in childbed the baby was christened on her coffin.[140] Chrissom children buried numbered nine in the crisis year 1623–4 at Ashton, when fifty-eight was the total of those conceived. They were even more numerous in 1621, the first of the two years of high mortality, when they reached nearly a fifth of all conceptions. The increase in babies buried in the first year of life can also be seen at Greystoke at the same time, at its worst when persons were actually dying of starvation.

Infantile mortality has a wider significance than its relationship with periods of want and starvation in the traditional

[138] *See page 265.*   [139] *See page 265.*   [140] *See page 265.*

world. It enters into our general attitude in the twentieth century towards the world we have lost, because of the widespread belief that industrialization in its early stages had a disastrous effect on the health of the newly born. It seems to be supposed that only recently and in only the most advanced industrial countries has the mass of the population been able to go back to anything like healthy, natural conditions under which the peasant woman had her babies, and therefore only recently has the tragic waste of infant life which comes from industrial conditions begun to be stemmed. Even historians have sometimes referred in an ominous way to some isolated index for the mortality of babies in an early industrial suburb, and the national proportion of 153 per thousand dying in the first year of life in the decade 1841–50 has occasionally been cited as an indication of a general deterioration. Nothing we have yet found confirms this view of what happened, and everything points to a somewhat different conclusion.

The French historical demographers, in fact, tend to suppose that a figure much greater than 150 per thousand, a figure nearer to 200 per thousand and probably even higher, was typical of rural villages in pre-industrial France in normal times. Since this may seem a startling proposition a few of their results are listed in the table which follows.[141] They have been worked out after intensive study of their more detailed and reliable parish registers, and using methods not yet put into practice in England.

Infantile Mortality, France and Belgium

Crulai, Normandy	1675–1775	210–230
Auneuil, Beauvaisis	1656–1755	288
Saint-Laurent-des-Eaux, Sologne	1st Quarter 18th century	326
Paris Region	1750–1789	230
Vieuxbourg, Belgium	1700–19	206·7
	1720–1739	193·9

Even these figures from France may not state the true position all over the country, and there were, as we have seen, enormous variations in infantile mortality from time to time, in accordance with nutrition and with general health. But it seems unlikely that the figures cited, or the general average, exag-

[141] *See page 265.*

gerate the probable mortality amongst the newly born. If anything it may understate it, for even in France the sharp eye of the curé might occasionally fail to observe an unwanted baby stealthily disposed of, or a careless family might fail to report it.

Certainly in England we have found it difficult to confirm an infantile mortality as high as 200 per thousand, and though our cruder methods undoubtedly tend to underestimate the figures, the actual rates cannot have been much higher. At Wem in Shropshire for example the figures show a minimum of 120 in the 1670's and of 139 in the 1680's, though they reached occasional peaks, numbering almost 300 for a year or two in the 1660's.[142] At Ashton-under-Lyne, where registration went into such rare detail and was apparently so reliable, the minimal rate certainly rose above 200 in years of crisis 1622, 1623 and 1624, but over the whole decade 1615–24 it comes out at only 141. Though it was 176 for the five years 1629–34, it never reached 200 for any prolonged period in the seventeenth century.

The largest sample available known for any European country for so early a date is contained in Graunt's study of the bills of mortality in London. His tables can be made to yield a rate of infantile mortality of over 200, but only on the assumption that all those he records as 'Chrissomes and Infants' at their burial were in fact less than twelve months old. Between 1629 and 1632, for example, there were 9,277 such burials out of a total of 36,024 baptisms, which would mean a rate of 257 per thousand. Even this estimate leaves open the question of whether any of those he classifies as dying of 'Convulsions' or 'Teeth and Worms' were in fact under one year of age.[143] The evidence best suited to the purpose, and probably the most reliable, once again comes from Clayworth during the pastorate of William Sampson, and it is interesting to find that in his village over the whole period infantile mortality was on average 215, not so very different from that at Crulai. Since such details are rare at the present stage of research, it might be as well to present them in full, together with some rough indication of the prices the villagers were paying for the wheat, rye or barley they made into bread, those of them, that is to say, who had to buy their food rather than living off their own crops.[144]

[142] *See page 266.* 　　[143] *See page 266.* 　　[144] *See page 266.*

Registered Infantile Mortality at Clayworth, Notts, rate per thousand live births. (With a crude index of prices of cereals.)

1680–1682	385	Price Index 1676–85	64·5	(1682	77·0)
1683–1685	300				
1686–1688	350				
1689–1691	242	Price Index 1686–95	53·4	(1690	43·7)
1692–1694	185				
1695–1697	168				
1698–1700	117	Price Index 1696–1701	68·4	(1698	103·5)
1701–1703	174				

If it had not been for the very unfavourable years in the 1680's, it will be seen, registered infantile mortality even here would have been on a somewhat lower level than it seems ordinarily to have been in contemporary France. Nothing can be made of the vague tendency of the level of local cereal prices to vary with the numbers of babies dying. But it is not without interest, that the number of baptisms, marriages and burials as a whole shows that there was something of a demographic crisis in the years 1678–81 with its peak of thirty-one burials in 1679, whilst the average during Sampson's time was under five overall. He never mentioned hunger during the twenty-eight years he lived in Clayworth, but he does record November and December, 1679, as 'sickly months', when, after 'a very wet time about autumn . . . the quartan ague was almost in every house and none in some escaped it.'[145]

Mortality at Clayworth interests for other reasons which will appear in the next chapter, but it would be difficult to use it even as a token demonstration that the liability of infants to die in their first year of life was increased by the coming of industry in England. The truth seems to be that infantile mortality cannot have been higher under Queen Victoria than it was under the Stuarts, and the first rough indications are that it was lower; fewer babies certainly died in industrial England in the 1840's than in peasant France in the 1670's, 80's or 90's. No doubt the early industrial suburbs did show a lamentable death-rate amongst the very youngest of their inhabitants, and the conspicuous fact about them was that in the areas of the same cities where the richer people lived infantile mortality was very much lower even in the early twentieth century. It seems true to say that a baby born into the

[145] *See page 266.*

Gorbals of Glasgow in 1879 probably had a better chance of surviving to its first birthday than a baby born into the entirely rural, open-field village of Clayworth in the fairly prosperous county of Nottinghamshire in 1679. These may be extreme examples, but it is unlikely that the traditional association between early industrial conditions and high infantile mortality can stand up to close investigation.

Therefore, even at the outset of the systematic study of the conditions of life of our forefathers, we have a rough idea of the general facts about the loss of infants. It is not possible to give precise reasons why the peasantry found it so difficult to keep their babies alive, or whether the food supply was the governing influence. The relation between the amount and cost of food and the variations in the level of mortality, of men and women as well as children, must remain an open question for the time, along with that of whether crises of subsistence were a present possibility in the English towns and country-side. One further plaintive query may be addressed to the historians of England, rather than to the slightly exasperating records of their doings left by our predecessors.

Why is it that we know so much about the building of the British Empire, the growth of Parliament and its practices, the public and private lives of English kings, statesmen, gene-rals, writers, thinkers and yet do not know whether all our ancestors had enough to eat? Our genealogical knowledge of how Englishmen and their distant kinsmen overseas are related to the Englishmen of the pre-industrial world is truly enormous, and is growing all the time. Why has almost nothing been done to discover how long those earlier Englishmen lived and how confident most of them could be of having any posterity at all? Not only do we not know the answers to these questions, until now we never seem to have bothered to ask them.

Personal Discipline
and Social
Survival
Chapter 6

Prone as we are to be sentimental about our ancestors, we are also quite prepared to believe that they were often wicked people, at least on the standards which they set for themselves. When bastardy comes into the conversation, we suppose that country people, and our forefathers in general, were far more likely than we are to bring illegitimate children into the world and far more tolerant of bastardy as a condition. It is widely supposed too, that no shrewd, hard-working peasant or craftsman, to whom strong, hard-working sons and daughters were a tangible asset, would ever undertake to marry a girl unless he knew from his own sexual experience that she was capable of bearing children. If she did prove barren (this implies) no marriage would take place, and the poor girl would have lived out her life as a reject.

This element of suspicion in our attitude to the world we have lost is probably complicated in its origins. So sudden and complete has been the desertion of the countryside for the cities in our recent history, that it was to be expected that those who remained behind were, and are, the inferior people – in aptitude and intelligence, and therefore, presumably, in moral calibre. Though this impression is faulty in its supposition of what actually happened, since the towns and cities have been recruited far more from their own natural increase than is often thought, it has had some little justification from surveys of the condition of rural communities in recent times; the village idiot, who was also a half-wit and a degenerate, is not entirely a fiction.[146] But to this must be added the outlook every emigrant tends to adopt towards those who lacked the energy and foresight to leave with him. He has to assure himself that the people he, his father or his grandfather had lived amongst in the green countryside, in the idyllic village community, were also people without initiative, inbred and not entirely desirable.

This unappealing attitude may perhaps seem to be confirmed

[146] *See page 267.*

to some degree by the suggestion a French historical demo-
grapher made to explain the occasional conditions of crisis
which concerned us in the last chapter. These periods of disastrous death-rates, of rising infant mortality and of high
rates of abortion, were, he thinks, also periods when bastardy
was commoner and when more children were conceived before
marriage; they may therefore possibly be explained as intervals of moral collapse as well as of scarcity of food and widespread infectious disease. At these times, so the suggestion
goes, the peasantry broke free to some extent from the strict
rule of sexual continence outside marriage which the Church
universal and established opinion prescribed for everybody at
all times. Hence a dangerously large number of children with
no hope of survival, leading to infanticide as well as to a sudden
growth in numbers of children not within the familial system.[147]

This hypothesis has met with little approval from other
students of the problem. Its rejection is due to more than a
dislike of its apparent desire to convict the suffering populations of moral obliquity. Though we shall find the issue of pre-
nuptial conception – the tendency of brides to be already
pregnant when it came to the celebration of the marriage
in Church – is a complex and interesting one, in England
at least the general proposition is easily disposed of.
Our English ancestors cannot have been generally guilty
of sexual irresponsibility of the kind which has just been
described.

The peasants and the craftsmen of Tudor and Stuart times
seem on the whole to have been cautious about the procreation
of children and the formation of families. All the facts we have
surveyed about the late age of marriage amongst them, and
the circumstances which surrounded every decision to set up a
new household, seem to imply that they were well enough
aware that the fund of food and conveniences of life were
strictly limited even if starvation did not ordinarily have to be
reckoned as a possibility. Their marked success in finding
themselves new partners when they were widowed is another
sign of recognition that the position of a child was precarious
indeed without a father's support, or a mother's care. The
registers demonstrate how soon neglected orphans or illegitimate children found their way in to the churchyard. They show

[147] *See page 267.*

signs also that the offspring of too young a marriage could easily share their fate.

It might perhaps be better to say that it was custom, traditional conduct and the regulations of the Church which took these dangers into account, rather than the deliberate reflection of men and women, whose only action was to do as others did and as always had been done. The code of moral behaviour in the traditional world can be looked upon from this point of view as an essential part of the workings of the general social scheme. Here was a nation-wide community of persons, not the local community of a village, living under agrarian conditions and not far above subsistence level. It was a community which made of the nuclear family the unit for nearly all activity, only adding other persons to it as servants, when that was necessary. If the shape of the society was to be maintained, Pauline morality had to be enforced.

Generally over the whole society, this code of conduct was strictly obeyed. Nothing approaching promiscuity can be inferred from the evidence in either England or France at any time or for any age group, and the whole issue seems peculiarly inappropriate to the study of life in the traditional world. As far as we yet know, the illegitimacy rates of English people two centuries ago and more were rather lower than our own; abortion and infanticide seem not to have been excessive amongst them. Whatever the final conclusion as to pre-nuptial pregnancy, the noticeable thing about the figures in general is how infrequently the regulations were infringed amongst a body of persons deprived for so much of their lives of sexual satisfactions. It would seem impossible to cite statements which contemplated permissiveness of any sort in such matters except for those which made full use of poetic licence, and except for some of the speeches heard in the London Playhouses during the Restoration period. Ordinary people can rarely be heard on this subject. But when they spoke their minds as witnesses in ecclesiastical courts they left no doubt that sexual intercourse outside marriage was universally condemned.[148]

Even the more light-hearted beliefs we have entertained about this intriguing subject seem to be unjustified. The tumultuous weeks of Charles II's Restoration to the throne do not seem to have been marked by any perceptible increase in the

[148] *See page 267.*

conceptions, legitimate or illegitimate, recorded by implication in the registers of baptisms nine months later. Nothing in the documents confirms that there was a change in sexual habits to correspond with that licence and licentiousness which has always been associated with the Restoration as a whole period of time.[149] The very interesting literary thesis recently advanced by Mr David Foxon, which would place the beginnings of prurience in the decade 1650–60, cannot be confirmed in the recorded doings of the ordinary men and women of the time, nor even in those of the nobility and gentry, as a whole.[150] Like Juliet's marriage, this literary fact, if such it was, must have been a change of style and emphasis which can only deceive the inquirer into what living people actually did.

The impression left by the beginning of research into the sexual conduct of the men and women of pre-industrial England is as follows. They obeyed the code. They did so whether they were Protestants or Catholics, Anglicans or Separatists, townsmen or countrymen, commoners or gentry. Closer research may well reveal that urban centres were more scandalous than country districts, and that the privileged were less inhibited than the respectable poor, but the differences are too slight to impress the general observer. Hypocrisy was presumably as widespread then as it always is, and indifference to religious sanctions was no doubt common and getting commoner. Fornication and adultery took place of course, and were often conveniently camouflaged by the low fertility of very young women and by the regularity with which babies came to married women in the ordinary course.[151] It can be assumed that much was concealed from the neighbours, and more from the parish priests, probably more in Protestant England than in Catholic France.

Certainly the English of Stuart times seem to have been less stringent about base-born children than the French of Bourbon times. Whores seem to have been an acknowledged feature of the social scene; the earnest ministers might deplore their existence, but when they talked of behaviour in a wife which might lead a husband to seek satisfaction elsewhere they accepted the brothel as a fact.[152] Certain women seem to have played the harlot's role in the countryside as well as in London;

[149] *See page 267.* [150] *See page 267.*
[151] *See page 267.* [152] *See page 267.*

in Ludlow, for example, in the early seventeenth century, one or two girls brought a succession of bastards to be baptized.[153] These unfortunate prostitutes, if such they really were, seem often to have been the daughters of widows, as was Anne Bacon at Clayworth. But by and large men and women lived what the respectable call respectable lives. They were chaste until marriage came, or perhaps until it was in certain prospect in the very near future, and then they begot children very quickly indeed. Thereafter they cohabited and they only seem very rarely to have indulged themselves outside marriage.

These statements, of course, are intended as overall generalizations, and apply to the majority living in the countryside, and not to the minority living in the towns, at least not with the same conviction. Difficult as it may be to confirm in accurate detail the principles laid down here for villagers, it will be even more difficult to do so for townsfolk.[154] It may be a long time, for instance, before we can confirm for London or for any other English town the practice of contraception which Louis Henry has discovered amongst the Calvinist burghers of Geneva as early as the last years of the seventeenth century. The villagers of France are known in two communities anyway, to have followed this example by the end of the eighteenth century, but we cannot yet say whether the rural English had adopted the practice by that date.[155] The uniform regularity of the sexual conduct of our ancestors means more to the historian than the fact that the Christian or Pauline code was strictly enforced amongst them. It is an extraordinary thing that we can investigate these, the most intimate, doings of our predecessors and discuss them with some confidence, whilst many of their more public actions and attributes are still mysterious and will probably remain so. When we analyse what happened between man and woman lying together in the little parlours of their cottages, for the parlour was the bedroom before the ordinary man's house acquired an upstairs, we are in fact observing the purchase over what they allowed themselves to do of a whole social system.

It was a system, as we have said, which proscribed promiscuity, which frowned on all sexual relations outside marriage, and which was particularly severe with bastardy. Every historian has met instances of this, nevertheless. The records of the magistrates are studded with examples made of unmarried

[153] *See page 268.*   [154] *See page 268.*   [155] *See page 268.*

mothers, and sometimes of unmarried fathers too, with provision for the upkeep of the child:

Jane Sotworth of Wrightington, spinster, swears that Richard Garstange of Fazarkerley, husbandman, is the father of Alice, her bastard daughter. She is to have charge of the child for two years, provided she does not beg, and Richard is then to take charge until it is twelve years old. He shall give Jane a cow and 6s. in money. Both he and she shall this day be whipped in Ormeskirke.

So ordered the Lancashire justices at the Ormskirk Sessions on Monday, April 27th, 1601, though the language they used was Latin and lengthier. At Manchester, in 1604, they went so far as to require that Thomas Byrom, gentleman, should maintain a bastard he had begotten on a widow, and be whipped too. On October 10th, 1604, he was whipped in Manchester marketplace.[156]

Not many 'gentlemen' can ever have suffered this indignity. But the frequency of these cases in the records, even the number of times behaviour of this character has appeared in the present essay, must not be allowed to create the impression that illegitimacy was commonplace, more often to be met with than it is in our own day. The trouble taken over each instance by the justices is an indication that it cannot have been a regular, accepted thing, and when their care grew less obvious in later Stuart times, the figures in the records of baptism marked 'illeg.', 'base', 'spur', or plain 'b.' for bastard did not markedly increase.

Illegitimacy is recorded in the parish registers, with a consistency which makes it seem clear that where they appear at all the entries must be taken seriously as an indication of the extent of the practice. This in itself is a demonstration of the power of ecclesiastical regulation and opinion because it must have taken some courage to offer a base-born child to the priest for baptism, though something must surely be allowed for the mother's concern for the baby's immortal soul. Evasion may have been common of course, and it is probably wise to reject as testimony those parish registers, or those periods of registration, in which bastardy appears not at all, or only at very long intervals. The fall in the number of illegitimacies which might come under a strong-minded parish priest, a man like William Sampson, could have been due to the fact that the

[156] *See page 268.*

cowering culprits fled the village to abandon their offspring
somewhere else, rather than to the restoration and maintenance of moral discipline. Still, he would be a bold man who
claimed that more illegitimacy was concealed then than now.
Assuming that figures are in some way comparable, let us take
a few comparative examples.[157]

Registered Illegitimate Baptisms, England, Wales and France.
(per cent of all baptisms)

		Mean %	Maximum % for a Particular Year	
Ludlow, Shropshire	1590–1640	3·8	1593	9
	1748–1774	7·8	1759	14·8
Kerry, Montgomeryshire	1610–1619	1·6	1619	11·5
	1620–1649	6·06	1624	10·2
	1670–1689	0·4		
	1690–1699	4·1	1691	10
Ashton-under-Lyne, Lancs.*	1594–1640	6·82	1594	16·6
Stoke-on-Trent, Staffs.	1660–1711	2·5	1687	8·6
Clayworth, Notts.	1676–1701	1·9	1686	8·3
Manchester, Lancs.*	1654–1665	1·38		
St Lambert-des-Levées, Maine-et-Loire, France	1650–1750	0·3–0·4		
Paris Region, France (41 villages)	1740–1789	0·5	5 villages show rates above 1·5	
England and Wales	1920–1930	3–4		
			1941	5·4
			1945	9·3
			1955	4·2

* The Ashton and Manchester registers also show numbers of bastard
children buried who do not appear in the baptismal registers.

It would not be easy to read this table in such a way as to
suppose that illegitimacy was generally higher in England and
Wales before 1700 than it is today. But there seems to be no
doubt that bastard children were commoner with us than they
were with the French. The very large sample from the Paris
region in the eighteenth century makes this conclusion almost
inescapable, since the rate in that area was lower than has
been found for any set of records of an English village. These
figures may perhaps give an unfavourable impression of the
record of our own ancestors, since in many registers decades
pass by with only a scattered bastard or two appearing. There
is now no way of deciding whether this was due to evasion and

[157] *See page 268.*

to lenience, or whether it was due to a genuine restoration of behaviour to the expected pattern.

The parish of Kerry in Montgomeryshire shows the most remarkable variation. Though this looks as if it must have been due to vagaries of registration, there is nothing in the published Welsh registers that we have seen to confirm a belief that the Welsh were more tolerant of illegitimacy than the English. The record of Ashton-under-Lyne in the 1590's remains the highest we have been able to find in Britain before 1700, over a group of years, and the individual year 1594 there is the peak for bastardy; both percentages, it must be remembered, leave out of account the unbaptized bastards amongst the burials. The comparison of figures from France and England is complicated by differences between town and country in both countries. Across the Channel foundlings, *enfants trouvés*, were a particular feature of baptismal records in the great cities, especially in Paris in the eighteenth century. There are traces of them in English registers, particularly in the capital and its environs, where the registrars exercised a banal ingenuity in inventing surnames for the deserted infants. But the tradition that a fallen woman went to the city to be delivered of her burden seems to have been commoner in France than in England. The illegitimacy and foundling rates of Paris, if ever they could be analysed, would no doubt look alarming; but the parish registers of Paris were burnt in the war of 1939–45.

In our own country, where pregnant spinsters seemed to have preferred to stay at home and brave it out, even to the vicar, the scattered figures for urban areas are comparatively low, as can be seen from the example of Manchester in our table. Registered illegitimacy at St Margaret's, Westminster, is known for a much longer period; between 1539 and 1648 it never exceeded 2·5 per cent and showed remarkable consistency in an area where population was growing rapidly and contained a large number of transients. The parish of St Augustine at Bristol, for all its numbers of sailors, had a low bastardy rate in the sixteenth and seventeenth centuries.[158] It would be unwise to treat either figure very seriously, but this early evidence faces us with an intriguing dual possibility. Not only does it look at first sight as if there was a significant difference between England and France in respect of babies

[158] *See page 268.*

born outside marriage, with the prize for continence going to the Catholic country rather than to the Protestant, Puritan, ascetic English. It also looks as if it may be difficult to demonstrate that the wicked, worldly city of London, the despair of the earnest preachers, was, along with the other English towns, more given to sexual irregularity than the countryside.

In spite of the difficulties of these fragmentary figures, the idiosyncrasies of parish clerks and the differing responses of errant peasant girls to the frowns of the parish priests, there may yet turn out to be some historical consistency in the bastardy rates for our country. The tendency seems to be for figures to be higher in the late sixteenth and in the middle eighteenth centuries. Now these were times when historians believe that population was rising, when perhaps the age of marriage was generally a little lower and when more people were getting married. They were times, in fact, when we might suppose that conditions were favourable, certainly not times of frequent dearth. In France the low rate of bastardy is understandably used as evidence for the stability of the rural social structure. But it will be much more difficult to use illegitimacy rates as indications of social dislocation in England if it does turn out that they tended to be highest in times of prosperity and not conspicuously higher in towns than in the countryside. Numbers of bastards should no longer be thought of as the necessary outcome of political crisis or even the movement of armies in England. The illegitimacy rate certainly does not seem to be positively related to scarcity of food and demographic crisis. But even these very preliminary suggestions may have gone too far. The two observations which can now be made with something approaching confidence are that bastardy seems to have been commoner in Protestant England than in Catholic France, and that it was no more characteristic of life in the world we have lost than it is of our life today.

Suicide is the most usual index of social demoralization, of *anomie* as the sociologists call it. If ever we could get to know anything reliable about it in these earlier times, it would probably be an even more sensitive index than it is now, indicating the relationship between personal discipline and social survival. Killing yourself was a far graver sin in the traditional world than fornication or adultery, and it was punished by the denial of Christian burial. We need go no further than the story of Hamlet to discover this fact.

Isolated records of suicides in the parish registers have occasionally been commented upon, and the extraordinary custom of burying the offending corpse at the crossroads survived into Tudor times, and perhaps later. At Ashton-under-Lyne there seems to have been a more humane attitude. On June 11th, 1683, for example, the following entry appears in the register for that parish.[159]

Roger Peake of Treehouse Bank, who hanged himself in his own barn the 9th day and was stolen into the churchyard and buried on the north side about one of the clock in the morning.

In hugger-mugger they had to inter him, just as they did Ophelia.

The parson must have connived at this neighbourly defiance of the church's rules, since the register is so frank about it. Suicides appear with what looks like fair regularity in the Ashton register throughout the seventeenth century. Most decades passed with only one suicide or none at all, but in the 1610's and the 1680's there were two, whilst in the 1620's there were four. Nothing like a suicide rate can be guessed at from figures of this isolated character, but it is at least worth remembering that the 1620's were times of depression in the textile trade, and of dearth; the probable crisis of subsistence at Ashton itself in 1623 and 1624 has already been discussed. The actual years in which suicides occurred there, however, were spread evenly out over the decade; 1623, 1625, 1626 and 1628.

Suicide in this one settlement, then, does not seem to have been very closely associated with demographic crisis, though it might possibly be connected with economic fluctuation. The French sociologist Durkheim introduced the concept of anomie, and established suicide as the most sensitive indicator of that condition. He noticed that suicide increased at times of economic depression, but he also related it to many other social phenomena which are often thought of as leading to disintegration of social life. Urbanization is one of them, and it so happens that a little can be said about suicide and the life of cities in Stuart England because Graunt's study of the bills of mortality can be made to yield a suicide rate of sorts for the middle decades of the seventeenth century, and the bills themselves could be used to continue the series up till the end of the eighteenth century. Taking the population as 400,000, a working minimum, something like 2·5 people per hundred

[159] *See page 268.*

thousand 'Hanged and made away with themselves' during the twenty years preceding 1660 for which Graunt prepared figures. This is a low rate as compared with those which obtain today, when a figure of 10 per 100,000 inhabitants is regarded as favourable, and when in a city like San Francisco the rate can rise as high as 25·9, as it did in 1950. It is probable, however, that many or even all of the people classified in the Bills of Mortality as lunatic at death were in fact suicides, and if this was so the suicide rate might well have been as high as 4 or 5 per hundred thousand in London in Graunt's day.[160]

Though we have no means of comparing these very vague estimates with suicide rates in rural England at that time, these first, preliminary figures do make two things clear. One is that suicide was a known and even a familiar phenomenon in traditional society and is not a peculiarity of our own highly urban, industrialized era. The literature of our ancestors could be used to confirm this essential fact, but it is very important that such evidence can now for the first time be related to actual happenings. The second point is that the enormous growth of London in Stuart times with all the disorganization of the pattern of people's lives which it must have brought with it does not on the face of it seem to have been accompanied by a suicide rate which was high on our own standards. Further work might establish some correlation between urbanization and anomie in pre-industrial England, but unfortunately so few parish registers record suicides that a credible rate for rural areas may never be a possibility. It is perhaps worth mentioning that suicide rates in London varied from year to year and decade to decade as they did at Ashton-under-Lyne. The years 1648, 1657 and 1660 seem to have been the bad ones in the seventeenth century. In the eighteenth century suicide in London was consistently higher than in the seventeenth, and from about 1735 it shows a steady tendency to rise.

Perhaps too much attention has been given to these particularly sketchy and unconvincing figures, especially since it seems so unlikely that we shall ever be able to follow Durkheim into those subtleties of social analysis of the incidence of suicide which would so illuminate the society of our ancestors. The last of the possible indices of demoralization is far more easily prepared, though its interpretation turns out to be much more difficult. This is the proportion of the chosen brides of

[160] *See page 268.*

English peasants and craftsmen who had been got with child before ever they took their parts in the rites of matrimony performed inside a Christian church.

It is quite a simple matter to work out a very approximate index for this phenomenon. All that has to be done is to observe the date on which a marriage was performed and then look up the date at which the first child was brought to the font for baptism. Over a given period the number of those baptisms which take place eight months or less from the date of marriage provides the index of pre-nuptial pregnancy, when divided into the number of marriages which are certainly known from entries in the register to have given birth to children in the parish. In England we find that there was an interval of something like a fortnight on average at most times in most parishes between the date of birth and date of baptism. In the following table, therefore, a column has been added for a period of eight and a half months.

Pre-nuptial Pregnancy (England and France).[161]

	Percentage of First Baptisms recorded (in months from date of marriage)					
	8	8½	9	10	11	12
Cartmel (Lancs.) 1660–75 (173 cases)	13·2%	17·8%	24·7%	35·6%	47·7%	57·5%
Wylye (Wilts.) 1654–1783 (76 cases)	28·9%	34·2%	40·0%	48·5%	63·0%	66·4%
Clayworth (Notts.) 1650–1750 (127 cases)	10·2%	13·4%	15·7%	22·0%	44·9%	49·8%
Colyton (Devon) 1538–1799 (976 cases)	46·2%		61·3%		83·4%	
Crulai (France) 1674–1742 (323 cases)	9·5%		20·3%	33·0%	42·2%	45·4%
3 villages in the Ile de France Late 18th century (206 cases)	19·90%		35·9%	47·1%	54·4%	63·6%
Gosforth, Cumb. 1920—50 (247) (Farmers only)	40% (53·2%)					
England and Wales 1938	18%					
1950	16%					

% of all brides pregnant at marriage.

[161] *See page 269.*

Less work has been done as yet on this point in France than on illegitimacy, and the figures for Crulai may be exceptionally low. But it is known that they vary very considerably in that country between parish and parish, just as they obviously do in England. The group of villages from the Ile de France may be exceptional too, and the figures are of later date. But they are well below those from Wylye and nowhere near those for Colyton. So the indications are that the French rates may have been lower than the English ones though the difference may turn out to be nothing like as marked as it is in the case of illegitimacy. It is also obvious that our record today is not all that different from that of our ancestors, except perhaps in some rural areas such as Gosforth. The indications are that English peasant society was less, not more, prone to pre-nuptial pregnancy than English industrial society.

Once we start asking for the reasons why Catholic France had a different record of bastardy and pre-nuptial pregnancy from that of Protestant England we find ourselves in the midst of an intricate discussion which would soon take us a long way from our present purpose. Some importance must surely be attached to the different positions of the clergy in the two countries. The *curés* of the French villages, celibate and officially without possessions, were no doubt much closer to the everyday lives of the peasants than the beneficed rectors, the substantial, housekeeping vicars and sometimes conscientious but seldom respected curates of the English Church. The English clergy moreover had to depend far more than the French upon opinion and conscience to keep discipline. In so far as the English Puritans were responsible for sexual prurience – their responsibility has probably been greatly exaggerated – this may be one of the reasons. They tended to emphasize subjective authoritarianism in sexual matters because they had to rely so heavily upon persuasion and verbal threat. They lacked the sanctions of the Roman hierarchy. Meanwhile, habits of the English seem to have become laxer than those of the French.

But, as we have already noticed in respect of illegitimacy, they had not become lax enough to imply anything like free love. The most regular feature of the above table is found in the percentages in the final column which show how many fertile women had their first baby within the first year of marriage. More than half were born within twelve months, and the full figures show that in both countries by the second anniversary three-quarters or four-fifths of all these couples had produced a child. In maintaining a late age of marriage, our ancestors were in fact holding down the number of births, and it is difficult to assume any degree of promiscuity among single people. Although women may have become mature rather later than they do today, being low in fertility until the early twenties, any general approach of sexual licence would have led to a far higher rate of bastardy than has yet been observed, even in England. Moreover more than half of those babies who arrive early had been conceived within the three months before the marriage ceremony and not earlier. If there had been any form of trial marriage in our country, this proportion would presumably have been lower. Babies would surely have arrived within a month or week or two of the ceremony, not occasionally but as a regular thing.

Nevertheless these first results of study show that premarital pregnancy was common in England, so common in Colyton and Wylye that it hardly seems possible that an affianced couple was everywhere expected to maintain chastity until after the church celebration was over. We saw how difficult it was to tell from the account of marriage in a Yorkshire rural area in the 1640's exactly when it was that a man and woman caught up in the process of getting married actually began to cohabit. The fact seems to be that in many places in England in the sixteenth, seventeenth and eighteenth centuries, and perhaps in France too, the older customs of Western Europe still appear to have persisted.

The striking difference between these customs and those which are now universally regarded as standard and required practice amongst Christians can be seen from the following quotation from the proceedings in the Registry of the Archdeaconry at Leicester, the case in question dating from July, 1598.[162]

The common use and custom within the county of Leicester, specially in and about the town before mentioned (Hoby and Waltham) and in other places thereunto adjoining for the space of 10, 20, 30 or 40 years past hath been and is that any man being a suiter to a woman in the way of marriage is upon that day appointed to make a final conclusion of the marriage before treated of. If the said

[162] *See page 269.*

marriage be concluded and contracted then the man doth abide the night the next following after such contract, otherwise he doth depart without staying the night.

It is plain that no ceremony in church, no ecclesiastical marriage, is in question here, but a contract to marry – an espousal, a troth plight, a *handfasting* as it was called in some localities – what we would term an engagement. The custom of Leicestershire and of a particular group of villages implies two rather surprising features of peasant behaviour. One is that marriage procedures were looked upon as liable to differ considerably from place to place, and even conceivably in the same place from time to time. The other is that in this particular custom sexual intercourse did not have to await the conclusion of the church marriage; it was expected to take place directly the contract was definitely concluded. Brides in Leicestershire at this time must normally have gone to their weddings in the early, and sometimes in the late, stages of pregnancy.

Espousals cannot be discussed in any length here, and a special study would be necessary in order to decide how widespread was the customary assumption that they permitted cohabitation and to estimate their consequent effect on vital statistics. It is suggested that their persistence in England has given rise to the belief in the existence of trial marriage amongst our peasantry. Marriage contracts of this sort were abolished in the Catholic world by the Papal Bull confirming the decree of the Council of Trent in 1564, making privy contracts null and void and directing that all marriages should be performed by a priest in the church of the parish where one of the parties dwelt. This would help to explain the apparently stricter discipline maintained in France. It is perhaps surprising that espousals continued so long in England after this date, and that our customs should have remained so localized. They were in a sense officially abolished here by the act of 1753, usually called Hardwicke's Marriage Act, but it seems improbable that so deep-seated a usage ever completely disappeared from the countryside.

It would be a nice study in social development and local variation, to discover how it was that the rule of the Catholic Church established itself as a moral imperative for the Protestant Christian, since this process must have been complete by the Victorian age. If local oral tradition is to be trusted, and this is obviously dangerous, the older practice was in full control in the remote hillsides of Cumberland in the early eighteenth century. The following is recorded in the guide to one of the lonelier churches –'The Kirk of Ulpha to the pilgrim's eye. Is welcome as a star'.

A story often told by the old folks, relates how a certain parson, before the days when marriages must necessarily be held in church, gathered together those living together and not yet legally united, and performed the wedding ceremony over seventeen such couples who assembled at Frith Hall on one day in the year 1730 for that purpose.[163]

Frith Hall was the largest house in that scattered hamlet on the Duddon.

In spite of local variations in the words used and the actions taken, it is possible to make the following tentative generalization about espousals or contracts in England in relation to marriage. A contract publicly entered into before witnesses and marked by two overt actions, the kissing of the woman by the man and the presentation of gifts – often a gold ring, or, oddly enough, half a gold ring – constituted a binding marriage, provided only that the couple then proceeded to sexual intercourse. In the Roman Church after 1564 such an action between an affianced couple was a grave sin. In the English church it was a much less serious matter. In extreme Protestant practice, amongst the sects in America as well as here, the whole issue was different. For the nonconformists marriage consisted simply of a promise followed by consummation: church ceremony was irrelevant. Since in our day Puritanism is closely associated with sexual authoritarianism perhaps an example ought to be cited from the works of an English Puritan divine on this interesting point. William Gouge had this to say in 1622:

I would advise all Christians that desire a blessing and good success on their marriage to be contracted before they are married. Contracted persons are in a middle degree betwixt single persons and married persons: they are neither simply single, nor actually married. Many make it a very marriage, and thereupon have a greater solemnity at their contract than at their marriage: yea

[163] *See page 269.*

many take liberty after a contract to know their spouse, as if they were married: an unwarrantable and dishonest practice. The laudable custom of our and other churches showeth, that at least three weeks must pass betwixt contract and marriage. For the contract is to be three times published, and that but once a week before the wedding is celebrated.[164]

If three weeks and more were added to the figures in the table we have printed, the intervals between marriage ceremony and first birth in Crulai and in an English village would begin to look a little more alike. Gouge's advice in favour of a definite contract confirms what is known from other literary and legal evidence, that the formal practice was on the way out in his time. The informal act of affiancing no doubt continued without document or sworn witnesses, but marked by social celebration and having the same effect on the behaviour of the parties. The really significant revelation in this passage is in the words used about sexual intercourse during the period of the contract, whilst the banns were being called and the actual marriage ceremony prepared. Though ascribed to the temptation of Satan, though 'unwarrantable and dishonest', such an action was not described as sinful.

No hard-headed peasant would have let his daughter get to the point of espousal until a firm agreement had been made between the two families. Still some risk remained that the banns might be forbidden from the body of the congregation on one or other of those three successive Sunday mornings. William Perkins was a better-known spokesman of the Puritans in the years of their rise to power in the seventeenth century, and he also skirts round the awful word 'sin' when he reaches this point, though he used it freely enough elsewhere. He talked in frowning disapproval of affianced couples 'seeking to satisfy their own fleshly desires, after the manner of brute beasts' but he goes no further than that.[165] Towards the end of the seventeenth century the nonconformist view of marriage as a personal matter, not a sacrament of the church at all, evidently grew much more influential in our country. In 1680 one, William Lawrence, a Scottish Presbyterian, published a long treatise insisting that all ecclesiastical matrimony was unnatural outrage, and that the indissoluble partnership between man and woman began whenever the first sexual union

[164] *See page 269.*   [165] *See page 269.*

took place, needing neither witness, nor confirmation, nor any public celebration. It is true that this highly unconventional book ends on page 422 with the confession 'By the interruption of the Press I am compelled to break off this book abruptly'.[166] Still the outlook he defended is close to the secular conception of marriage so prevalent in our own century. In registering his protest against what might be called the authoritarian orthodoxy being established in his time, he cannot be said to have been expressing anything like relaxation of moral discipline or anomie in English or in Scottish society.

The marriage customs of the English peasantry may have been variable and complicated, much more so than those of their Catholic French contemporaries, but they expressed and maintained personal and social discipline nevertheless. Still it remains the case that pre-nuptial conception may never provide the sort of index of social dislocation in England which it perhaps already provides in France. When they discovered that the proportion of brides having babies within eight months of marriage rose to 30 per cent at Sotteville-les-Rouen towards the end of the eighteenth century, the French historians might have concluded justifiably that some important social difference had appeared there to bring about so marked a contrast with the record elsewhere.[167] In England we shall have to look more closely at the actual length of the interval after marriage before making any such inferences. The significant fact about the figures from Colyton may not be so much that nearly two-thirds of the brides had children baptized within nine months as that one third of those already pregnant were delivered within three months of the ceremony. It seems as if the young men in that parish found themselves making honest women of the girls rather more often than was necessary elsewhere, and this might possibly have important implications about the age of marriage and the effectiveness of regulation.

The consideration of the relationship between personal discipline and social survival must be left at this point. It may perhaps be felt that the evidence at present available is almost as challenging and inconclusive as it had to be on the subject of starvation. But the belief that the defiance of Christian injunction and social regulation was very common in the world we have lost would be difficult to sustain in the face of the figures we have quoted and it seems unlikely that 'moral'

[166] *See page 269.*   [167] *See page 269.*

breakdown can have been of much importance in bringing about demographic crises. In trying to decide what significance is to be attached to figures of bastardy and pre-nuptial pregnancy amongst our ancestors, there is one salient fact which must never be overlooked. Enforced chastity affected a far greater proportion of people's lives than it does today. This was because so many of them were too young to be married, the age of marriage being so high, and because marriage if and when it came was likely to last for a shorter time.

It may have been noticed that no room has been found to discuss the best known of all vital statistics, birth-rates, marriage-rates and death-rates. Crude rates of this sort, numbers per thousand of a population being born, married or dying in a period of twelve months, are somewhat deceptive indices. They have some usefulness, especially when the crudity is refined out of them, but they are extremely difficult to obtain for the time before the census gives totals, because to calculate them at all the total numbers at risk have to be known. When these numbers can be obtained at all, death-rates generally turn out to be high, marriage-rates about the same as ours, and birth-rates very high in comparison. These rates also varied from place to place and time to time; it will be many years before any accurate general impression will be available. Even then statisticians will prefer to use more revealing measures, such as age-specific fertility and mortality. Nevertheless it may perhaps be just worth-while glancing at the birth- (baptismal), marriage- and death- (burial) rates where they are known with something like twentieth-century accuracy. Thus we can take Clayworth and Cogenhoe as examples. In 1676 Clayworth had 401 people and 412 in 1688; Cogenhoe had 185 in 1618, 180 in 1628, and varying numbers in between.

The birth- and death-rates were high at Clayworth over the relevant years, the baptismal rate being about 35 or 37 per thousand and the burial rate 40 or 42. These are both above the peak rates reached in Victorian times, when the birth-rate was about 35 over the whole country and the death-rate in the 20's. Clayworth seems to have experienced very high mortality indeed, even if no demographic crises can be confirmed for these years, though we have seen that something very like it occurred between 1678 and 1680. In Cogenhoe on the other hand between 1613 and 1628 rates were lower; the baptismal-rate was somewhere between 26 and 35, the burial-rate as low as it is today, at 13½ to 18; nowadays both rates vary at about this level for the whole country. The experience of these communities then, as to general mortality and fertility, is contradictory and tells us very little about conditions in the world we have lost as a whole, except that, as might be expected, they could be extremely unfavourable. They illustrate, in fact, the uselessness of trying to argue overall from a sample too small to be free of extreme random variation. But there is another and more important reason why they are of interest to us.

We have to admit that we are still at an inconclusive stage in answering questions about starvation and comparative sexual discipline. Our colleagues in France are something like half a generation ahead of us in the study of these questions, but we have been able to demonstrate one striking and entirely unexpected feature of the life of the English village community at that time. The turnover of population in these settled, agricultural, traditional communities was remarkably high. No less than 61·8 per cent of the people living at Clayworth in 1688 had not been there in 1676, and something like 50 per cent of those living in Cogenhoe in 1628 were not there in 1618. Most of the movement was clearly local and larger areas would show much less. In these two communities, people were moving to and fro, society was changing, whole households were coming and going and both villages were in perpetual exchange with their neighbours. All this went on quite independently of the level of birth- and death-rates, though if this were the opportunity, it could be demonstrated how intimately this movement must have been connected with the low expectation of life. In fact every feature of pre-industrial society could be shown to fit in with this somewhat unexpected characteristic of peasant society, and especially the migratory activities of servants.

Some of these details of life at Clayworth and Cogenhoe have been printed in a preliminary form. These are the first public results of the attempt now at last being made to understand the social structure of our peasant forefathers in something like numerical form. We may finish this chapter of our essay by quoting the concluding paragraph of what was written about these two villages when these facts were announced in 1963.[168]

[168] See page 269.

In spite of sudden change of this sort, and of the more gradual change which came about through the succession of son to father, nephew to uncle, kinsman to kinsman, the impression of permanence in the constituent households which composed a Stuart community is easy to understand. Nearly half of the heads of households at Clayworth had either died or had left the village by 1688, nevertheless their successors presided over units of persons which were mostly recognizably the same. And at Cogenhoe, where eight out of thirty-three households failed to survive a decade of change, it is still true that over three-quarters of them did survive, often with different heads, with a membership sometimes extensively revised, but still the same households, inhabiting the same buildings, working the same fields. The system, that familial, patriarchal system which dominated and gave structure to pre-industrial society, had succeeded in maintaining permanence in spite of the shortness of life, the fluctuations of prosperity, the falling in of leases, the wayward habits of young folk in service, and the fickleness of their employers.

The institutions of the old world must be looked upon in this way, as expedients to provide permanence in an environment which was all too impermanent and insecure. The respect due to the old and experienced, the reverence for the Church and its immense, impersonal antiquity, the spontaneous feeling that it was the family which gave a meaning to life because the family could and must endure, all these things helped to reconcile our ancestors with relentless, remorseless mortality and mischance. But they must not deceive the historian into supposing that the fixed and the ancient were the only reality: an unchanging, unchangeable social structure may well be essential to a swiftly changing population.

The historical observer in an inquiry of this sort can only feel himself to be in the position of the scientist in his bathyscope, miles beneath the surface of the sea, concentrating his gaze for a moment or two on the few strange creatures who happen to stray out of the total darkness into his beam of light. Where have they come from, and what will happen to them? he cannot help asking himself. What did happen to poor little Copperwhite Mastin, son of Elizabeth Mastin, spinster, and seven months old in May 1688, the only bastard alive in Clayworth? Or to the Coles household, thirteen strong, which appeared at Cogenhoe in 1623, no doubt as tenants of the leased-out manor, was there in 1624, but had disappeared by 1628? Even more puzzling and challenging is to ask whether these two communities are in fact typical of the whole. On this the historian can only talk as the scientist might. Here are two samples of communities in motion, two tiny globes of light disposed at random a little way down into the great ocean of persons who lived and died in our country before records of persons in general began to be kept. These samples may be ordinary enough, but they may be quite extraordinary. We cannot yet tell: we may never be able to tell.

Elizabeth Mastin was a widow's daughter. We may not know enough yet to decide whether the English peasants literally starved, but we do know what was likely to happen to a fatherless boy who, because his parents had broken the disciplinary rules, had no regular home in the world we have lost. He was almost certain to die before he was mature, just as so many millions will die in our own world, unless the age-old problems of subsistence and population are somehow finally resolved.

Social Change
and Revolution
in the Traditional World
Chapter 7

In spite of the smallness of its scale and the simplicity of its economics, the society we have been describing was a highly complex arrangement of persons. The kings and queens of the old order, the lords, knights, master-craftsmen, bishops, yeomen, apprentices, and the rest were all disposed in intricate, traditional order and based on the patriarchal family. But as we have said, the whole structure was subject to conflict and change.

Up to the end of the feudal era proper, civil strife was commonplace all over Europe. Shakespeare still preserves for us the interminable quarrels of the fifteenth century, when the houses of York and Lancaster embroiled baronage, knighthood, church, citizens and people in a dreary contest for dynastic power, only occasionally a matter of open fighting and never as dramatic as Shakespeare had to make it out to be.

But the contest which sticks in the imagination and which the whole world immediately associates with civil war and revolution in our country is the last which ever occurred, that between Roundhead and Cavalier, when Charles I was defeated and beheaded by the Puritans. The years between 1640 and 1660, when desultory fighting turned into desperately serious campaigns, and constitutional crisis led to usurpation and to an irregular régime, is conventionally called the Puritan Revolution. After the much less romantic embroglio which took place in 1688 and 1689, ending as it did in the exile of the Catholic Stuarts, was added to it, the whole English Revolution had run its irregular course. This *English Revolution*, needless to say, along with the *French*, *American* and *Russian Revolutions*, is one of the great historical realities in accepted parlance.

In this interlude between our discussion of the personal, everyday life of the traditional world and the brief description we shall attempt to give of its political workings, it is necessary to analyse the reasons for the Civil War and to ask whether the word Revolution can justifiably be used of seventeenth-

century England if anything of Social Revolution is intended.
This necessity arises from the persistent preoccupations of the
historians, rather than from the subject itself. It is always
interesting and important to know the circumstances under
which a society will be at war with itself, but social description
can be undertaken without entering into the issues of any
particular crisis, however fundamental it may have been.
Dwelling on the seriousness of the differences over which men
fought at Naseby and Sedgemoor has helped to distort the
shape which that society has taken up in the minds of men in
our time. But since this question is so often put to the evidence
by historians and learners alike – 'What was it in Stuart society
which led to political disaster and fighting?' – it can scarcely
be evaded here.

The historian, as we shall see in our last chapter, is something of a nuisance to the sociological inquirer, just because
it is his habit to ask questions of this blank and simple sort.
What is much more confusing is that he expects to be able to
get swift and straightforward answers to them. In the present
case, because of the form which an answer is ordinarily expected to take, the question itself is not simple at all. Along
with a request for the social origins of a particular political
crisis, there is usually also a demand for a descriptive response
of a kind which would relate the English Revolution with the
long-term social transformation which finally gave rise to the
modern, industrialized world. Can any connection be traced,
it is required to know, between Cromwell and his Roundheads
on the one hand, and the social forces which led to the de-
thronement of the patriarchal family in economic organization
on the other? Or between the Glorious Revolution of 1688
and the coming of the factories?

We shall not attempt to deal in this preliminary essay with
the course of the secular, overall change which brought about
the contrast between our world and the world we have lost.
Our subject is rather the comparison of the two, and all that
we shall need to do is to dwell briefly on the England of the
early twentieth century in order to point the contrast as
sharply as we can. The task of the present chapter will have
to be entirely analytical, therefore, and at a rather more
academic level than the rest of the book. The reader who
wishes simply to get to know some of the facts about the
comparison as such may safely pass it by.

The subject begins with a curious uncertainty as to the actual nature and extent of that contrast itself. This uncertainty attaches to the most conspicuous feature of all in the industrialized world – the factory, that instrument of mechanical and mass production. No one seems quite to know exactly when the factory appeared.

Final origins of things like this are in fact much more difficult to trace than might be supposed. Like the source of a river, the institutional story as you trace it back first branches into numbers of streams of similar size, so that you are puzzled to say which is the one you should follow, and then finally disperses into the runlets and the raindrops of the distant and misty heights of time.

The *ergasterion*, or slave work-centre, where these human chattels were congregated for collective work in the Ancient World is one such tributary. Another, in the analysis laid out by the great sociologist, Max Weber, is the *fabrica* or cellarden, found in the medieval town as the collective property of a group of masters, or deep in the countryside as part of the lord's property in a manor. Though Weber and the more learned and cautious of the other writers express surprise at the absence of evidence for factories in earlier times, when they get to Tudor England they feel at last that they are on firm ground.[169] Listen to this:

> *Within one room being large and long*
> *There stood two hundred looms full strong*
> *Two hundred men, the truth is so,*
> *Wrought in these looms all in a row.*
> *By every one a pretty boy*
> *Sat making quils with mickle joy.*
> *And in another place hard by*
> *An hundred women merrily,*
> *Were carding hard with joyful cheer*
> *Who singing sat with voices clear.*
> *And in a chamber close beside*
> *Two hundred maidens did abide*
> *In petticoats of Stamell red*
> *And milk white kerchers on their head*
> *These pretty maids did never lin*
> *But in that place all day did spin.*

[169] *See page 270.*

And so on; 'quils' were needed by the men for the loomwork, as was the carded twine: the maidens who did not 'lin' did not neglect their work as they sat in the coarse (Stamell) red petticoats. Here was a building large enough for two hundred looms, with two hundred men, a hundred women, two hundred boys, and a hundred girls all employed by Jack of Newbury, the famous clothier of England. The poem comes from the novel by Thomas Deloney, published in 1619 and dedicated to the Clothworkers Company of London. Jack's great establishment, Deloney tells us, became so famous that it was actually visited by the reigning King and Queen, Henry VIII and Katherine.[170]

It all looks very much like a factory, and this piece of verse has often been quoted by historians and other authorities to argue that factories existed before the coming of modern industry.[171] Jack of Newbury has been classed with the large-scale clothiers, one of whom is known from historical documents to have made use of buildings which may well have been of factory size. This was Stumpe of Malmesbury, who took over the abbey in that Wiltshire town, deserted and forlorn after the dissolution of the monasteries; he negotiated for Oseney Abbey at Oxford also. But intensive search has yielded no other examples, and nothing directly is known about what actually went on in those immense workrooms, so strikingly different from the little shops at the side of the house where the individual Tudor weaver worked, if he did not have his loom in the *hall*, that is the living-room, of his cottage. Deloney's description has filled in a very important gap in the account of social and economic organization as its development has been traditionally reconstructed.

But the fact seems to be that this Jack of Newbury was as much of a myth as Jack and the Beanstalk, and the 'factory' he is supposed to have set up as deceptive as Juliet's marriage, if it is used as a guide to the institutions and behaviour of our ancestors. Throughout Deloney's ribald and formless work, the manufactory is referred to as a household: he tells us at one point that 'This great household and family had its own butcher, who killed ten oxen a week for its members to eat.' It soon becomes plain that Deloney was engaged in making up a story about a fabulous clothier's household for the diversion of the London clothworkers; his subject was a Panurge

[170] *See page 270.*   [171] *See page 270.*

amongst craftsmen, not perhaps capable of drowning a whole city when he made water as Rabelais's character could do, but certainly recognizable in the master-baker with whom this book began, built on Gargantuan lines, with his household enlarged to impossible size. If the grave and famous scholars who have cited the Royal visit to the 'factory' as evidence of its importance to English economic development had actually read Deloney's book, they would have found that the King took away some of the poor children working for fabulous Jack. Some of them were made Royal pages and others the King 'sent to the Universities, allotting to every one a Gentleman's living', an interesting piece of make-believe. This fragment from that fascinating half-world between literature and folklore, does not show after all that factories existed in Tudor times. What it does show is that the successful clothier could be idealized as a hero and his household poetically exaggerated. But it was a household still.

This may set us on our guard once more against literary evidence even when used by professional historians. It does not by itself prove that factories were entirely absent in the world we have lost, but we can say with confidence that large-scale undertakings for the purpose of manufacturing goods are conspicuously lacking in all descriptions of life in England before the late eighteenth century. The traveller of that time was particularly interested in objects and institutions of exceptional size; royal palaces, cathedrals, bridges, vessels of outstanding dimensions are always being commented upon, along with every 'curious engine' which that inventive age brought forth. From Leland to Defoe, in the books of Evelyn, Pepys, Locke and such an exceptional horsewoman as the peripatetic Celia Fiennes, things seen are meticulously recorded, even by measure.[172] Some authors, especially Defoe, show a special interest in manufacture and manufacturing processes. Yet not one book can be made to yield a description of what we should call a factory.

Approaches to that peculiarly industrial form of social and economic organization certainly existed before the great Industrial Revolution, and some of them were listed in the first chapter. Mining, building, shipyards, saltworks and a whole list of other forms of manufacture certainly brought together dozens and sometimes scores of workers and placed

[172] *See page 270.*

them under some sort of discipline. Contracting for military and naval operations, turning out tapestries and other articles of refined manufacture needed for monarchical and aristocratic purposes led to the establishment of royal workshops all over Europe, and in England to such institutions as the Mineral and Battery Works set up by Queen Elizabeth. But a complicated system of definitions has to be adopted before it can be decided how far such institutions could be called factories, and the part which all of them put together had to play in the whole economy of the country was exceedingly small. Interestingly enough the closest approximation is to be found in the municipal workhouses, established under a succession of Acts of Parliament and as part of various bursts of energy on the part of municipalities to 'set the poor on work'. In its prehistory the factory was associated with poverty and destitution, just as manufacture generally was universally regarded first and foremost as a means of keeping people occupied who would otherwise be idle, perhaps even keeping them alive when otherwise they might die.

A great deal of post-industrial history has had to go by before this association could be outgrown and before the factory could take its place as a human grouping in its own right, still perhaps the typical institution of the industrialized world though said by some to be at the end of its career in that position. When at last a document appears which belonged to an organization justly described as the first English factory the emphasis on poverty and remedies against it are a conspicuous feature. Winlaton iron mill at Swalwell in the County of Durham, where ironmaster Ambrose Crowley began work in about 1691, turned out metal for the Navy in William III's war with the French; within a few years Crowley was literally employing workmen by the hundred. The 'Law Book' which he left behind makes it evident also that many of those workers were banded together in one building; certainly they were treated by him as a single labour force, a platoon in an industrial army.[173] The provisions against poverty were many and various and there was a Clerk of the Poor who also ministered at a chapel for the workpeople and kept school for their children. Something of the atmosphere of the factory as it was deliberately established in the close-knit, patriarchal society of Japan under the Meiji emperors in the 1890's is already present here.

[173] *See page 270.*

But the point which impresses the twentieth-century reader in this lengthy and complicated document is the extraordinary mixture in its provisions of elements of the old order with those of the new, the family workshop with the communal workroom. Much of the actual production for Ambrose Crowley was obviously still being done in the homes of the workmen under conditions which had prevailed since the beginnings of history. The problems of disciplining those who did work together on the premises and of co-ordinating the efforts of everyone were evidently exceedingly difficult; they seem to have become an obsession of this earliest factory-owner and organizer to have left his records behind him. The resistance which had to be overcome, if resistance it can be said to have been, was not that of machine breakers, for there seem to have been extremely few machines to break. It was rather the reluctance of an immemorial social order to accommodate an institution so alien in its assumptions about the way in which people should spend their lives.

In the present state of the evidence the arrival of the factory in the earliest country to become industrialized must be firmly placed in the middle and late eighteenth century and it is exceedingly difficult to imagine the discovery of documents in such quantities as to make it necessary to revise this conclusion. Those changes of scale, that sense of alienation of the worker from his work, that breach in the continuity of emotional experience in which we have sought for the trauma inflicted at the passing of the traditional world, cannot be referred to Tudor or to Stuart England. When factory life did at last become the dominant feature of industrial activity it condemned the worker, as we can now see, to the fate previously reserved for the pauper. But the threat of this did not become apparent until the early nineteenth century.

It is still possible, however, that those lesser changes in scale which went forward five or six generations before large-scale industrial organization began may have had some little part to play in the political malaise which then prevailed. An exhaustive understanding of politics and social change in the world we have lost, ought presumably to take every little influence into account which might have made more difficult the preservation of political stability. Perhaps the intensification of trade and commerce could be called divisive, because of the differing relationships it presumably brought with it, and because of the operation at long last of an institution entirely alien to the traditional structure, the joint stock company. This new principle of economic organization was present before 1700; the East India Company and the Bank of England had already set up the model for those institutional instruments which were to bring into being 'business' as we know it. The impact they can have had before the early eighteenth century was infinitesimal in relation to the whole of commercial and industrial activity. Still, in the vocabulary of current expressions now used by historians 'the commercial revolution of the sixteenth and seventeenth centuries' is a recent but fairly respectable phrase: if there was such a thing, it must supposedly have had some effect on politics.

It could be shown, however, that enormous commercial expansion was possible under the old order without a change in the scale of institutions or even of undertakings, and that the major social outcome of growth of this sort was in the mobility which it gave rise to. The same can be said of manufacturing activity and wealth, as it is known to have developed in Tudor and Stuart times, even though mining was growing so fast and other industries too. There was another area of social relationships which can be thought of in the same way, though it may turn out that here expansion in size was in fact accompanied by a change in structure of much greater strategic significance. This was governmental administration. Samuel Pepys of the Navy Office may prove to have a claim to be a forerunner of industrial England as important as that of Samuel Smiles.

If, as we shall try to show, social mobility was a constant feature of traditional society, then neither commerce, industry nor bureaucracy need be thought of as always disruptive because of their expansive tendencies. But there was one current in economic development which affected many more people than all these put together, in ways which clearly led to unrest. Although we were disposed to play down the enclosure movement as a solvent of the village community, there can be no doubt of the social displacement which it caused, even though only a small proportion of villages was concerned. Any considerable change in land-distribution, anything which bore on the crucial question of access to the means of growing food, was bound to be important. But even when all these influences are added together it seems entirely unlikely that a situation which could be called a social crisis or which might lead to social revolution, could have been brought about by them. Discussion of why civil war happened in seventeenth-century England which is confined to such slight effects as these lacks all conviction.

The truth is that changes in English society between the reign of Elizabeth and the reign of Anne were not revolutionary. The impression left by this first attempt to survey the fundamental framework during these generations is of how little, not of how much, evolution seems to have taken place. Nothing in economic organization or in social arrangements seems to have come about which would have led of itself to political crisis, and the changes that did go on seem to have been gradual over the whole period rather than sudden.

This is a hypothetical claim of course and no historian can prove a negative, especially in an area so elusive as the development of social structure. He can be certain of only one thing, which is that interpretation will always incline to exaggerate the next discovery about social change into a revolution. The vagaries in the fortunes of the nobility, for instance, or the success of a particular textile innovation, or the possibility of marked progress in literacy and education will tend to be made into that one crucial social change which explains everything. But once it is recognized that the rise-of-a-capitalist-class interpretation can be misleading as well as informative, and that social mobility was present in the traditional world, then the idea of a social revolution however occasioned becomes an embarrassment rather than a help towards understanding political breakdown.

It might be very different, if for example, the few facts so far discovered did indicate the possibility of fundamental change in the size, structure and function of the family over this period. Or if the growth of town life had looked as though it must have led to social dislocation on an impressive scale. Or if there were unmistakable evidence of class-consciousness and collective resentment building up over the generation in question amongst a group of persons increasing in power, number and organization, though always frustrated in their expressed aims.

None of these things seems to have happened. There were changes in all these respects, perhaps some overall changes in the atmosphere of family life. The movement of population and the transformation of environment associated with the enormous growth of London must surely have led to *anomie*, even though there does not seem to have been an obvious increase in suicide, and so on. But these long-term, gradual tendencies cannot in principle have been the cause of political upheaval in the middle of the seventeenth century. The famous ructions which led to the execution of Charles I and the exile of James II, the two outstanding episodes in 'The English Revolution', seem therefore to have little relevance to the passing of the world we have lost, to that contrast between our world and the world of our ancestors which is the subject of this essay.

Nevertheless it is understandable that historians should always strive to relate political frictions to what is called 'underlying social change'. If this is to be done, great care must be taken to avoid the pitfalls which words like 'underlying' or even words like 'expressing' carry with them when society as a structure is contrasted with its political and intellectual life. Religious and political beliefs have tended to be looked upon as displaced symptoms of something in the material structure of society, manifesting itself in what is called ideological terms. It will be a long time, so it seems, before historians recognize that no simple, powerful, universally adaptable mechanism capable of bringing about such effects ever existed in any society.

If we are to understand how violence and military contest did fit in with social arrangements we may be able to learn from the attitude which professional sociologists are now developing towards social conflict. After long years of insisting that stability was the normal state of human society, and that integration was the function of every distinguishable element in the social structure, they are now prepared frankly to accept the existence of conflict as a permanent and even a necessary element in every social system. Some emphasize the social purposes of conflict to such an extent that conflict itself appears to be functional: 'where there is no conflict, there is no change, no progress', is the point they make. Others feel that this is unnecessary, and suppose that in all societies at all times there are disintegrative tendencies, some of which have the final effect of furthering social purposes and others which do not. If the problem of relating political crisis in Stuart England with long-term, overall change is approached along the lines of this second attitude, these seem to be the conclusions which may be reached.[174]

In the first place the tendencies to disruption and disintegration which were obviously at work at that time need no longer be regarded as abnormal, in the unexpected sense. The unruliness of the Puritan clergy and gentry, the obstinacy of the common lawyers, the arrogance of the parliamentarians in the early 1600's, cease to be things which have to be explained because they existed at all. Historians need no longer go on looking at all contradictions as peculiarly significant, on all conflict as the exception to what is to be expected, and on anything which could be described as 'revolutionary' as very special indeed, requiring the most determined effort of understanding. Once it is realized that all societies, including those as stable as the England which was described in our first chapter, are liable to break down into conflict, sometimes armed, it becomes possible to look at political violence with a cooler eye. This can be done not only in our country in the 1640's, but in France in the 1790's, and in Russia in the years after 1917.

Conflict, as has been said elsewhere, is a common enough form of social interaction.[175] Since nearly everybody has an obvious interest in preventing differences from becoming collisions all parties will take strenuous avoiding action when collisions threaten. But collisions sometimes take place in social and political life, just as car collisions do, and there is a logical resemblance. When accidents happen on the roads, it makes sense to look for long-term, even 'deep-seated' causes, as well as for the errors of the drivers concerned; the continued growth of traffic, the increase in its speed, the progressive inadequacy of the roads may all have to be analysed. But it does not follow that the more dramatic the crash and important its consequences the more profound its causes must be and the more likely to be the climax of some perennial 'process'.

Now it is natural, though it may not be justifiable, to suppose that great events have great causes. The Civil War and the Puritan Revolution, together with the Glorious Revolution of 1688, are so conspicuous, so interesting, so momentous in their consequences and fraught with the origins of our liberties and of our political values, ours and those of the rest of the world, that they have inevitably been looked upon as cata-

[174] *See page 270.*   [175] *See page 270.*

clysmic, the apex of some mountain-building movement in historical evolution. And this from the very time of their occurrence. 'If in time as in place,' said the acutest of all contemporary observers, Thomas Hobbes, 'there were degrees of high and low, I verily believe that the highest of time, would be that which passed between 1640 and 1660.'[176] The parliamentary struggle and the bloodshed on the battlefields must have been the final outcome of a process going deep down into the social fabric, and extending over many generations, backwards and forwards in time. This assumption comes the more easily to the English because we pride ourselves on the continuity of our political life, and believe it to be unbroken except for these particular events. What could be more understandable than that the historians should have set aside a whole century, from 1540–1640, for the causes of the Civil War, and the whole period 1640–88, or even 1625–1714, for 'The English Revolution'?

But what is true may also be trivial, which is perhaps why the discussion of this portentous question has become by now so tedious. Nothing, beyond a fuller demonstration that conflict was everywhere, necessarily follows from showing that the causes of war between Roundhead and Cavalier can be infinitely extended into areas 'social', 'economic' or even 'social structural', for every event that ever happened can be treated in this way, and be made to appear culminatory. The simple and over-dramatic question: What was it in English society over these years which led to open fighting? has encouraged the tendency to inflate the importance of the next little piece of evidence on social development into something crucial to disaster. Hence the persisting search for the one final cause of catastrophe, the unwitting acceptance of the stale paradox about the nail in the shoe of the horse of the rider whose presence might have won the battle and changed the world.

But the most constrictive effect of the conventional assumption about the relation of the struggle in Stuart England to social structure and change has yet to be mentioned; it leads us on to the second lesson we can learn from the sociology of conflict.

The habit of expecting to discover that 'revolution' was a geological catastrophe, when a situation of ever-increasing instability suddenly gave way to a situation of rock-like

[176] *See page 270.*

permanence, obscures the possibility that society at that time had what might be called a conflict-mechanism built into it. This oversight is the more extraordinary since the supreme achievement of the whole epoch was the adaptation of a medieval institution into a classic conflict-defining, conflict-restricting and conflict-resolving social instrument, that is to say the Houses of Parliament with their Oppositions, their motions of censure, their parties and their unending, superbly conventionalized political battle.

Once the imagination is set free, there are many possible comparisons in social organization which spring to mind for Stuart England. There are, for example, the segmented societies described by anthropologists. Professor Gluckman's examination of African communities shows how a fight over the dynastic succession is a permanent feature of political life. Far from weakening or destroying the whole, conflict actually confirms its solidarity. This fits some of the features of political life in England aptly enough, from Tudor, to Stuart, to Hanoverian and even to Victorian times.[177] The segmented characteristics of the political community of our country in pre-industrial times, its division into a network of small county communities which were also conflict arenas, will concern us in our next chapter.

The picture of political institutions and political life which might finally be adopted is one where the stream of variation was wide enough to include the 'despotism of Charles I' as one extreme, and the rule of the Parliamentary Army as the other. Both were unlikely to be permanent but both nevertheless belonged within the definition, each as possible, if not quite as to be expected, as the traditional King-in-parliament arrangement. But the most useful concept to be borrowed from the sociological study of conflict in industrial, as opposed to pre-industrial, society does not concern itself with extreme situations as such but with the reasons why they alternated with each other. 'Revolution' as meaning a resolution of unendurable social conflict by reshaping society as a whole has been rejected here as impossible in pre-industrial times. But what Ralf Dahrendorf has to say about the process which occasionally brings it about in the twentieth century has its value in understanding irreconcilable conflict as it happened in the seventeenth century.[178]

[177] *See page 270.*   [178] *See page 271.*

Political breakdown is only likely to come about when it happens that several sources of conflict become *superimposed* – Dahrendorf's word. To the permanent divisive influences in the society are added specific issues about which the men of the time care so passionately that they are prepared to fight about them. The particular reason why political agreement becomes impossible is often that forces of conflict which at other times tend to modify each other, even to cancel each other out, all conspire together to make compromise impossible. This is no very novel nor perhaps a very subtle way of looking at things, but its important virtue is that each individual conflict, each pair of antagonistic forces, is looked upon as for the most part an independent variable. None of them is taken as an 'expression of' another, or as necessarily 'underlying' one or all of the others.

Of course, a difference of opinion or a collision of interest at one point in the structure will have a greater divisive effect than at another. If the King fell out with the Common Council of the City of London over monopolies (conflict of economic interest with obvious political potentiality) more disruption occurred than when a Bishop insisted that the surplice be worn in all the churches in his diocese (religious conflict with only a slight possibility of affecting any but the participants). But a simple scheme of this sort excludes altogether any explanation which insists that the whole complex interaction was 'really' religious, or 'really' economic, or 'really the rise of the social class', and that the 'real' contradiction was somehow resolved in the process of open violence.

In the particular case we are examining, it could be said that the so-called Puritan Revolution happened when a desperately acute religious controversy was superimposed upon a fierce dispute over political organization, and upon much more than that. A number of other sources of conflict were polarized at the same time, and complete knowledge would presumably show that some of them were what we should call conflicts of economic interest; many of them might well deserve the title of challenges by capitalistic organization and the values of a market economy to traditional organization and assumptions. But the discontinuities which had arisen to commercial, industrial and administrative life which were referred to above were decidedly not all of this character, and can only, as we have said, have had additive effect of problematic and perhaps negligible importance. When after a year or two of Civil War the Levellers raised their platform and the Diggers added a tiny scrap of plain communist protest over the distribution of property, then it could be said that something like a conflict over membership of the ruling *élite* became involved. To this limited degree the description 'conflict over a class differential' might be applied to part of the general disagreement.

Using a word like superimposition for all these elements of conflict emphatically does not imply that one underlay all the others, or was expressive of it, or that some aggressiveness was the displaced symptom of something else. A general release of suppressed resentment was apparent in the events of the 1640's nevertheless and there is truth in the claim that, like other movements of political disruption, the whole episode had a certain dynamic of its own. Contemporaries at the time and the observers of our day have reason, moreover, to believe that as the struggle intensified, social structural friction became a little more apparent. When the Clubmen appeared in Dorset, that latent fear of the *jacquerie*, that betrayal by those in superior positions that they were well aware of the resentment of those beneath them, had something tangible to fasten upon. But not all the sources of stress were at play in the struggle, and it is quite unjustifiable to exaggerate their breakdown into a general social structural cleavage. Of this, let it be repeated, there is no indication, and the notion of a social revolution is not permissible.

So much for the relationship of political violence in the seventeenth century to the structure of society in the world we have lost, and to the overall transformation which at the time of the military battles and the constitutional crises was still well in the future. Before we inquire why it was that our ancestors endured the supremacy of the very few, and why it was therefore that they showed so little disposition to challenge authority, social or political, we ought perhaps to complete the story of what happened in seventeenth-century history in a very summary form. We shall have to anticipate what will be said in our next chapter about the county community of country gentry, but the suggested mechanics of constitutional crisis under the Stuarts can be understood in a formal way without knowledge of the nature of political associations as it then existed. We shall be quoting once again from the context in which the comparison of political breakdown with accidents on the roads was first suggested.[179]

The political stability of England in Stuart times depended on two things, on the maintenance of ordered responsibility within each county community of politically active gentry, and on the interplay between those county communities and the central organization, that is the Crown and its institutions. The occasional meetings of Parliament were opportunities for local and national political awareness to be merged for short periods; the politics of Parliament when it was in session were national politics, the stuff of constitutional development. Far greater in extent and absolutely unbroken were the politics played within each county community. It was there, for example, that the collective memory of Parliament was to be found between its sessions.

This last point may need a little explanation, for in our day Parliament is a more or less continuous affair, and intervals of two, five or seven years are a constitutional, administrative and political impossibility. Apart from the very brief life of the Short Parliament from April 13th to May 5th 1640, no less than eleven years had elapsed since the last foregathering of Knights of the Shire and Burgesses for Parliamentary towns when Charles 1's Long Parliament met in November of that year. The previous experience of 167 of the 547 members of that remarkable assembly, which was to lay down the general lines of the Anglo-Saxon model of representative government, was confined to the three weeks of the Short Parliament. Of the remainder 161 were newcomers altogether.

Though many of them had presumably met and discussed parliamentary affairs before, and though the London season had probably brought a good number together for very different purposes, the reason why this new House of Commons was able to take up just where its predecessors had left off must be sought away from the centre of the country. It was at their meetings as justices of the peace, at the Quarter Sessions in the country towns, at Petty Sessions in the smaller places, over their morning draughts as they called them when the militia was exercised or sporting engagements took place, that the gentry of England talked parliamentary affairs. The truly political among them, of course, must have met for the purpose in their own manor houses. But however its continuity

[179] *See page 271.*

was maintained the memory of Parliament was dispersed during the periods when no sessions took place and only became collective again when the M.P.s, new and old, appeared at Westminster with the years and years of conversation with their neighbours, friends and rivals in the shires reverberating in their minds.

In the county community of gentry local offices were intrigued over, parliamentary seats were lost and won, family rivalries were created, intensified and handed down from generation to generation, changing their objects of competition and their ideological content with the times. Continuity was kept up over the whole area of national politics and within each county because differences were resolved by argument and compromise, by the victory in the political struggle of one official, or of one man over others, or of one family or faction over others.

This is only the beginning of an anatomy of political consciousness at that time, and we shall have to go into it a little more closely in our next chapter. For the moment let us turn our attention to what happened to this complex of relationships in the year before the Civil War. As the Tudors gave way to Stuarts, politics, national and local, began increasingly to include the politics of intellectual difference, of argument about theory or something approaching it. This may be recognized as the beginnings of constitutionalism, told however without supposing that the occasional and intermittent life of the House of Commons was the whole political life of the English gentry. In the counties from day to day, as well as in the Palace of Westminster once every three, five or seven years, men differed volubly over issues which were brought up for discussion, as well as combating each other over matters of prestige and office, matters of economic interest and policy, matters above all of family aggrandisement. The overriding issue which was tearing them apart during the early Stuart reigns was of course religion. Differences over the content of the faith and the proper organization of the Christian church set man against man and family against family. Some of them wrote about these bitter controversies, some published what they had written and others even preached about them, so little did the clergy retain their function as the official intelligentsia.

Naturally only a small minority within every community took to argumentation in this way, but politics are always a matter of the articulate, vigorous, able few at work amongst an inert majority. The questions which the vocal ones chose to raise and to become indignant about may not all have been those which most of their companions would have thought the most important. But anyone who resented the activities of the proselytising Puritan gentleman, or of the fanatical defender of the Ancient Constitution, or of the grim-faced Lecturer expounding the necessity of restoring the constitution of the Primitive Church, found himself drawn into argumentation too. Under such circumstances each county community, and the ruling segment as a whole, found it increasingly difficult to maintain political continuity, to contain their frictions. Even the men who sincerely wanted to be loyal and to main-tain traditional arrangements, which for the most part every-one protested he wished to do, became exceedingly difficult to manage. Even if they agreed on fundamentals, as they all perpetually claimed they did, what now interested them was their differences, and there were always arguers on hand to exacerbate them.

As disaster and ineptitude succeeded each other in Charles I's conduct of affairs, the royal task of maintaining assent to policy became hazardous. In the crisis of the 1640's, after long years of difficulty over the national finances, this task became at last impossible. What wonder that the Stuarts wished to dispense with Parliament, and so added to the turbulence by giving the gentry reason to believe that their liberties were indeed in jeopardy. Since two of the Stuart House were in fact Roman Catholic in their personal convictions, it is not sur-prising that the less scrupulous leaders were able to convince themselves that a Bourbon solution was in store. Government by discussion is not the correct way to describe what went on in Tudor, Stuart or Hanoverian times. But it may be quite accurate and very important to lay it down that government, agreement and civil peace in England did involve the resolution of differences of opinion, which must sometimes be called intellectual. Political breakdown, when it occurred in the 1640's and again in the 1680's, was an event, intellectual as well as political and constitutional, for those with the greatest power to disrupt or to settle English political life.

This analysis might perhaps look like one further attempt to assign a new meaning to that controversial yet appealing phrase 'The Rise of the Gentry'. Certainly the appreciation of political and constitutional issues in something like intellectual terms by the communities of gentry in the counties may turn out to be a crucial development for the conduct of political life in late Tudor and early Stuart times. The communities of gentry themselves had an origin and a history, and it might perhaps be possible to reserve the expression to the story of that particular process. But the associations of the phrase with the pattern of interpretation which has become misleading seem too strong for it to be worth while to keep it at all. It would, if it were possible, be far better to lay 'The Rise of the Gentry' carefully alongside 'The Rise of the Middle Classes', and to place them reverently together in the great and growing collection of outmoded historians' idiom. There they might long exercise the ingenuity and delight the hearts of the historians of historiography.

Once the limitations of this way of thinking about the last generations of the traditional world have been recognized, a different view will have to be taken of its other attributes, some of them even more important to us in the twentieth century. This was after all the 'century of genius' for Englishmen, and the social structure which we have been discussing formed the surroundings of Shakespeare, Milton, Locke and Donne as well as those of Cromwell and Charles I. Even more significant for the world as it has developed since their time are the names of Bacon, Boyle, Harvey and Newton, for this was the era when the new 'natural Philosophy', natural science, came into being. In so far as historians generally, and historians of science in particular, have thought of the final causes for this astonishing departure in human activity, they have tended to suppose that it all was in some sense an expression of the rise of the bourgeoisie, just as the rise of the gentry is supposed to have been.

Only the most ingenious manipulation of the theory of ideology could possibly make such a final explanation sound at all convincing. But though it seems to be unwarrantable to suppose that any overall evolution like 'the rise of the bourgeoisie' was in fact characteristic of England at that time, which means that the new natural philosophy cannot be thought of in any convincing sense as its ideological expression, this does not settle the question of the relation between science and social arrangements. Scientific activity, as has been said elsewhere, during the heroic generations when Englishmen were so prominent in it, was heterogeneous, so various that it can scarcely be called an activity in itself. It has to be sought in the tiny interstices, the nooks and crannies of the social structural whole, for the number of people able to contribute to it was tiny even on the scale of their own small society, and their activities were remote from each other. The study of an activity of this sort is a study of what might be called residues, minutiae, not of a general preoccupation which can be easily associated with the trend of overall, widespread social change.

If, therefore, we are to inform ourselves with any accuracy about the origins of the most remarkable of all our inheritances from the world we have lost, we shall have to get to know the map of English society in Stuart times in very intimate detail, and decide with clarity on the principles of its structure. Very small tendencies, forces of negligible strength may have been the promptings behind this particular intellectual tendency. These residual influences could in principle be related to some process of class formation, though no persuasive evidence of this seems as yet to be forthcoming. When simple-minded argumentation from material and economic substructure or background to cultural and intellectual result is abandoned, the challenge to the imagination and subtlety of the socio-logical historian is indeed acute.

The Pattern of Authority and Our Political Heritage
Chapter 8

Hatfield House still stands as the embodiment of the political importance of the famous house of Cecil, a symbol and an instrument of their enormous political effectiveness, and a reward from the Crown for services rendered. What the Marquess of Salisbury says and does there is of consequence in Hertfordshire, in the House of Lords, in the Conservative Party and in the British Commonwealth. They are not to be compared, of course to the actions and attitudes of his great ancestor and founder of the name and lineage, William Cecil, Lord Burghley, minister to Queen Elizabeth, but they are of importance all the same.

A little way across the suburbanized Hertfordshire country-side Cassiobury House has long since been blown up to make way for semi-detached residences. This was where the Earls of Essex and of Shaftesbury once plotted the expulsion of the Catholic Stuarts. Nevertheless the political life of the country houses and the pattern of political consciousness which made of the county community of gentry its local instrument, still affects our life and conduct. This pattern did not vanish at once before the advance of the factories, firms, railways, schools and building estates of industrialized society. For the political system which the Cecils, the Churchills, the Pitts and the Walpoles worked in and through became after all one of the most efficient, formidable and humane that the world has ever known. Nevertheless, in spite of certain seemingly happy and permanent survivals like Hatfield House, this powerful political inheritance from the world we have lost was based on a set of social institutions which has disappeared.

So completely have these attitudes, practices and relationships vanished from our society that their surviving physical remains often embarrass us, just as the huge crumbling ruins of the buildings from the late Roman Empire embarrassed the Goths and the Saxons. Where the mansions have not succumbed to the swift and final fate of Cassiobury House, they have been put to incongruous uses.

Something of their prestige-conferring and status-symbolizing virtues are being set to work of course, if rather clumsily. They can be seen at play on the puzzled faces of visitors, as they wander through the stately homes of England each summer, listlessly pursuing a gabble of unknown names and old, unhappy, far-off things not worth the entrance fee to hear about. Elsewhere they are lending a very welcome dignity, of sorts, to brand-new universities, or to university departments of adult and extra-mural education. But to be the scene of earnest, self-improving communion in entirely over-impressive surroundings is scarcely ignominy. Royston Manor, the home of the family of that name in 1676 and in 1688, when Parson Sampson made his lists of his parishioners, certainly survives in the village of Clayworth. But its windows have been boarded up and its rooms are filled with the warm stench and perpetual scrabble of fowls being fattened for broiling.

The last peer to be Prime Minister, as a peer, was a Cecil, and Hatfield House was at the hub of the political life of the country only sixty years ago. The continuing political leadership of the very rich and prestigious is a paradoxical feature of other democratic countries than our own, even of the United States. Therefore the succession in the 1960's of the fourteenth Earl of Home to the office held in the 1900's by the third Marquess of Salisbury should perhaps be looked upon in that light rather than as direct evidence that country house government still persists. But it is surely a sign that that tenacious system is not entirely lifeless even yet.

Nevertheless the political machine of the landed families had its origins in a social situation entirely different from our own. It could only work fully when men's assumptions about political organization were of a kind which now we can only imagine. This was the time when the great house in the park was the sole centre of political authority away from the Royal Court; when its size and magnificence were the one means of expressing political influence and achievement in monumental form. The influence and achievement in question here were those of the resident family and its reigning head, for in that age these things belonged to families alone. 'Family' here has a dual meaning; the actual group of persons living in a mansion, along with the retinue of servants, and the complex of blood relatives of the same lineage scattered across the face of the county, or of several counties, and inhabiting many seats. For if it was not true that the individual household in the traditional order was ordinarily an extended group of kin living together, it was true that political relationships went with kinship. The Cecils, as Cecils, were a political complex of their own, a very intricate one, from the sixteenth to the eighteenth centuries and beyond.

As a matter of fact the great aristocratic household in the great house was more likely to contain grandparents and grandchildren, nephews and nieces, young married couples not yet in their own establishments, cousins, aunts and in-laws generally than the less conspicuous household. This seems to have been so with the gentry also. For one thing there was room enough and to spare in those rambling and towering structures to accommodate the relatives, and servants in plenty to wait upon them. For another thing rich people had more children and lived longer and so would tend to have more relations alive – the Duke of Omnium's huge establishment was not typical of Victorian life and Victorian politics alone. Since all these prominent people were well aware of the world, they were likely to know who were their kinsfolk and to be acquainted with them. How important this could be may be illustrated by an incident from the court history of Queen Anne.

In self-defence against the bullying of Sarah Churchill, born Jennings, but known to posterity as the wife of the distinguished soldier John Churchill, Duke of Marlborough, Queen Anne finally took into her favour one of her dressers, Abigail Hill, whose duties were to lie on the Royal bedroom floor at night and empty the slops. Abigail had been given this humble post by Sarah herself, because the duchess had been told that one of her great band of relatives was living in complete penury; Abigail and Sarah were in fact first cousins. No sooner had this high-church chambermaid whom Sarah had raised 'from a broom', been taken into the Royal confidence, than Robert Harley, master as he was of political intrigue, discovered a blood relationship with the new favourite. His actual connection with her has never been worked out. Hence the final fall from favour of the Churchills and hence also the Treaty of Utrecht in 1713. The French dramatist Scribe once wrote a play about the negotiations for this treaty, which he made out to have been held up because of the cup of coffee being spilt down the dress of Abigail, now the Lady Masham.[180]

Though it underlines the intimacy of kinship and politics, the story of Abigail is in no way typical of the workings of court patronage, and (as we have already seen) the family of the possessing minority is a deceptive guide to the family in general. Once more, since it was families like this which interested people, and since most writers came from them or from those near to them in the social structure, the literary evidence on family and household in the world we have lost is deceptive too. The analytical questions about the role of kinship in political life, as well as the size and structure of the household, must be left to a more academic discussion. Some notion has already been given of the function of the varying size of household within each village community in maintaining social authority, in keeping the hierarchy in being and ensuring submission on the part of peasants and craftsmen. This is obviously of importance when we approach once more the question of the reasons for obedience.

Pre-eminence of the rulers in virtue of the size of their families was only one feature of a system of authority whose overall description, as we have already repeatedly insisted, must be patriarchal. This final chapter on the nature of the traditional world and the contrast it presents with the world we now inhabit, will concern itself first with that unquestioning subordination which marked relationships then, and which marks them no longer. From a short survey of the political education of our ancestors, the conditioning process as we might say, we shall proceed to a brief exploration of the actual mechanics of political life. Three characteristics are important to our purposes: social mobility, geographical isolation of all below the level of gentleman, and illiteracy.

The study of these characteristics belongs to the subject which is still in its earliest phase of development, now known by the ugly phrase political socialization. Only the most general reflections are therefore possible as yet. A beginning may be made with a statement about the predominant tone of social and political life at that time, and of almost the whole of political literature. In this society, subordination and politics were founded on tradition. Therefore critical examination of the reasons why some men were better placed than others was

[180] *See page 271.*

unlikely to come about. This submissive cast of mind is almost universal in the statements made by the men about themselves. 'There is degree above degree, As reason is . . .' 'Take but degree away, Untune that string, And hark what discord follows.' It would seem that once a man in the traditional world got himself into a position where he could catch a glimpse of his society as a whole, he immediately felt that degree, order, was its essential feature. Without degree, unquestioning subordination, and some men being privileged while all the others obeyed, anarchy and destruction were inevitable. Any threat to the established order was a danger to everyone's personality.

There are two reasons why this is what might be expected to have been the almost universal attitude. One is implied by the word traditional itself, which meant that the set of standards used to make judgements about society and varying positions within it stayed constant for almost all people at all times. Put into more technical language, it must be presumed that neither peasant, pauper nor craftsman nor even gentleman in the pre-industrial world ever changed his reference group in such a way as to feel aware of what is called relative deprivation.* Directly this assumption is recorded, it raises questions about those occasions on which change of reference group did come about in seventeenth-century English society. It could be argued, for example, that the disturbances caused by the Civil War and especially those connected with the recruitment and activities of the parliamentary army, did bring humble people into contact for the first time with those who were better off and had a more aspiring outlook. Indeed the isolation of individuals from their counterparts in other village communities was so marked a feature of the society we have described that the very fact of bringing them together to share a common, vital purpose for months and years together might be expected to have some crystallizing effect on their attitudes to their social position and political rights.

If for example the literature of the Levellers of Cromwell's army and of the city of London could be shown to have arisen to any extent from such circumstances as these, it would provide a fascinating parallel with events in our own century. National war, conscription and disbandment are now com-

* *The developing theory of relative deprivation and reference groups is admirably described in his book* Relative Deprivation and Social Justice, 1966, *by W. G. Runciman, where English social history since 1918 is analysed in these terms.*

monly assumed to be associated with intense feelings of relative deprivation and revolutionism. Social mobility in industrial society is also known to have the expected effect on reference groups. Once the opportunity of rising in society is envisaged, and once its actual fulfilment begins to look possible, then men do become aware that they are being deprived of what their superiors enjoy, and may well begin to question the rationale of the established social order. Now that we have reason to believe that social mobility was present in pre-industrial society as well, we must suppose that some discontent and criticism was engendered in traditional societies for similar reasons. Social quiescence, therefore, should not be regarded as quite fully descriptive of England or of Europe three hundred years ago, especially of the kingdom which Oliver Cromwell found himself responsible for.

Interesting as these possibilities are, they can hardly have been of much importance. The second reason why the society we are so hastily describing must be presumed to have been nearly always socially quiescent is that the phrase stable poverty does on the whole seem to be a fair description of most of its area. It is a commonplace of social observation that stable poverty means resignation to the situation as it is. Such an impression seems the only possible one to gather from Gregory King's table, in spite of the political, military, even commercial and industrial energy which was displayed by the England of his century. Though we have nothing like the amount of evidence which de Tocqueville assembled for the *ancien régime* as it was in France just before the fatal year 1789, it seems entirely unlikely that anything like a revolution of rising expectations could have been contemplated by the peasants and craftsmen of our country in Stuart times. Further information and more determined analysis may modify this claim, but an acceptance of unvarying, even poverty seems to be as much a characteristic of those local village communities we have yet been able to examine as it seems to be of King's description of the whole nation.

Nevertheless it is generally supposed that a society in such a situation will have its share of desperate men, and that the downtrodden pauper if ever he does find an opportunity will express his resentment of the hardships he is forced to suffer. We have cited a little evidence of the awareness of contemporary observers that the deprived in their society might be expected on occasion to break out into violence. Quite apart from those in extreme situations, some rationale must have been present to settle the doubts of those who were disposed for any reason to question the rightness of arrangements as they were and the duty of submission and obedience. Social superiority and political authority did to some small extent depend for their maintenance on outside sanctions.

The outside support for authority in the traditional world was religious, though 'outside' scarcely expresses its relationship with the social system. We can gain a little somewhat unexpected insight into the way in which attitudes of obedience were inculcated into every personality in the formative years.* The stated duty of each parish priest was to teach the children of his flock the catechism. After matins on Sundays in every one of the 10,000 parishes of England there gathered, or should have gathered, the group of adolescents from the houses of the gentry and the yeomen, the husbandmen, the tradesmen, the labourers and even the paupers to learn from the priest what it meant to be a Christian. This is what they all had to repeat after him: every single one of them had to get to know it by heart:

My duty towards my neighbour is to love him as myself, and to do to all men as I would they should do unto me: to love, honour and succour my father and mother: to submit myself to all my governors, teachers, spiritual pastors and masters; to order myself lowly and reverently to all my betters; to hurt nobody by word nor deed: to be true and just in all my dealings; to bear no malice nor hatred in my heart: to keep my hands from picking and stealing, and my tongue from evil-speaking, lying and slandering: to keep my body in temperance, soberness and chastity: not to covet nor desire other men's goods: but to learn and labour truly to get my own living, and to do my duty in that state of life unto which it shall please God to call me.

These words are still familiar and evocative because they come from the catechism of the Church of England, originally composed in 1549 and still in use. Some effort of the historical imagination has to be made to recognize how important they were at the time when every living person in England was both a believing, fearing Christian and also by compulsion a

---

* *I owe almost all of what follows on the subject of catechizing to the work of Prof. Gordon Schochet, Rutgers University.*

member of the national church. 'We hold,' said Richard Hooker, the official spokesman of the established order, 'that there is not any man of the Church of England but the same man is also a member of the Commonwealth. Nor any man a member of the Commonwealth which is not also a member of the Church of England.'[181]

What is more this was the only thing that young people were ever told about obedience, authority and the social and political order. It was solemnly inculcated on one of those few public occasions when, as we have seen, they left the circle of the household and the authority of its master, to find themselves in the church under the authority of the priest. Many of these youths and maidens, moreover, had no means of confirming or revising what the grave minister had to tell them, for they could not read. He had to teach them by word of mouth what they would have to say before the formidable figure of the Lord Bishop when it came to their service of Confirmation.

Lest it should be thought that only the orthodox had this formal lesson so firmly impressed upon them, here are the words adopted for the *Shorter Catechism* in the year 1644, when the Puritan clergy were taking control of the Church of England at the height of the war between King and Parliament.

Question 64: What is required in the fifth commandment?
Answer: The fifth commandment requireth the preserving the honour and performing the duties, belonging to every one in their several places and relations, as Superiors, Inferiors or Equals.
Question 65: What is forbidden in the fifth commandment?
Answer: The fifth commandment forbiddeth the neglecting of or doing anything against the duty which belongeth to every one in their several places and relations.

In this case the English Presbyterians were overtly stating the position universally adopted in the traditional interpretation of the Bible, by separatists and sectarians as well as by the hierarchies, that the duty of Christian obedience rested on the commandment *Honour thy Father and thy Mother*. It was a nonconformist minister who wrote the exhortation to the husbandman which we quoted in our first chapter, reminding

[181] *See page 271.*

him that obedience was due to his landlord because of the
fifth commandment. What more familiar sentiment for the
beneficed rector or the itinerant preacher to appeal to when
the children of the village community were being instructed
in their Christian duties? Submission to the powers that be
went very well with the habit of obedience to the head of the
patriarchal family, and it had the extremely effective sanction
of the universal fear of damnation to the defiant. 'Short life,'
so the doctrine went, 'was the punishment of disobedient
children.'[182]

Of course the tenant obeyed his landlord for what may be
thought were much more tangible reasons than his early
training and his care for the salvation of his soul. He might be
evicted if he showed insufficient respect, especially in what
was his clear political duty when, providing that he had got a
vote, he came to exercise the franchise. His landlord was also
very likely to be a justice of the peace, with all the forces of
the established order on his side. As for those below the landholders, there was the relationship of menial service, past,
present and to come, which was described when we talked of
the village community. A labourer, or a craftsman, a cottager
or even a lowly husbandman could very well have been a
servant in one of the larger houses in the locality, and his sons
and daughters might in fact be in that position at the time.
Each of them might well have to look to those same substantial
householders for a day's work all his life.

There is no need to labour the point about the familial basis
of society and submissiveness further than this. It may begin
to look strange that any one was ever bold enough to escape at
all, impossible that ideas of individual rights, of the account-
ability of superiors, of contract as the basis of government
could ever have occurred to the men of seventeenth-century
England.

This is one more of the paradoxes which urgently await
systematic study by the sociological historian. If we are to
begin to understand why it was that a society so static and
authoritarian in its attitude to social discipline, and so strict
in maintaining it, could be at the same time so free and inventive in its political ideas and institutions, we must turn our
attention to the actual mechanism of political life. There can
be no doubt of the strangeness of the contrast between what

[182] *See page 271.*

men said about the rights of individuals and what those rights actually were.

All and every particular and individual man and woman, that ever breathed in the world, are by nature all equal and alike in their power, dignity, authority and majesty, none of them having (by nature) any authority, dominion or magisterial power one over or above another.[183]

This is a famous statement made by John Lilburne, gentleman, the Leveller leader in 1646, and it reads very strangely in view of all that has been said here about universal subordination and inequality.

The Levellers were of course an extraordinary phenomenon. Their appearance in the parliamentary army and in London during the later years of the Civil War and the earlier years of unkingly government certainly provides us with the most revealing evidence we have or ever shall have of life below the level of the *élite*. Here, if anywhere, we must look for those sentiments which did take all the people into account and were not distorted by supposing that the claims made for the few need never be supposed to apply to the many. There are grave difficulties in deciding exactly how many Levellers there were and how they were placed in society; whether they really were confined to London, the army and a few of the home counties, or whether every intelligent villager with a smattering of education would have supported them if he had been given the opportunity. Perhaps some sort of half-collective life, quasi-political life, of this kind was present well before the Civil War, and maintained itself all the way through the centuries until the Chartists brought Leveller demands again into the public arena, and finally the Labour Party developed them into an attitude which is supported by at least half of those with political personality in our country today.

If anything of this last statement could be shown to have been true, a quite different strand of interconnection between the political outlook of the old world and our own might come into view, this time not confined to the fully literate minority and not providing reasons why we should respect and obey our traditional leadership, but grounds for criticizing and replacing it.

[183] *See page 271.*

But in the world we have lost, as had already been laid down, an entity like 'England' lived its whole life within the confines of a small, select minority. Even a critic of political arrangements, a man who, like Lilburne, had come to believe that most institutions were the unjust result of conquest and usurpation, of the 'Norman Yoke' thrust upon the free English in the year 1066, himself belonged to that fraction of society which alone possessed political awareness. It was therefore perhaps possible even for him to say things which seemed to affect every living individual without his actually contemplating more than a small proportion of them. Political humanity to John Lilburne presumably meant far more people than it did to John Locke when he wrote out thirty years later something with a marked resemblance to Lilburne's statement in the measured tones which were to make it the classic text for the liberties enjoyed by the gentlemen of eighteenth-century England and the citizens of eighteenth-century America.

To understand political power right, and derive it from its original, we must consider what state all men are naturally in, and that is, a state of perfect freedom to order their actions, and dispose of their possessions, and persons as they think fit, within the bounds of the law of nature, without asking leave, or depending upon the will of any other man. A state also of equality, wherein all the power and jurisdiction is reciprocal, no one having more than another.[184]

Though the cautious Locke omits women, and later excepts children from natural equality, he sounds as if he meant literally all humanity in this statement. Indeed he may well have supposed that he did mean such a thing, provided only that the ordinary assumptions of his day about who was in fact concerned in political matters were maintained by his reader. In fact almost everyone did stay within these limits at that time. Very, very few ever found themselves wondering whether a government literally having consent from every breathing, responsible human could or should exist, so far were the assumptions of twentieth-century democracy from their minds. One of Locke's associates, James Tyrrell, did get into a position where this possibility crossed his path, but it will be seen how peremptorily he dismissed it.

There never was any government where all the promiscuous rabble

[184] *See page 271.*

of women and children had votes, as not being capable of it, yet it does not for all that prove that all legal civil government does not owe its original to the consent of the people, since the fathers of families, or freemen at their own dispose, were really and indeed are all the people that needed to have votes . . . Children in their fathers' families being under the notion of servants, and without any property in goods or land, have no reason to have votes in the institution of government.[185]

Locke and Tyrrell were both answering Sir Robert Filmer, the Kentish squire and apologist for the Crown, who wrote out his defence of absolute monarchy before ever the Civil War came about and called it '*Patriarcha, or the Natural Power of Kings*'. This document, a codification of unconscious prejudice, as it has been called, was addressed to his neighbours, to the other members of the Kentish community of county gentry, and not to the intellectuals of a later generation who made of it the most refuted theory in the history of politics. Locke, Tyrrell and even Lilburne were as much gentlemen of England as the Filmers of East Sutton Park, though Lilburne was no scion of an established family like the others. Filmer's patriarchalism, for all its oddities and its entirely uncritical acceptance of the Scripture – he really believed that Charles Stuart was the literal heir of Adam among the English and so entitled to exercise upon them all the prerogatives conferred on the first father of mankind – provided a reason for the duty of everyone to obey, whilst his critics could justify the right of only a minority to resist. There is however no need to suppose that Filmer took any more account of the really humble mass of the people than his opponents did. Nobody took much notice of them when politics were in question.

Perhaps Colonel Rainborough came nearest when he made his oft-quoted statement to the victorious Parliamentary soldiery at Putney in 1647, when they were debating the future of English state and society: 'For I really think that the poorest he that is in England hath a life to live as the greatest he.' The response of the weighty champions of authority was just what we might expect: they invoked the fifth commandment: 'Honour thy father and thy mother', said Ireton, Cromwell's son-in-law, 'and that law doth extend to all that are our governors.'[186]

[185] *See page 271.*   [186] *See page 271.*

Rainborough's response was nothing like as confident as the emphatic challenge with which he had begun, for he found himself denying that the people of England were bound to obey any [political] parent who had not been elected, though parenthood and election go very uneasily together. What is more we can be fairly certain that Rainborough himself did not really mean all the poor people of the country. Like the rest of the Levellers he presumably excluded both servants and paupers from the franchise. We have seen that together these made up a considerable proportion of the whole population.* But Rainborough had no occasion to refer specifically to them, and like everyone else he seems to have had no very clear picture of what the *whole* people of England, every single one of them, can have looked like. For even in 1647 the facts of political life and the workings of the political machine were against it.

In our analysis of the political breakdown which occurred in Stuart times something has already been said about that wonderful contrivance, that ingenious instrument for maintaining political participation over the whole area of society. The crucial part of the mechanism, the community of gentry in each county, has as yet only been examined from this point of view for one county in one year and this happens to have been Sir Robert Filmer's own county of Kent. In sketching the human geography of our country as it was in pre-industrial times, we have already insisted upon the universal presence of the gentry, noble and merely gentle, over its whole area, pressing evenly everywhere, like the atmosphere, or resting like an iridescent film on the entire surface. This was certainly true of Kent in 1640, and the interrelated, interacting inhabitants of the manor houses there can be seen to have been active in every possible direction.

When the Civil War came, it led to the formation of County Committees in Kent and all over the kingdom: once the central administration was withdrawn, that is to say, the local administration took its place as a matter of course. The running, recruitment and financing of the hostilities were conducted on a county basis. But in Kent anyway, the county community was also an intellectual society, which was why Sir Robert

* *I owe the point that the Levellers excluded servants and the poor from political society to Brough Macpherson, though I cannot agree with him that the word servant then included many wage-earning householders.*

Filmer wrote his theory of politics for his companions in the manor houses, not for publication in London. In fact in his county in his time something like a dispersed university could be said to have been in existence, whose research workers found their material not simply in their own libraries of classical and scriptural authorities, but also in their own boxes of title deeds.

Family relationships kept the whole institution in working order, and the genealogical interrelationships between the manor houses were extensive, complicated and meticulously observed. It is astonishing how distant a connection qualified for the title 'cozen', and obvious that those in London, or in any part of the country where a living was to be got from commerce or from any other activity which a gentleman might take up, was as much a member of the society as those in permanent residence in the country houses. In Kent, in fact, these outlyers stretched a very long distance indeed; by the year 1660 quite a high proportion of the county families had offshoots in the plantations of Virginia.

The essay from which this description of Kent is drawn makes the following general reflections about the activity which went on within the communities in the middle of the seventeenth century.

There are two characteristics of English society at that time which may prove to be more important to the world than the tensions which ended in fighting. One is that persistent preoccupation with political speculation which was a dominant trait of intellectual life in England in 1640 and for two generations thereafter. This finally gave us the theoretical presuppositions which now underlie our institutions and those of the whole English-speaking world. The other is that urge to create new societies in its own image, or in the image of its ideal self, which appeared in the self-confident years of Queen Elizabeth, though its first momentous consequences became apparent by about 1640 – when the Colony of Virginia was beginning to show the characteristics of American society in infancy. [187]

Fifteen years have passed since these words were written, and the shape of political society in the country as a whole in 1640 seems to have turned out to be much as might have been expected from the rough model worked out for Kent. Though

[187] *See page 272.*

emigration was a special feature of certain maritime shires, and though intellectual interchange may not have been as common between the country seats in other counties, political England does appear to have been a reticulation of such familial network as the one in which Sir Robert Filmer lived his life.

If we had time we could fill out the details here, beginning with the life of the village community which was earlier described, which was politically isolated save for those at the head of the community; the squire and sometimes the parson were the links between the village and the nation. More important to the present purpose is the manner in which the political game was played between the manor houses and the lordly seats: how even a minor gentleman in a new family might win one of the political prizes if he had the skill; how even an ancient lineage and a baronial estate could not help a lordling with the wrong opinions, or lacking a head for management, intrigue and plain political aggrandizement. Not many of the gentle families were of great political importance at any one time, we may notice, and very few from any one county counted nationally: like other political societies, most of the units were inactive, in reserve for a new occasion, another generation. But each genteel establishment always possessed political potential, and, when crisis came, support or resistance could be expected from almost every cell in the battery.

We cannot dwell on the relationship of our own political universe with its party caucuses and its central offices, with its state primaries and its national, presidential conventions, to their ancestors in this vanished political arena. Nor can we go further in exploring what happened when passion was released and political potential became active participation, of the kind discussed in the last chapter. One suggestion must be made, in order to fulfil a promise made there. If it is justifiable to look upon the total system, social and political, as having any sort of conflict mechanism as a permanent part of its workings, then the county community must be thought of in that light. For the county community, the local political society, was a permanent, everyday affair, of which any qualified person could make himself an active part, and everyone of suitable status was by definition a member; this was not true of any national institution, and particularly of Parliament whose intermittent life depended on the whim and policy of the Sovereign. It may be remembered, however, that the presence of institutions for conflict does not necessarily mean that *all* friction was institutionalized.

Considerations like this belong rather to a general theory of political and social interaction, than to a comparison of the kind which is our proper subject. Any suggested similarity of Stuart England with the segmented societies of contemporary Africa must be left on one side for the same reason, though once again the community of county gentry turns out to be the important point. Stuart England, and perhaps England at any time before industrialization, might begin to be looked upon as something of a permanent federation of segments, within each of which rivalry, almost entirely symbolic and peaceful, was perpetual, and between which open conflict was always a possibility. On those rare occasions when it happened it need not have been simply a weakening of the national political consciousness, but rather an assertion and intensification of it. This would make political and constitutional history read rather differently than it has done, especially the history of 'revolution', in our country and in others.

But this is not the last word to be said about authority in the world we have lost and our political heritage from it. There remain two questions to be touched upon, both of which are rather difficult and have been referred to once or twice before. One is social mobility and the other the extent of literacy. Each is open in principle to numerical investigation of the kind which we have been able to use in a very preliminary way in discussing such things as size of household and sexual conformity. The relevant evidence is much more elusive, however, and has yet scarcely been tackled at all, particularly for literacy. The considerations then must be very rough and provisional indeed.

The indications they seem to imply for social and political change may be thought to be rather surprising, especially in the case of social mobility. The expectation must be that movement both upwards and downwards was normal rather than exceptional in the society of our ancestors, though it was of course a marginal effect. There is at present no way of telling how great the movement was but it seems certain that it was commoner at some times than at others. Nevertheless some motion both ways, upwards and downwards, seems likely to have been going on all the time. Put into the language of traditional discussion, there always was a rise of the gentry and always a (slightly larger) fall of the gentry, though 'rise into' and 'fall out of' would be a more accurate way of putting it. This expectation arises from what is known and what can be inferred about the vital statistics of the population as a whole in relation to the privileged minority. It is certainly not contradicted by other evidence, and once the possibility that this was the ordinary pattern is recognized, the known facts of all kinds seem to fit in quite well.

Common sense and the little we have found out go to show that the gentry must have lived a little longer, married a little earlier and had a few more children who survived to adulthood than other people. We may even suppose that it will turn out that they had children more often, since genteel mothers did not have to suckle their babies and so could conceive sooner after childbirth. Wet nursing (not however entirely confined to the gentry) was probably bad for their babies, but this effect was amply offset by their generally higher standards of welfare. It seems that the net reproduction rate, as the demographers say, must have been higher amongst privileged people than it was amongst the population as a whole. They more than replaced themselves at every generation.

Hence downward mobility; hence the individuals born into the manor-houses who found themselves marrying into the houses of the yeomanry, the clergy, or even the husbandmen, as well as of the city tradesmen. The numbers of such cannot have been large even when social mobility was at its most intense. But we may suppose that the proportion of those on the way down in the world was never negligible in relation to the size of the privileged minority and its existence was certainly noticed by contemporaries. An example may be taken from a book published in 1656, *The Vale Royal of England, or the County Palatine of Chester*:

In no country of England, the gentlemen are more ancient and of longer continuance than in this country. I have thought good to set down all such arms, as I find them to bear, or to have borne. And not by order or in degree, but after the manner of the alphabet. It goeth with such matters in other countrys of England. For riches maketh a gentleman throughout the realm, which is contrary to the manner of some other countries beyond the seas. So you shall have in this country, six men of one surname (and peradventure of one house) whereof the first shall be called a Knight, the second an

Esquire, the third a Gentleman, the fourth a Freeholder, the fifth a Yeoman, and the sixth a husbandman.

So convinced was this urbane author of his main point that he put in the margin against this passage: '*Riches maketh Gentlemen in all countries of England.*'[188]

He was an acute observer who could recognize that the identity of wealth with status meant that a poor man, even if of gentle birth, might go down in the world. His other statements illustrate many of the claims we have made about the social order in the English counties, whilst the habit of calling the shire by the word we reserve for the whole national area must not be missed. The truth of the observation that the name of the gentle family within a village community was often the same as that of much humbler families can be confirmed from many of the listings of persons in village communities which we have recovered and examined. Indeed many a gentleman's son at his marriage called himself a yeoman, just as the yeoman's son often called himself a husbandman. Although almost unnoticed by the subsequent historian, social descent was something like an institution of the traditional order in England.

This may have distinguished our country from the rest of Europe, as we have already stated and as the writer just quoted also realized. The complaint that the social system played cuckoo to the superfluous children in a privileged family is far more often met with in the perennial form of the younger brother's lament. Here is one from 1600, written by Thomas Wilson:

I cannot speak of the [number] of younger brothers, albeit I be one of the number myself, but for their estate there is no man hath better cause to know it, nor less cause to praise it. Such a fever hectic hath custom brought in and inured amongst fathers, and such fond desires they have to leave a great show of the stock of their house, though the branches be withered, that my elder brother forsooth must be my master. He must have all, and all the rest that which the cat left on the maltheap, perhaps some small annuity during his life or what pleases our elder brothers worship to bestow upon us if we please him, and my mistress his wife. This I must confess doth us good someways, for it makes us industrious to apply ourselves to letters or to arms, whereby many times we become my master elder brother's masters, or at least their betters in honour

[188] *See page 272.*

and reputation, while he lives at home like a mome [a buffoon might be our word for this] and knows the sound of no bell but his own.[189]

The industrious younger sons of the manor-houses of Kent were those who went and carved out a career for themselves and a new future for the family name in the southern colonies of North America. They were impelled to do so both by the status consciousness of their elder brothers and by the overriding sense of dynasty which led each successor to a manorhouse to identify himself with his lineage, past and future.

Patriarchal custom and authority enabled an unfeeling heir to treat his brothers and sisters badly, and his younger children also. A legal system imbued with such attitudes helped him too, though English law was not as emphatic about *patria potestas* as the Civil or Roman law which Wilson professed. But not all heads of families could find it in their hearts to behave in this way and the dignity of their house often led them into actions which depressed the fortunes of the line.

Here we meet a whole series of possibilities arising out of the vital statistics of each lineage, complicated by all the vagaries of personality and predilection. A man might have a large number of children, mostly sons, whom he could, if he wished, either set up in the City, the Army or elsewhere, reasonably cheaply, or else, if they would stand for it, quietly neglect. On the other hand he might be affectionate and indulgent, unwilling to allow dependents to fall into penury, or unable to prevent them from insisting on a maintenance. In the first case the family fortune would be handed down intact, provided always that he had been a good manager, and in the second it might be dispersed. If daughters predominated amongst his children, inroads into capital would be more difficult to resist, because without dowries daughters, even below the level of the gentry, could not be married at all. Many a bearded patriarch besides King Lear was ruined by his daughters.

This is only the beginning of what went on, and it must be noticed how much difference numbers of births and expectation of life made in any such situation. Economic historians have studied the market in dowries and jointures (these were the amounts which had to be settled on a son's bride to maintain her if he should die) and shown how the price of a good

[189] *See page 272.*

match for a child varied over time. Naturally the situation would be very different for a family where there was only one child, and a male at that; or where a great deal was unexpectedly inherited from the early death of the wife's father and only brother; or where the wife died early, and a new marriage brought in a rich heiress; or where a ne'er-do-well cadet suddenly returned from the Indies with a fortune and added it to the main stock. In the eighteenth century this went on offstage in India perhaps or the Navy, and in Victorian times in New Zealand, or in South America. This is the stuff out of which the plots of novels and plays were woven; in the end they mostly consist of a study in the ups and downs of the fortunes of a family. The perpetual presence in these stock situations of impoverished relatives now begins to look significant. Not all of the grandchildren, not to speak of the nephews and nieces, could possibly expect the golden prospects of the hero and heroine when finally they settled down to live happily ever after.

But we have learnt to mistrust literary evidence on matters of this kind. It should not be long before we have reliable figures on the differential fertility of the various descriptions of people in the world we have lost, and particularly on the larger group of children born and brought up in the manor-houses, for it was this rather than the longer life of each individual which determined that there should be a surplus of gentry.

Nevertheless mortality was exceedingly high there, even amongst the titled people: the mean age at death of all the English aristocrats dying in the sixteenth and seventeenth centuries was in the early thirties. What is more, slightly higher overall fertility emphatically does not mean that every privileged mother had a large number of children who survived to adulthood, particularly when expectation of life remained modest. Some would have a child and die; some would lose their husbands after one or two births; others would have daughters only; a few, even at this time, would be unable to have children at all. Even allowing for remarriage and collateral succession, the perpetuation of a male line was uncertain; exactly how uncertain will presumably soon be worked out numerically. Therefore for reasons of vital statistics alone, there must have been upward social mobility.

But the facts about the rise of fortunate persons in traditional society are not as clear as those about the fall of unfortunate ones. Some of the people who would otherwise have lost their status in the ruling segment were certainly able to step into the places of those required to keep a failing lineage in being. In this way, for example by the judicious marriage of a girl destined to become the final representative of a particular name to an impoverished younger son of a flourishing brood, replacement could take place without social ascent. But this could only happen to a limited extent, and although by adoption of surname it might save appearances it could not save a hereditary title from extinction. In any case it depended on the efficiency of the market, so to speak, on being able to find just the partner for your child or more likely for your ward.

If mismanagement had been a major reason for decline, moreover, nothing less than the sharing out of property, with a near-certainty of serious losses, could have saved the day. No privileged order seems likely ever to have gone as far as this to preserve its exclusiveness, especially in the face of pressure from outside of men with money to spare. Least of all would this have happened in the England which we have described, and where we know that recruitment went on from below. Marriage was the approved method of bringing it about, and it was for the most part marriage which set the seal of familial relationship on the arrival from below of property and power.

Much of the mobility must have been what might be called semi-circular. A younger son of a manor-house moved into the town; or had to satisfy himself with a parson's or a yeoman's house and duties in the country. Then after a series of deaths in the family his son or grandson found himself moving back into the family mansion. Often it was a different house from that of his direct ancestors and often the perpetuation of a 'family' in the records found in the county histories is a matter of different branches flourishing and languishing, though the final diminuendo is almost never worth recording. City money was very frequently the reason why an obscure branch became the major line, but careful historical study has shown that it was not the only one and may perhaps have been exaggerated, along with the importance of enclosure and capitalist farming, in its effects on social ascent and a family's fortunes. This semi-circular motion is not particularly special, for all social mobility takes place backwards and forwards, or up and down, just across the specified dividing line.

We have already referred to this whole mazy process as the way in which the bourgeoisie kept on a level with the others in the ruling minority, discriminated against for a time by other, older members of a county community of gentry, but always acceptable after the passing of a generation. When the sparse evidence so far collected is examined for signs of the movement roughly described, it seems to conform well enough. Taking a sample of some fifty bridegrooms and over sixty brides described as belonging to the gentry in the Lincoln marriage licences between 1612 and 1617 we find that almost a third of the men and over two-fifths of the women married outside their social order. When clergy and the obviously bourgeois occupations are taken into account the indication of social mobility is rather less; only about 20 per cent in the case of men though still over a third of the women married outside what we have called the ruling segment. Nearly a quarter of the women and over 15 per cent of the men married into yeomen's families; one gentleman married a daughter of a waterman, another the daughter of a pursemaker, whilst one gentlewoman married the son of a barber, another the son of an apothecary and a third the son of a husbandman.

These fragmentary indications have the disadvantage that they only imply change, not its direction. We do not know whether the eight clergymen who took gentlewomen to wife were on their way up in the world, or whether they themselves were sons of gentry marrying on their own level. Some at least of them may have been taking a daughter off the hands of a squire fast succumbing to the burden of trying to maintain too large an establishment for his failing means. The daughter of an alderman to be found in the sample, and the merchant's daughter, seem rather more certainly to have been on their way up in the world. But even they may have belonged to bourgeois families failing in their fortune, and have been joining genteel families unable to find better alliances. We have found gentry marrying people beneath them in Manchester in the 1650's, allying themselves with clothiers, drapers, mercers and tanners, even husbandmen. In the Gloucestershire marriage allegations in the 1660's a 'gentleman' appears who was apparently unable to sign his own name. He at least seems unlikely to have been climbing the social ladder.

There is plenty of evidence from other contexts to confirm what the actual records have to tell us about social mobility.

It would be inconsistent of us to take the literary evidence too seriously after all that has been said about its capacity to deceive the social historian. But it is difficult not to mention the trading and manufacturing families of the city of London as they are portrayed by the Elizabethan and Restoration playwrights. Their children seem to have been brought up to marry into the gentry; the decayed gentleman anxious to wed city money by fair means or foul is a stock figure too. Still it comes as a surprise to see 'John Cockeshutt, gent.' licensed in 1591 to the drover's trade by the Lancashire justices.[190]

That particular county may have been exceptional in the use made there of this most important social description. But the existence of a considerable number of families and persons who were either just about to move into or were in process of falling out of the privileged group is what we ought to expect in a society arranged as this one was. Some of these people must have been gentlemen for life. They were persons whose fathers had been landed proprietors, but whose own sons would be virtually landless: or those who had risen by their own exertions but not built up enough to found a gentle line.

John Lilburne may have been a member of this penumbra of the ruling segment as we called it when it was first mentioned, and its possible importance in movements of critical unrest in the social structure opens up a whole vista of possible speculation. It must not be overlooked, however, that the members of this fringe area of society were sharply contrasted in their social experience. Some were on the way up and others on the way down, whilst many of the lineages would be up in one generation and down in another. There would be little justification for making this social area into a 'middle class', certainly not one which could be described as rising or falling as a whole. We cannot linger over the very important issues which social mobility raises, and the whole discussion requires a great deal more evidence and much closer analysis than we have yet been able to undertake. But there is one question which cannot be entirely neglected.

This is the size of the privileged minority, which is after all critical to the fact of social mobility. Did it remain fairly constant in relation to the population as a whole, expanding with a general expansion and contracting in a time of falling numbers overall? We have tended to assume such a steady

[190] *See page 272.*

relationship and the consistency in titles given to persons in, for example, the lists of burials, seems to confirm it. But this is after all a very rough sort of calculation and we do not even yet know whether the numbers of gentle persons and families tended to grow in times of economic expansion and contract in times of depression, as common sense might make us expect.

More interesting and significant perhaps is to ask exactly how the numbers were kept in steady relationship with the numbers of the whole society, if indeed they were. It could be suggested that this was indeed one of the perennial sources of conflict in the social structure, but extremely intermittent in its operation. Whatever the mechanism was it seems to have resembled in its operation there the crisis of subsistence which afflicted the peasantry in France. It must have made itself manifest quite unexpectedly and then, after doing its work, when conditions changed, vanished again. A society retaining the general shape this one is observed to have done could only afford a certain number of privileged persons, just as with its given resources of food it could only afford a certain total population.

But all this is guesswork only, in a field where guesswork has been only too common. In our present state of ignorance and in the infancy of studies of this sort speculation about possible changes in the structure of the ruling segment, about the probable effects of more small estates and families and fewer large ones, or of more great nobles and fewer small ones, seems premature. Nevertheless generalizations of this kind have confidently been made about such things as the 'rise of the gentry', or 'the crisis of the nobility' and so on. No doubt such events and tendencies were real enough, and their historical implications may have been important. But it must now be clear that it is no more than a preliminary exercise to prove that certain families rose and others fell within the social structure. Only if it could be shown that the movement up or down was truly excessive, very much more than might be expected in view of what was normal, could it enter into any explanation of critical social change. Even then, if something to correspond with revolution is to be supposed, it would also have to be demonstrated that the movement in question was such as to defeat the resources for compromise in the political system. This system, it must be assumed, was adapted to disturbances of such a kind. The same consideration applies to the gentry themselves though not as a community, and to every other distinguishable part of the ruling minority. Internal changes amongst the gentlemen or the nobility would have had to be truly novel and unexpected if they were to have led to changes in the general shape of the whole society.

The exchange of persons between the privileged minority and the rest shows us something of how the whole was related to the all-important part. This does not go very far towards explaining why it was that those within the network of gentle families, when they thought about politics, believed that they were thinking for the whole society. Far more revealing, however, is the recognition of the situation of most of the great majority of people whose existence, attitudes and desires could be assumed, or ignored, by their superiors. Ordinary Englishmen three hundred years ago lived in an oral culture, that is to say one where most transactions went on by word of mouth, yet they belonged to a society whose politics were run in writing. This is the most conspicuous reason why the peasants of one village were politically and socially isolated from the peasants of all other villages; and why the literate few could feel that they were thinking for the whole mass. Without access to books, without always being able to write as much as their own names, how could the husbandmen of a village where the politically active gentlemen lived be expected to think at all? And if so many of the landholders were in this mute and unreflecting situation, what about the labourers and the artificers, the millers, the wheelwrights, the weavers, shepherds, drovers, masons, shoemakers? What about the paupers?

Not all of these men were entirely unlettered, and it may be that more cobblers could read than husbandmen or even yeomen. It is evident that tradesmen had more occasions to use written and printed material than landworkers did, and the tradition of radicalism amongst these trades, especially the cobblers, reveals at once the possible association between literacy and thinking for yourself politically. Since tradesmen were so much greater in numbers and in importance in the towns than in the countryside, the extent of literacy must have made a great difference between the urban and the rural population. In Norwich in Elizabethan times, systematic arrangements seemed to have been made to provide even paupers' children with some sort of instruction. This attribute certainly divided the sexes; in every type of evidence we possess which bears upon the issue, more men turn out to be literate than women. Every historian has met ladies in very high stations who could scarcely spell, to whom writing was evidently a painful ordeal and this continuing into the nineteenth century. It divided the household in another way too, for reading was no common accomplishment amongst servants, even those in genteel and literary households.

The discovery of how great a proportion of the population could read and write at any point in time is one of the most urgent of the tasks which faces the historian of social structure, who is committed to the use of numerical methods. But the challenge is not simply to find the evidence and to devise ways of making it yield reliable answers. It is a challenge to the historical and literary imagination. What we have to recall, to reconstruct, to make a present reality to ourselves is a time when most men and women could only think, and talk, and sing and play, and make things, and till the soil, whilst only some men could also read and write, and record, and refer again, and criticize, and tell others what was the truth of the matter and what should be done about it. Up till now history had indeed been literally history, the record of men who have been able to leave written records behind them. The rest has been left to the expert in folklore, or to the propagandist for a particular message about 'the people'. What has now to be done is to recognize what it means to observe only the literate activity of a society most of whose life was oral, above all to try to get the feel of how the attitude of the illiterate mass affected the literate few, and so was allowed for, taken into account, in the social process as a whole and particularly the process of politics.

After Hardwick's Marriage Act of 1753 each bride and bridegroom was required to sign or make a distinctive mark in the marriage, just as they had done in France for 150 years and more. In East Yorkshire two-thirds of all bridegrooms could sign their names in the 1750's, but only a half of the brides; a hundred years later bridegrooms unable to sign had fallen to a quarter.[191] This fragment of evidence reveals a level of literacy of the same order as that from France, where something over a half of men and something over a quarter of women signed the register at the village of Crulai in the 1750's, though the proportions had risen to 80 per cent and 64 per

[191] *See page 272.*

cent by 1790. In France generally this accomplishment grew
steadily in the eighteenth century: in the 1680's a fifth of
brides and bridegrooms were able to sign the register but in the
1780's over a third.[192] But there was great variation from area
to area of that country, as there seems to have been in our own.
English evidence moreover is so sparse that it may be misleading, especially for the years before 1700.

About a quarter of those applying for marriage licences in
the 1660's in Gloucestershire, all men, were forced to sign their
applications with a cross. But those married by licence were,
as we have seen, more likely to be educated than the population as a whole. In a part of the county of Surrey in 1642, no
less than two-thirds of the males over eighteen found it
necessary to make marks rather than sign a protestation of
loyalty to the embattled Parliament against the King.[193] All this
evidence, English and French, presents considerable difficulty
to the interpreter, because we do not yet know what the mere
ability to sign, often very shakily and sometimes probably by
tracing or copying, really meant at these times. It is just con-
ceivable that there were those who could read and share in
literate life to some extent, who could not sign their names,
but the opposite interpretation seems much more probable.
This would insist that ability to sign cannot be taken by itself
as implying that the signer could take any part in the written
and printed activities which governed the society. In order to
have an opinion of this character, and to take part in political
discussion, habitual reading must have been necessary, as well
as daily familiarity with the task of recording by writing. A
life of this sort may be supposed to imply the ownership of
books, and this was very much less common than even the
lowest figures for the proportion of signatories might imply.
The inventories attached to wills suggest that something like
one in ten propertied persons possessed books before the year
1700.

No woman could sign the marriage register at Crulai in the
1680's, and very few in the early eighteenth century, but the
proportion rapidly rose to over a half after 1740: it is known
that a school for girls had been opened in the village. Where
there were schools undertaking the instruction of a good proportion of the community, male and female, then perhaps we
can assume that the monopoly of literate communication held

[192] *See page 272.*   [193] *See page 272.*

by the ruling minority was broken down to some extent, especially in the eighteenth century. But it would be more than usually misguided to make general statements about effects of this kind before the numerical exercises, only now beginning, have been taken a great deal further. Contemporary statements and the rapid growth of schools in Tudor and early Stuart times have recently been used to make out the case for yet another revolutionary process in England over these years, an educational revolution between 1550 and 1640 which made English society into the best instructed of all societies up to that time, where in certain favoured areas up to a half of the whole population were properly literate. The whole movement has been linked with changes in higher education over the same period of time.[194]

There can be no doubt of the development in higher education, the education of the gentry, the clergy and the others, however uncertain the claim about a general rise in literacy may turn out to be. We have already referred to the growth of an intellectual interest in political matters amongst the gentry of England at this time, and the story of the universities over the relevant period is now well known. Interesting evidence is beginning to come to light which links educational change of this kind with social mobility downward from the higher levels. It would seem that in the largely illiterate society of England in early Stuart times there may have been for a generation or so too many highly educated people, and in particular too many university trained clergymen for the number of livings available to support them adequately. This paradox has its parallel in Africa and India in the 1960's, where there is also a surplus of highly educated professional people, although the general educational level is extremely low. 'Alienated intellectuals' is the phrase which has been applied to the unwanted graduate priests of Charles I's reign but in assessing their possible significance we must once again bear in mind the fact that such a surplus is exactly what might be expected to appear from time to time. There is no necessary connection between the presence of professional men without a proper livelihood and a general raising of educational standards, except in so far as they took to teaching the poor their letters as a means of keeping alive. In order to make a perceptible impression on social and political life, furthermore, they would

[194] *See page 272.*

have had to have brought about in large numbers of communities a substantial increase in the numbers of reading, writing, book-owning households.

If such a hypothetical argument as this is to be pursued, it might be said that in the eighteenth, though not in the seventeenth century, there may turn out to have been just such a development. The freeholders of the county of Middlesex, already to some extent a suburban county, who repeatedly defied their traditional political rulers and managers in the 1760's to elect the incredible John Wilkes as their member of Parliament, were beginning to dissolve the immemorial pattern. Wilkite radicalism may therefore rightly be heralded as a sign of an altered relationship between the common man and his gentleman superior, in which quiescent political ignorance had begun to give way to demands for a share in the national political life. If we go back to the technical language, it could perhaps be rightly said of them that they showed signs of relative deprivation of political power, taking as their reference group the members of the ruling minority rather than their own companions. If this is what took place, it seems extremely likely that they were better informed than their ancestors, less completely lost in a world where inability to share in literate life cut most men off from even contemplating a share in political power.

But Middlesex in the 1760's does not belong in the world we have lost as we have used that phrase in this essay. It may be appropriate to bring to an end this hurried survey of that world with the words scrawled on a piece of paper by a Luddite and sent to a clothier in Gloucestershire in 1803:[195]

Wee Hear in Formed that you got Shear in mee sheens [shearing machines] and if you Dont Pull them Down in a Forght Nights Time Wee will pull them Down for you Wee will you Damd infernold dog.

Here is a barely literate man, the lilt of his ordinary speech showing through his pathetic attempt to make himself understood in writing, struggling and just succeeding in expressing his passionate resentment. We can look on it as a sign of the terror which the coming of the factories and the machines struck into the hearts of ordinary people, those village crafts-

[195] *See page 272.*

men who have occupied us so much. We can also look upon it as a token of what it meant to live an entirely oral life in a world dominated by reading and writing. Surely this is the most compelling of all the contrasts between our world and the world we have lost.

After the Transformation:
English Society
in the Early
Twentieth Century
Chapter 9

1. The Working Class since 1901

> *Rattle his bones, over the stones*
> *He's only a pauper whom nobody owns*

When Queen Victoria died at the very outset of the twentieth century one person in five could expect to come to this, a solitary burial from the workhouse, the poor-law hospital, the lunatic asylum. On the whole the first year of our century, 1901, was a prosperous time for the English, one of the twenty good years not marked by Depression or by war to the death which they were to have in the fifty which followed. There was a war going on, it is true, the South African War, which, if men had but known it, was the beginning of the end of the English as a people of commanding world-wide power, but its social effects at the time did not go very deep. The huge coal-fields of Yorkshire and Lancashire, the great shipbuilding towns, the acres and acres of factory floor given over to textiles, were made busier by the demand for armaments and uniforms and machinery. Nevertheless something like a quarter of the whole population was in poverty.

Poverty, we must notice, was no vague condition then, nothing like as uncertain as the state of 'decreasing the wealth of the kingdom' has to be for the historian looking back to England in 1688 through the eyes of Gregory King. Families were in poverty 'whose total earnings are insufficient to obtain the minimum necessaries for the maintenance of merely physical efficiency'.

Those precise syllables come from Seebohm Rowntree's book called *Poverty* which appeared in 1901 and which published the sombre results of a house-to-house survey carried out with monumental thoroughness in his native city of York, a railway centre, where the family firm of Rowntree manufactured chocolates as it has ever since. Confectionery is perhaps as representative a light industry of the twentieth century type, as railways were of the heavy industry of the nineteenth century, which had given England and especially the north of England her world-wide manufacturing supremacy. Young Mr Rowntree had done his work in order to find out whether a reasonably typical provincial city was like London. He had discovered that 27·84 per cent of the citizens of York were living in poverty according to his definition. In London 30·7 per cent of the people were in poverty as his predecessor and mentor, Charles Booth, had already shown, London which was the richest city in the world and a fifth of the whole kingdom.

Englishmen in 1901 had to face the disconcerting fact that destitution was still an outstanding feature of fully industrial society, a working class perpetually liable to social and material degradation. More than half of all the children of working men were in this dreadful condition, which meant 40 per cent of all the children in the country.

These were the scrawny, dirty, hungry, ragged, verminous boys and girls who were to grow up into the working class of twentieth-century England. This was the generation which was to man the armies of the First World War, although they were inches shorter and pounds lighter than they would have been if they had been properly fed and cared for. Those who were left of them became the fathers and mothers of the working people who endured the Depression of the 1920's and the Great Depression of the 1930's, and who saw at last the squalid streets in which they made their homes luridly lighted up by Hitler's bombs. They were also the men and women who nurtured the Labour Party, the working-man's party, and brought it to maturity in the 1920's, and to overwhelming, if somewhat short-lived political victory in 1945. They are still, it could be claimed, the most easily neglected element in English political and historical consciousness even today.

We might take a very well-known example to demonstrate this fact, though the tenacious memory of labour politicians and labour voters for the terrible days of not so long ago might seem to prove it straightaway. Young Beatrice Potter was an assistant in Booth's survey, as gifted and extraordinary a member of the governing minority as ever took to 'Social Reform' as the Edwardians called it. But she did not go as far as a year or two with the Charity Organization Society, and then marry one of her own set, compounding for a series of

subscriptions to worthy causes as so many of her fellows seem
to have done. She became the wife of Mr Sidney Webb, of the
London County Council and the Fabian Society, and the two
of them founded the London School of Economics as well as
the New Statesman. As Lord Passfield and Mrs Webb – for the
aristocratic Beatrice would have nothing to do with Sidney's
silly title – they visited Russia in the early 1930's. Hence the
title of their final book, the last of a long series, *Soviet Communism, a New Civilization.* Irreducible poverty, that of London in the 1890's and of all the English unemployed forty years
later, had helped to turn them from liberal socialism and the
most successful movement of gradual reform that the world
perhaps has ever seen, into prophets of communism.

In this final mood, and perhaps only then, they ceased to be
typical of the attitude taken up by their countrymen to what
was ordinarily known in their youth as the 'condition of England question', one question amongst the many others that the
eminent English political leaders had to deal with. The exact
percentages in Booth's and Rowntree's figures make uneasy
reading in our generation, when statistics are so much more
cautiously handled that two places of decimals almost never
appear in sociological percentages. An attempt at a scientific,
a physiological definition of poverty, one graduated in terms
of the biological needs of an ordinary man in performing his
day's physical work, would never be attempted today. It will,
therefore, perhaps be doubted whether the shift from 1688 to
1901, from counts of parishioners and Gregory King, to house-
to-house surveys, Mr Booth and Mr Rowntree, makes much
difference as to reliability. Can we really be so certain that the
problem of poverty was still so urgent after a century and more
of miraculous economic growth and change? Our traditional
picture of England in 1901, the first year of the golden Edwardian age, is altogether lighter than this.

What about the countryside, and the country towns? What
about the really prosperous manufacturing areas, which were
to make the England of Edward the Seventh more expansive
economically than it ever was to be again until George VI was
on the throne and Mr Attlee became his Prime Minister? The
actual condition of the population as a whole of course will
never be known, though in the succeeding two generations
many cities were submitted to the treatment given to London
and York, using an ever-more realistic criterion of prosperity

and poverty. But Rowntree had thought of agricultural England.

Some years were to pass before his analysis of agriculture was to be completed, but in his book on York he pointed out that in 1899 over three-quarters of the population of England lived in 'urban areas'. The time in fact had already almost arrived which we talked of when discussing the village community of the traditional world, when the balance between town and country would be completely reversed, and the typical Englishman would be brought up amongst bricks and mortar, and only the exceptional amongst trees and fields. Moreover Rowntree was probably right to assume that those who had remained in the country after three or four generations of steady emigration from it lived rather below the standards endured by their grandchildren, great-nephews and cousins in the city streets.

In 1903 the little village of Ridgmont in Bedfordshire, over the wall from the great park at Woburn, the seat of the Duke of Bedford, was investigated according to the principles of Booth and Rowntree. The Dukes of Bedford were doing very well in that year, with income tax at elevenpence in the pound and death duties at a maximum of 11 per cent. Like most noble families they had urban as well as rural property, industrial and commercial wealth as well as landed. In fact the Fabian Society alleged that the Bedford Estate was receiving £15,000 a year from Covent Garden at the time that Professor Higgins met Eliza Doolittle outside the Royal Opera House. Still the estate was managed in an exemplary way and Ridgmont was being rebuilt cottage by cottage; the tall red-brick roofs of that time of expansive if cumbersome domestic architecture are still to be seen in the village. Yet the investigator found that 41 per cent of the population living there were in poverty, the sort of poverty which left biological need unsatisfied.

We cannot linger long in Ridgmont, though the facts about countryside and town, about inequality in income and about the persistence of the country house as the political instrument of a very different society are all very important to our subject. In October, 1900, the Marquess of Salisbury submitted the name of the Duke of Bedford to Queen Victoria when he was reconstructing the Cabinet, and his Grace declined because of his interest in estate-management; Woburn remained a centre of political power nevertheless. Perhaps the annual income of this great noble family was some £100,000 and it must have ranked with the largest in the country, even with the huge industrial and commercial fortunes, though an English duke might already find it advantageous to marry an American heiress, as the Duke of Marlborough had done in 1895. Here was a splendid contrast with an income of about £50 which was what was earned by a farm labourer in Ridgmont. In Gregory King's time the average nobleman had £3,000 a year and a labourer £15, which was a similar disproportion if a Duke then possessed double the ordinary noble income.

But though agricultural labour was still the biggest occupation in England in the early 1900's, it cannot have been any longer true that the country could be divided, as King divided it, into a large minority receiving six times the income of the bare majority. We cannot tell how the £6 10s. a year which King reckoned to be the resources of that quarter of the people in his day whom he called cottagers and paupers compared with Rowntree's £100 a year, or rather less, which he reckoned to be what a family needed to be above the poverty line in 1899. Still it is clear that the traditional, agricultural society as it had survived in Ridgmont was not more prosperous than the commercial and manufacturing society of the city of York. Nothing went on in this part of Bedfordshire except the tilling of the soil and the keeping of beasts; rural industry was already almost entirely dead. A few cottagers still plaited straw, but lacemaking had disappeared completely. The making of hats had gone off to the factories of Bedford and Luton. Not so much as a loaf of bread was baked in the village; it all came in horse vans from the towns. And every single village child was living in poverty.

To the historian of an earlier England it is a gross and telling contrast that Ridgmont should have belonged in 1901 to a residual area of rural society within an expanding industrial whole, an area already not much more than a fifth and still getting smaller. This made English society different in order from anything which had ever gone before, in Europe or in the whole world. It means that the process of social and economic transformation which we call *industrial revolution* was already virtually complete in our country. This distinguishes the society of England as it now is, very sharply from other societies. English social experience since the death of Victoria is the only lengthy experience any country has ever had of really mature industrialization.

It has been in fact experience not of a state of things exactly, but of a perpetual tendency towards continuous change. For industrialization is not a once-for-all process and it is an English error to suppose that it is. Since 1901 our country has tended to fall somewhat behind others in the race to re-industrialize with every new technique, but our history since 1901 has been a history of successive transformation all the same. The question of importance for the contrast we are trying to draw in this essay is the question of welfare. In so far as the industrializing process is to be described above all as a change in the scale of living, such as we dwelt on in our first chapter, only in England does it seem to have been virtually complete by 1901. What has happened since then has been a matter of the levelling up of standards, the lengthening of life, the diminution of poverty, the universalization of education. This may not have been the result of what became so suddenly and shockingly apparent after Booth and Rowntree had done their work. But since that time, intentionally or not, the spread of the benefits has gone on both by political compulsion and perhaps also of itself.

This may seem an easy and too comforting a generalization, since the contemporary world is even now discovering that in rich societies great hidden areas of poverty go on persisting. The conclusion that we shall reach about the Welfare State which arose in England out of the attitude which Rowntree represents, will not be that it was completely successful in abolishing want in an industrial society, rather perhaps that it was just the last and most effective way of convincing the conscientious that it had been abolished. But when all this has been said there is a difference between Rowntree's revelations and those which shocked the 1960's about the condition of the old in Britain and of the coloured in the United States. It is difficult for us now to realize what it meant in 1901 for England to have to recognize that after a century of leading the world in economic matters, when she was still undoubtedly the world's greatest political and military power, still in many ways the world's wealthiest power, a quarter of her population was living in poverty, in something like destitution.

If King's figures are comparable with Rowntree's, and if both are somewhere near the truth, then the growth of wealth brought by industry did succeed in reducing dependency and destitution by more than half in two hundred years, from the 1690's to the 1900's. If this was so, then it accomplished a great deal, especially when we remember how little sign has ever been found that progress of this sort was ever possible in the world we have lost, where the text 'The poor ye shall always have with you' was a truth not worth the disputing. But the difference in standard between these two observers, the Stuart pursuivant-at-arms and the Edwardian industrialist with a conscience, is so enormous that this most challenging and difficult of questions must be left on one side for the present as unanswerable.

Unfortunately the same objection, that of a difference in standard, can be urged against the known facts about the subsequent history of poverty in the England of the twentieth century. The truly remarkable thing about Seebohm Rowntree was that he lived long enough to satisfy himself by personal investigation that poverty of the hopeless sort had virtually disappeared. In 1936, thirty-seven years after his first survey of York, he examined the city again. This time he used a much more sophisticated method of survey, impelled as he was by the disaster of unemployment which made him expect rather less of a reduction of poverty by 1936 than he had hoped for. Things were even worse than he feared, for on his new and more realistic standard 31 per cent of the working class of York were still in poverty in the late 1930's, as against 43 per cent in 1899, on the cruder standard he was then using.

But there were other differences between the two years. The greatest individual cause of poverty in 1899 had been insufficient wages, and no more telling indictment of industrialism could be imagined: but by far and away the greatest cause of poverty in York in 1936 was unemployment. When he was eighty years old in 1961, Rowntree was able to publish his last, and, it must be said, his least satisfactory, survey of poverty in the city. Using a new and still more sophisticated poverty line, he found that only 3 per cent of the population were in destitution, and that the great cause of poverty was old age. From being a predominant feature of our social life, poverty, so Rowntree tended to think at the very last, had been reduced to insignificance.

We must notice that the abolition of poverty, if abolition it was, came about not gradually over the years, but suddenly, between the late 1930's and the late 1940's, as part of the foundation and functioning of the Welfare State. Within half a generation of that time, in spite of the warnings of Rowntree's successors as investigators of poverty in our country, we have now begun to think of the problem of industrial society as a problem of affluence, of having too much leisure and too many goods.

This attitude may not survive for long. There are signs that the remainder of the twentieth century may also interpret its social mission as the equalization of wealth between every citizen, whatever his colour and his history. This time the redistribution will have to go on not only within so-called 'rich' societies, but between 'rich' and 'poor' areas of the globe as a whole. But gross and familiar contrasts between our country as it was in 1901 and as it is now are quite immediate nevertheless. If any such superficial attempt as this one is to describe the twentieth-century English working class is to be successful it must rely for the most part on the reader to make the comparisons from his own experience. Here is some of the obvious material.

In 1901 people in the upper class could expect to live for nearly sixty years, but those at the very lowest level for only thirty: paupers were still, in fact, as short-lived as the whole population in Stuart times. In 1901 you could tell at sight whether a man belonged to the upper or the working classes – bearing, dress and speech, size, attitude and manner were noticeably different. Some are still alive who remember seeing the Victorian farm labourer in his smock. School teachers then had an average of seventy children in every class. Only two-fifths of the population had the vote, and no women at all. Shop assistants worked an average of eighty hours in every seven days, and many of them lived in dormitories above their work, compulsorily unmarried. Since those who had no separate room were excluded from the franchise, a shop assistant living in voted only if the partitions between the beds in the dormitory reached the ceiling. So conscious indeed was this earlier England of social class that the bath-houses of London displayed the following notice:

Baths for working people, 2d. hot and 1d. cold.

Baths for any higher classes, 3d. cold and 6d. hot.

Of course such a crude method as this cannot convey any-thing like an accurate idea of what we are trying to show and

the choice of poverty as a starting point for our survey has
grave disadvantages. It distorts our picture of the working
people because it leaves out prosperous workers. A wrong
twist may have been given to the evidence a little while ago.
It was not those who were sunk in hopeless misery who founded
and ran the trade unions, who organized the Labour Party.
The submerged tenth, as they were sometimes and too hope-
fully called, were not pre-eminently the people who created
and transmitted the traditional culture of the working men
which interests our own generation.

We must never forget that well over half of the workers were
above the poverty line at any one time, though we are at the
great disadvantage of knowing very little from first hand evidence of how they lived. Poverty was on the consciences of our
fathers and grandfathers and it was poverty which they described for us. The working-class family, said Rowntree, pursing
up his lips, spent 6s. a week on beer, a whole sixth of their
income – hence a very great deal of secondary poverty, which
the people could have avoided, and which less sympathetic
people blamed them for. Now for 6s. you could get 36 pints of
beer in 1901, and a working family in the clear can get a great
deal of fun out of 36 pints of beer, even if it did sometimes
finally lead to the workhouse.

Nevertheless, as has been said, the most important cause of
poverty at the turn of the century was low wages. 'The wages
paid for unskilled labour in York,' Rowntree concluded, 'are
insufficient to provide food, clothing and shelter adequate to
maintain a family of moderate size in a state of bare physical
efficiency.' Here, then, was the proletariat of Marxian theory
and the Marxian law of increasing misery under capitalism
seemingly demonstrated for all to see, in the only mature industrial society then known.

The great puzzle about the English working-class may therefore seem to be why it was that the active, intelligent and well-
paid amongst them did not all draw the correct Marxian
inference, why it is that there has been no violent social revolution in England in the twentieth century. It cannot be said
that geographical and personal propinquity has been lacking
in anything like the way that it was lacking amongst their
ancestors in the Stuart countryside. Working-classness has
existed since well before 1901. It should become clear as we
go on that the issue of revolutionary action was never quite

as simple as this might make it seem, and that critical social change has in fact occurred without it. But though revolution in this latter sense is the subject of the last section of this chapter, the problem of the acquiescent attitude of English workers in the twentieth century goes beyond the limits of this essay. Let us turn our attention to the cyclical character of poverty in recent times, not so much the alternation of periods of prosperity and depression as the succession of events in the lifetime of an individual working man. This is one of the interesting points of resemblance between his situation and that of his predecessors in traditional society.

'*A labourer,*' Rowntree tells us, '*is in poverty and therefore underfed:*
In childhood, when his constitution is being built up.
In his early and his middle life, when he should be in his prime.
In old age.
And
The women are in poverty for the greater part of the time when they are bearing children.'

This is how the life cycle of working people went. Very few manual labourers in York in 1899 could have been without neighbours, friends, relatives struggling for subsistence. Infantile mortality was 94 in a thousand in the middle class, but no less than 247 amongst those in poverty. Again the resemblance with Clayworth in the 1670's comes to mind. One baby in every six died in the working class generally – the small coffin on one of the family beds, or on the table, or under the table when the family had a meal. This was a sight every working man must have seen and every working woman grieved for.

The discovery of the cyclic descent into the area of poverty was the most interesting sociological discovery which Seebohm Rowntree ever made, and has too often been forgotten. It meant that everyone in the working class had at some time in his life had personal experience of people living below the poverty level, even if he himself had never been so unfortunate. It meant in fact that the fear of poverty, the insecurity which that fear brought with it and the resentment against the system, all these things went deep down into the character of the English working man. It is not entirely fanciful to think of them as an inheritance from the traditional world of peasant, craftsman and pauper.

Those amongst us who now talk of the bourgeoisification –
the horrid word they use – of the working class should take due
note of this. Those who look for a centre for the sense of community in the working class should note it as well, the sense of
community which is forever being stressed as the heart and
soul of the Labour movement. The positive urge to remake the
world in a way which would abolish poverty has its spring in a
negative attitude, the fear which dominated the lives of grandfather, fathers, uncles, aunts and cousins. To call the prosperous working family of the later twentieth century simply
bourgeois or middle class is a superficial historical misconception. It is rather the working family of the 1900's, of the 1920's
or the 1930's with something of the horror of poverty removed.
'Workingclassness' in the social development of England in
the twentieth century has, therefore, an obvious justification
in attitude, in instinctive response, though of course it has
many other defining characteristics. It has an immemorial
history too.

So much for the English working class since 1901. For all
the over-simplification which the developing story of our own
century had brought with it, it must be obvious that no such
phenomenon could ever have existed in the world before the
coming of industry. The probable resemblances and direct
descents are fascinating to contemplate nevertheless.

ii   *The Solid Middle Class*

The solid middle class is a very familiar expression. It is surrounded by a cluster of clichés which reappear when the
English think of themselves as a society, and look back on
their history, particularly their recent history – the backbone
of the nation, the salt of the earth. The idea of a middle class
which was the anchor of a community's stability is not a recent
one. Aristotle first suggested the notion and it has been applied
to almost every political system and situation known to the
historian. We have seen how commonly the expression has been
used of England before 1700. But Victorian and Edwardian
England is usually looked upon as the outstanding example
of apotheosis of the middle class as a community and a
culture. The decline of that solid middle class has sometimes
been made into an account of the social development which
has gone on in England since the twentieth century began.

Meanwhile the working class has also supposed to have begun to become like the solid middle class, to be taking on its attitudes and values.

But when the evidence is closely scanned it turns out to be somewhat misleading to think of a solid middle-class community as existing in England in 1901, and even more so to suppose that social development since that time has been the story of its decline. The word *community* is the important word here. There most certainly was a lump of persons in English society in the age of Arnold Bennett and Thomas Hardy and George Meredith, to which they applied the phrase 'the solid middle class'. The question is whether it can ever have been so nation-wide a community.

The very fact that the phrase has been in perpetual use gives the solid middle class an independent existence of sorts. The people we shall be examining were, at least as individuals, solid in the substantial sense of the word. They were substantial because they were rich and had big establishments, and because they bulked very large in all the affairs of the nation. What we shall find is that the notion of a community at one level, more or less homogeneous in its consistency and composed of fairly equal units, is a very questionable one. The twentieth-century working class which has just been discussed has these two characteristics, although it is much less usually referred to as solid. But the facts about the middle class are rather different. Fortunately these facts are no longer guess-work and riskily made inference as they had to be when we were talking of the seventeenth century. By and large the evidence is reasonably well known.

Arnold Bennett recognized something of the truth in the suggestive and inexact way which is typical of the literary artist and which we have had to become so wary of. In February, 1909, this highly representative author wrote one of his many essays speculating about who bought and read his books:

'When my morbid curiosity is upon me,' Bennett says, 'I stroll into Mudies or the Times Book Club, or I hover round Smith's bookstall in the Strand. The crowd at these places is the prosperous crowd, the crowd which pays income tax and grumbles at it.' In February, 1909, we may notice, income tax stood at five per cent of earnings. 'Three hundred and seventy-five thousand persons paid income tax last year,' he continues, 'paid it under protest. They stand for perhaps a million souls, and this million is a handful floating more or less easily on the surface of the forty millions of the population.'

We ought perhaps to underline Bennett's words about income-tax payers being only a handful of the population: 'floating on the surface' is very significant too. His description continues thus:

Their assured, curt voices, their carriage, their clothes, the similarity of their manners, all show that they belong to a caste, and that the caste has been successful in the struggle for life. It has been called the middle class, but it ought to be called the upper class, for nearly everything is below it. I go to the stores, to Harrods, to Rumpelmeyer's, to the Royal Academy, and to a dozen clubs in Albemarle Street and Dover Street, and I see again just the same crowd, well-fed, well-dressed, completely free from the cares which beset at least five-sixths of the English race. I do not belong to this class by birth. I was born slightly beneath it. But by the help of God and strict attention to business I have gained the right of entrance to it.

In one nostalgic Edwardian image after another Bennett goes on to list the notorious characteristics of the solid middle class. He talks of its sincere, religious worship of money and success – the world, he says, is a steamer in which the middle class is travelling saloon. He talks of its barbarism, the barbarism which toasts the architect *and the contractor*, and might as well toast the poet *and the printer*. He talks of the dullness, the humourlessness, the unresponsiveness of that 'great, solid, comfortable class which forms the backbone of the novel-reading public'. How appropriate Rumpelmeyer's is, that Mayfair shop which catered only for the carriage trade, and which has not survived to share in our day the fate of the other exclusive Edwardian emporia.

Here, then, is the solid middle class of Edwardian times as a contemporary saw it. Here too we may notice a distant reminder of the shadow of poverty which we have just considered, that other community within the nation which had not been so successful in the struggle for food, housing, clothes and freedom from perpetual insecurity. Bennett's openness in telling his readers that he had not been born into the solid middle class is interesting, but should not be counted as all that revealing; although a solicitor by his best description, his father had kept a pawnbroker's shop at one time, at Hanley in the Potteries. His other uncertainties and inconsistencies are interesting too, for rather a different reason.

He talks sometimes of the *upper* class, as if that were the better term, of a *caste* rather than a *class*. Yet he is prepared to believe that a million people belonged to it, as if the crowd of faces which he saw so often at Rumpelmeyer's or the Clubs could possibly belong to as many as a million people. He was wrong about the figures, as will appear in a moment, but his instinct in thinking of the income tax in order to calculate the size of his potential readership was apt enough. If Bennett had been taken more seriously, if his hint about consulting the income tax returns had been acted upon and the figures they contained had been prominently displayed, then perhaps the numerical fallacy, as it might be called, about the solid middle class would never have come into currency. The other part of this particular illusion, that of a community on one level, might have been avoided too.

By the numerical fallacy about the solid middle class of Bennett's time is meant the uncritical supposition that the middle class can then have contained a sizeable section of the English population, an eighth, shall we say, perhaps even a fifth or a quarter, or a third of the whole population. It did not. It consisted at most of about a seventeenth. If we rely on the income tax figures by themselves it was even smaller. Only one person in twenty-five was rich enough in England in 1909, when Arnold Bennett wrote his essay, to enjoy the famous middle-class standard of living. The resemblance to the figures we have quoted for the privileged minority in the pre-industrial world may simply be a coincidence, but a very interesting coincidence it is.

Income is not the only way to measure such things as *class-membership*, and these few numerical facts do not prove that only this tiny minority regarded themselves as belonging to the middle classes. Quite the reverse. The truth seems to be that for the whole of this century some millions of people have been aspiring to live as only a few hundred thousand of people could in fact afford to live. The secret of the historian's stereotype about the solid middle class is imitation, what might be called in Arnold Toynbee's expression *mimesis*. Only if imitation, mimesis, is taken to constitute 'solidity' can the phrase the solid middle class be made to apply to any substantial part of the population, not only in Arnold Bennett's day but for most of the time since.

Decline of the middle class, which is how the historian has tended to look on social history since that time, could unfortunately mean many things. It is as elusive a phrase as the rise of the gentry. But if its possible qualitative meaning is disregarded and its numerical meaning only is retained, then it is completely untrue of England in the earlier twentieth century. There has been a completely uninterrupted growth in the numbers of those who could be called middle class in the economic sense since the year 1901. This growth was slowed down but not interrupted by successive depressions, and it has never been more rapid than it has been since 1945.

The numerical fallacy about the solid middle class, then, is very easy to see and to dispose of. More difficult is the fact that historians have allowed it to persist, as have some of the social scientists in spite of their repudiations. To see why the facts have been difficult to appreciate, we must glance at the figures of middle-class occupations as well as of middle-class persons.

It is difficult to decide how much money was needed to maintain the suburban villa which we associate with the solid middle class of Bennett's time, to pay the servants, to educate the children – five or six of them – to run the carriage, and to pay for Bennett's books. Seven hundred or a thousand golden sovereigns a year, shall we say, together with the expectation that the value of money would never go down. Though the precise numbers of tax-payers is not known for that period, it is known that there were about 280,000 households in England and Wales in 1909 with £700 a year or more. That is to say there were less than 300,000 families out of a total of 7,000,000 which reached the level necessary for comfortable middle-class living. Not that there was a plateau at this level, or at any level in British incomes over the century. Indeed, the variation above our chosen point was enormous, with gaps yawning far more widely than the gap between those who had enough to live adequately in the middle class and those who did not.

There were in Edwardian times 120,000 'capitalists' who were reckoned to own two-thirds of the wealth and they obviously constituted a large proportion of those with seven hundred or a thousand a year and above. There were something like forty thousand landowners who owned twenty-seven out of the thirty-four million acres in the country. Some of these of course were aristocrats and perhaps a case might be made out to show that there was a useful sense in which these people were upper class, not middle class. We have already seen that the very rich and powerful played a distinctive role especially in politics even after the transformation. In this arena, in the relationship between the country house and the suburban dwelling, there was a cleavage between the bourgeoisie and the landed families.

But Bennett's typical hesitation between upper and middle class shows how difficult the distinction was even in his day. In fact in the twentieth century the upper class has been a nullity, just as the second class was for so long on our railways. The only sensible course for the historian is to put the people at the very top in with the rest of the successful, and face the fact that this makes the whole an extremely various group of persons. We can now recognize the second misconception in the historian's stereotype of the solid middle class, that of homogeneity, in income, and in occupation. However vivid the impression which these privileged people give in the *sameness* of their attitudes and tastes, nevertheless their surroundings, their experience, their wealth, and its sources were all very various indeed – these lawyers, clerics, imperial officials, businessmen, doctors, professors and plain receivers of dividends and rents.

The confusion over class distinctions and their relation to political and other forms of power has led in the last decade to the appearance in English of a new word, beginning its career as such words often do as a piece of slang, a smart expression for journalists and satirists. This word is the 'Establishment'. Vague as its meaning is, if it yet has a settled meaning at all, this term seems to express what Bennett was trying to say rather better than anything else we have to hand. What he had in mind turns out to be very much more like an Establishment than it is like that class community which we found amongst the workers and the poor. Instead of a solid middle class, with an upper class above it, we should rather think of a minority of some 300,000 families which several million families were busy imitating, and imitating rather unsuccessfully because they had not enough money to do it well. The figure of 300,000 belongs to the 1900's; it is a much bigger number of families now and it is growing rapidly. It is still a small minority, to some extent an isolated minority, but nevertheless the goal of social aspiration.

The resemblances between this situation and that we have tried to describe for the traditional world are coming into view, together again with the very important differences. Mimesis, social imitation, did not first appear in England in late Victorian times. The perennial complaint against citizens and citizens' wives from the middle ages onwards was that they imitated their betters, the aristocracy. This was resented for more reasons than one, although the most important was no doubt ordinary snobbery and the contempt of those who could afford to live well for those who could only pretend to. There was also the knowledge that some at least of the imitators could in fact afford more than those whom they imitated, and would be in their places before long. In a society where downward mobility was, as we have seen, probably greater than upward, and where status was regarded as a fixture, part of an unchanging universe, this led to legislation as well as to satire. In high industrial times such an attitude has become impossible and movement in every direction is undoubtedly much easier. The perpetual growth of the privileged section of society has ˙become a possibility, even a reality, both because the whole population has been growing and because ever expanding wealth has made for an increase in the proportion of the rich to the whole.

There is a feature which the two systems manifestly shared, the presence of a large marginal area between upper and lower, a penumbra, as we have called it, to the privileged minority. This interesting region could only be very roughly sketched in indeed for pre-industrial society, but by Arnold Bennett's time its outlines have become fairly clear. In 1909 income tax began at £3 a week, and the figures show that there were 800,000 incomes between this, the lowest level, and the level where we believed true 'solid middle class' living was possible, that is at £700 per year. This was the area of the imitators, the people in between the working-class community below them and the privileged above them. To make it manifestly clear who these people were, let it be repeated that they were placed below those who could objectively afford a 'middle-class' standard of living, and above those who were by universal agreement working class, manual workers, men and women living under the threat of poverty.

These in-between families with £150–£700 a year were the chief of the aspirers, the Mr Pooters of the Edwardian world. They were the people whom Arnold Bennett missed out when he walked round London looking for his readers, and from whom he himself had his own origin. There can be little doubt that *Clayhanger* might well have been found on the mantel-piece of Mr Pooter's sitting-room, if it had been written in 1895, rather than in 1909. It would have found a place along with the rest of the bric-à-brac, not quite as appropriate as the two stone lions which, as Mr Pooter tells us, graced the flight of steps leading up to his front door, but a likely book for his rebellious son Lupin to be reading. George and Weedon Gros-smith who contributed their pieces on Mr Pooter to Punch in the 1890's were as shrewd in their observation of English life as Bennett, Wells or even Shaw.

There were nearly three times as many people of this type as there were with an adequate middle-class income. Some of them could justly be called more than aspirers, for even with four, three, or two hundred a year a man could do very well in 1909, especially if he belonged to a respected occupation like that of the clergy. He could often afford a servant, and some-times had expectations of succeeding Mama and Papa in their genuine establishment. Or he might resolve to make his own way up to solidity; opportunities were not wanting to the really vigorous and enterprising, especially those willing to go abroad.

Even if all the families of the imitators are added together only about a million at the very most, a seventh of the whole number in the country, can be made out to be middle class. Considering how this seventh now appears to be composed it would seem to be extraordinary to think of this section of society as a 'solid' community or even a community at all. Moreover it cannot have been true that the whole remaining part of the population was embraced within the working-class community, over 85 per cent of the whole country. There is yet another intermediate area, an area considerably larger than the one we have classified as the area of aspiration, which has to be traversed before we reach the working class proper. In order to observe the people living there it is necessary to go below the £3 level, beyond the realm of a somewhat uncertain light given out by the income-tax figures. Only if large numbers of people from this region of society are admitted into the middle-class could it ever become a fifth, a quarter or a third of the population.

Some of these people certainly had a claim to middle-classness. At least they felt themselves to belong to the professions, the lettered and liberal occupations, rather than with the manual workers. From the little which is objectively known about their way of life it seems that, although aspiration was out of the question for them, they also were subject to mimesis. Deliberately rejecting the artisan's outlook, what else could they do but model themselves upon their betters? But if for that reason we include them with the middle class, perhaps now dropping the adjective 'solid' as conceivably intended in some vague way to qualify one part of the middle class but not the whole, this is what we find in terms of income. 'Elementary schoolteachers' were a large element of this type, and three-quarters of them in 1909 were women, whose average income was £75 a year. The same sort of thing is true for office workers, in business and in government, especially local government, who made up most of the rest of the people in this category. White-collar workers they are called now, but it is worth mentioning that in the 1900's they did not contain many women. It seems quite out of the question to try to classify them on the conventional three-layer scale, especially if one layer is null. We need a wholly more realistic vocabulary.

This subject like all social description becomes tedious if it is pressed beyond a certain point. All that the reader is required to acknowledge is that the 'solid middle class' of the incautious historian and social commentator turns out on closer inspection about earlier twentieth-century society in Britain to be to a large extent bogus. Bogus is used here in its original technical sense, meaning blank types put in to fill out space. Perhaps it may be doubted, whether these claims have ever been seriously made about the middle class in our country over recent generations, and a reference or two is required here.

The late Sir Arthur Bowley was a distinguished statistician and social historian of the first half of this century. By reckoning in the white-collar workers generally and insisting that everyone who was not working class must belong to it, Sir Arthur fixed the middle class at 23 per cent of occupied men in 1901, 25 per cent in 1911 and 26 per cent in 1931, growing steadily as we have already noticed but checked by the blight of the Depression. Mr Bonham in his very interesting study of the *Middle Class Vote* decided that it comprised 30·1 per cent of the electorate in 1951 and was again growing rapidly. No less an authority than the late Professor G. D. H. Cole willingly accepted this figure for the class as a whole in the 1950's, though he admitted the difficulties about defining the middle class.

Perhaps all that it has been possible to do in this section is to convict them of the rather cumbersome and misleading use of an obsolete terminology. There are other ways of describing the 'middle class', and Seebohm Rowntree suggested and consistently used the expression 'the servant keeping class' for his purpose, which was to find a way of putting on one side all those who were neither in poverty, nor ever likely to be so. It has none of the political and other overtones of *the Establishment*. For that reason, because it lays the emphasis on the fact of social superiority alone, this is the phrase we shall have in mind as we turn to the issue about revolution in England since 1901.

iii The Social Revolution of our time

When we discussed social change in England 300 years ago, at a time of military violence over civil issues, it was concluded that to talk of revolution was inappropriate. Though there were breaches in the political fabric and constitutional changes which were so abrupt and sudden that the most extreme descriptions have always been applied to them, the notion that the social structure itself was radically changed had to be rejected. The third and last of the issues which has to be considered in this swift survey of English society in the earlier twentieth century is whether something which might be called social revolution has been happening in our time, although neither civil conflict nor, as yet, any sharp constitutional conflict has taken place.

The discussion has to go on in recognition that the general contrast between seventeenth- and twentieth-century English society is the one which seems to us now considerably more important than any other known to English history. If by the exercise of historical ingenuity it could be attached to a particular set of events, there can be no doubt that it would have been called revolution, *the* revolution in fact. This being so, any change confined to the period since 1901 could only appear as incidental. There is a further complication too. No one in the later twentieth century whatever his definitions could possibly decide whether a social revolution occurred earlier in the century, because everyone is still caught up in the process under description. Only the decision to defy convention and to choose deliberately to write history from the present backwards puts us in the uncomfortable situation of having to raise such a question at all. We must return to this crux in our final chapter.

Meanwhile we can address ourselves to the following possibility. Even in the light of the overall change which can be observed between the older, traditional social world and the industrial one which has succeeded it, a change of shape in the social structure of our country (which might turn out to be a critical one) does seem to have taken place since 1901. The argument will be that some sort of crystallization may have been taking place, with its apogee between the years 1940 and 1947. The result was a reduction in the social height, to pursue the spatial metaphor about social relationships: to go even further with the image, from a pyramid, lofty and slender, English society began at that date to look something more like a pear, tending to become an apple. Because it has an altered shape in fact, people have tended to change their image of English society, if only by very little. Englishmen, perhaps even more Englishwomen, have ceased to look upwards as much as they had always done; outward-looking has begun to compete with upward-looking.

These newer metaphors, directly they are written out on paper, begin to look even more gawky and inadequate than the older ones. Let it be clear before any attempt to justify them has been made, how modest is the claim being put forward. It is no cataclysm of the Eastern European type which is here at issue. The society described in the Jugoslavia of the 1950's by Djilas obviously differs from the Jugoslavia as it was in 1939 by a great deal more than our England differs from the England of Mr Neville Chamberlain, even of Mr Lloyd George.

The fact that productive capacity has stayed almost entirely in private hands clearly distinguishes the nature of the social change in the two countries. The change in Jugoslavia and in other countries has also been a change towards greater industrialization, a very rapid advance indeed towards a society dominated by the factory and the office. This has not been open to the English in the twentieth century to anything like the same extent because we have been highly industrialized all the time. Moreover the system of social status in our country is still officially much as it always has been, even if in fact it has become considerably less definite, whilst in the communist countries status has been completely transformed. If the height of the social ladder in England is now much less, the number of rungs is somewhat the same.

The inappropriateness of *revolution* to describe these changes is obvious when their nature is considered. It is a fact for example that in 1898 no less than 13,000 people in England and Wales died of the measles, and there are no doubt plenty of people still alive who can remember the terror which these infectious diseases caused, especially amongst families with children. By 1948 this number had dropped to about three hundred, and the other infectious diseases show the same amazing decrease in their incidence and in their power to kill. Deaths from diphtheria dropped from 7,500 to 150 over the same period, and deaths from scarlet fever show a hundredfold decrease.

Changes like these can only be counted as marking a deliberate transformation consciously contrived. It is tempting to call these things revolution, yet this merely makes us think of them in terms of a conflict, a turning point and final victory which is almost physical. And this is a nuisance.

There was, nevertheless, a critical point in these medical advances, when mortality really began to go down sharply. This point also came in the early 1940's, or somewhere near that time, for it was in 1937 that the effect of the sulphonamide drugs first began to be felt, and in 1945 that penicillin went into general action. But the experts count the new drugs as only one amongst a whole list of other changes, much more general and long-term, such as better sanitation, better housing, cleaner bodies and so on. All these tendencies combined then to produce this triumphant result in our country, though we must remember that they are features of contemporary Western industrial society as a whole. We may notice that this achievement marks the early twentieth century as a time of progress far more rapid and intense than any process of this kind which took place in the nineteenth century. Yet it was the nineteenth century which called itself the century of progress, and which historians have always thought of under this title.

Perhaps it may seem surprising that the point at which the shape of English society can be seen to have changed came during the last war. For this was when our country was in greater military danger than it has ever been, and under a government, the Churchill coalition, which certainly did not take office to bring about reform, least of all of the social structure.

But the sociologists have recognized for a long time that national warfare, especially warfare which requires a high proportion of citizens to participate, tends to produce changes of social attitude and policy, in the 'reformist' direction. The programme of the Levellers in the late 1640's has already been tentatively brought under the same heading. There was such a tendency during and after the war of 1914–18 all over Europe. Universal military conscription is one of the characteristics which distinguish twentieth-century societies from their predecessors and in Britain in the early 1940's participation in the national war effort was at a level probably unequalled anywhere at any time. Not only were able-bodied men conscripted to fight but all mature men were required to work. Not only were women enrolled voluntarily to help in a womanly way but all women were directed to some task useful to the war effort. Factories, institutions, communities, everything British was made to play its part with an efficiency and a success which is a high tribute to the British administrative skill, whatever its record since that time.

The impression should not be that under these quite unique circumstances the people of this country, or a particular number of them having support from many others, deliberately decided to introduce something like a new social order in the early 1940's, and that they succeeded. The overall changes we are discussing were not exclusively a matter of the social results of medical advances, of changes in mortality, of a rise in real wages and alterations in the distribution of income. Such advances might conceivably have come about without any governmental or political policy, being at play, as they did to a large extent in the U.S.A. over the same period. Deliberate shaping of social change did go on at the same time, however, in England. But before anything more is said about the causes of the transformation, a little more must be added about mortality and about the family.

We have talked at some length about the number of children born to peasant women 300 years ago, and made some reference to changes at age of marriage of women and numbers of children born to a marriage. These varied in ways which may turn out to be of great interest for the study of social and economic history and of social structure. The nobility and gentry showed similar fluctuations in these respects, but with them the process is clearer. It seems more obviously a question of deliberate policy in reaction to the changing situation. Over the last half-century and more there has been a very remarkable deliberative change in England of this kind, affecting now every level of society, almost every married couple.

In the later years of the nineteenth century over four children were still being born to every marriage. It should now be obvious why the size of the household grew in the eighteenth century and grew again in the nineteenth; the numbers of births remained much the same whilst child mortality went down. But by the 1950's the figure of births per marriage had fallen to two and a half, that is a decline of over 60 per cent in less than two generations. Although the family means something very different in the industrial world from what it meant in the pre-industrial world, this phenomenal fall in the numbers of children has meant an enormous change in the position and outlook of women. Together with the lengthening of their expectation of life, this change, in Professor Titmuss's authoritative opinion, has brought about something like a total transformation.

'At the beginning of this century,' he wrote some years ago, 'the expectation of life of a woman aged twenty was forty-six years,' and we may notice that it had increased by nearly a quarter since Halley made up his life table in the 1690's. 'Approximately one-third of this forty-six years,' Titmuss continues, 'about fifteen years, that is to say, was to be devoted to child-bearing. Today the expectation of life of a woman aged twenty is fifty-five years and of this only four years, about a fifteenth, is spent in child-bearing.' He also tells us that about half of all working-class wives had borne between seven and fifteen children by the time they had reached the age of forty, in the early twentieth century, that is to say. All this is entirely different today.

One is tempted to say of a society which has changed so far and so fast in such a fundamental particular is quite simply a new society. The emancipation of women, beginning with the right to vote, has meant the addition of a new and a different half to public society. Though the direct political effects have not yet been as dramatic as such language as this might lead one to expect, the final outcome is not yet apparent. For it has all happened very recently, within the twentieth century. Once again, the rate of transformation in Victorian times begins to look modest in comparison.

The change in the size of the family was undoubtedly deliberate, as deliberate as that which came about amongst the bourgeoisie of the city of Geneva in the early years of the eighteenth century, for it was likewise due to the use of contraceptives. It cannot however be dated to the 1940's, like so many of the other changes we have discussed. The lowest point reached by the biological family in England occurred during the Great Depression of the 1930's. Still freedom from the tyranny of repetitive child-bearing only means freedom to join in the world of work in times of full employment. And full employment only began in 1940. The proportion of English men and women out of work since 1940 has never reached for any full year the level at which it ordinarily stood over the whole period since the 1890's, excepting only the years 1914–18. It is possible, in fact, that more people have been continuously occupied in paid labour during the last thirty years than ever before in our history.

If full employment has been the crucial matter in the emancipation of women, it has played almost as considerable a part in the virtual disappearance of poverty from the lives of whole families which has been so marked a feature of twentieth-century English social development. Even full employment, however, has not prevented destitution among the aged. One reason for this is the presence of so many older people in relation to those in full vigour and earning power which has come about with increased expectation of life.

Legislative action in support of full employment has occupied the Parliament of our country a great deal during the twentieth century but it would be a bold man who claimed that full employment has been brought about by deliberate political action, or that unemployment will never return for the same reason. Nevertheless, bursts of welfare legislation have undoubtedly led to the intensification of the rate of social change, in education, and in the social services generally as well as in the maintenance of minimum standards of living. It seems just to say that the series of measures passed in the late 1940's has been so far the most conspicuous and the most effective. Under Churchill's coalition government a series of reports and of individual Acts began which continued almost without interruption into the years of Labour rule from 1945–51. The Butler Act of 1944 was looked upon for nearly twenty years as the charter of educational opportunity for our generation, for it instituted the principle that a secondary education, free of charge, was the right of every English citizen who could pass the proper examination.

We may already have outgrown this very moderate educational ambition, just as the classic of the British Welfare State, the Beveridge Report, published in that year now seems more than a little antiquated. 'Full employment in a free society' as Lord Beveridge's remarkable document was called, was a world best-seller in its time, as much read in the Western hemisphere as in Britain. Its great principle was that everyone in Britain from the Queen to the pauper child should be insured against financial misfortune, against the economic effects of loss of work, health and youth. Most of its provisions were enacted by the Labour Government. The National Health Service, like all the other enactments of those reformist years, codified and made into a culmination, all the earlier legislation of that kind. Then came the new towns, the nationalization of industries, the final democratization of the parliamentary system, and many other things – all of them having their origins in plans which were laid down before even the war was won in 1945.

The actual shift of opinion in favour of radical reform seems to have taken place about 1943. From that point on it might be said that 'ideological politics' became at last the accepted pattern in England. This seems to be the decisive argument in favour of the later 1940's as a time of critical social change and we must pursue it a little further.

The Labour Party began in 1901 as a practical political proposition, and its success was rapid for the first twenty-five years. This was not surprising since what we should quite spontaneously call the natural support of the Labour Party, that is to say the working people, constituted then and has ever since at least two-thirds and probably more like three-quarters of the whole population. With the great extensions of the franchise in 1919 and in 1929 the complete disappearance of the Liberal Party in favour of the Labour Party and a situation where Conservative and Labour governments alternated were to be expected.

But though the Labour Party did head minority governments in 1924 and in 1930–31, which were both in their own way political disasters, this did not occur. Nor did the Liberals take a final quietus. If we take a great gulp at a huge pudding of a historian's problem we might claim that what happened was this. The society of England was unwilling to accept ideological politics where there are two possible governments, one of the economically privileged and the other of the economically dissatisfied. Not until 1943. In that year apparently it did accept the possibility of Labour rule, the prospect of nationalization and of developing socialism. In the last decade it seems that even ideological politics has begun to look a little out of date. The effect of the great change we are describing has turned out to be a bringing together of the two opposed attitudes, not an intensification of them. But when every qualification is made, this shift still looks as if it was decisive, although the Labour government with a large popular majority only lasted for five years, and although there may never be such another again.

So much for an attempt to make the social history of England in high industrial times history of critical social change, in particular a reduction of the social height, if that patient metaphor will stand. If the exact meaning to give that phrase is still in doubt, we may pick out one last little strand from the bewildering tangle of social developments in twentieth-century England which may make it a little clearer. In 1901 personal domestic service was the major occupation of all the employed women of the country, a million and a half servants there were amongst the four million women at work. It was the largest occupational group for men or for women, larger than mining, engineering or agriculture. By the end of the First World War the numbers had fallen so far and so fast that there was an official inquiry. But even during the 1920's and 1930's when everyone, men or women, one might think, would have been glad of a job and when the demand was as great or greater, domestic servants continued to get fewer. By the 1930's they were down to half, though still a considerably sized occupation. By 1951 the female domestic servant had practically disappeared – all 'servants', men and women, in institutions and in houses numbered only about 175,000; in the same year the numbers of women in offices reached exactly the number of domestic servants in 1900. The price of domestic help had risen in the last twenty years more than almost any other item of household expenditure, but servants are still not to be had. English women simply will no longer do the personal work for other English women, whoever they are asked to serve. The social height is too low.

Understanding Ourselves
in Time
Chapter 10

It is very easy to show how important contrast is to understanding. The architect in his drawing and the painter in his picture both casually introduce some human figure, to give the onlooker a proper sense of scale and an opportunity to contrast the scene with himself. When the astronomer sets out to show us what our earth is like, he finds it important to talk about other planets, other sunlike stars, other solar systems. When he tells us that its diameter is 8,000 miles, he also tells us that the diameter of Jupiter is 86,800 miles, and this adds to our understanding. In fact we feel we can understand fully only when we can confidently say 'It might have been otherwise', and give the details – what it would be like if the earth were hundreds of times as big, and five and a half times as far from the sun; how heavy things would be, how long the day, how cold the night.

The astronomer is genuinely interested in Jupiter for Jupiter's sake, quite apart from the comparison which that planet and all the others offer to him with our earth. In the same way the marine biologist is interested in the plankton of the sea and the geneticist in the varying types of drosophila fly, interested in them dispassionately and not simply for what they can tell us about our own environment and about how to devise ways in which we can control it. We call this attitude scientific, and a scientist will often insist that he has no other reason for his interest in what he works on.

We may look a little quizzically at a man who says this to us, but we must freely admit that men do not find out about their world exclusively with themselves in view. Or rather, for the point raises philosophical questions, the sense in which all human knowledge is knowledge for human purposes can be very general indeed and can be virtually ignored in such activities as pure mathematics and general scientific theory at large.

But it is true nevertheless that all human knowledge gets caught up into the overriding interest which we take in ourselves and in our doings. Even the pure mathematician, if asked what he is doing with himself, will talk in this way. The sort of scientific endeavour which everyone is disposed to call really important brings the two elements clearly into view. The theory of continuous creation of matter, for example, very much of the mid-twentieth century, is extraordinarily satisfying to all of us simply in the scientific sense of adding to knowledge. But the other interest it arouses, its possible effects on ourselves and our own experience, is even greater than this. If the theory is true, then the world had no beginning and will have no end, just as the universe has no boundary. Neither the time sequence nor the space continuum in which men live have any sort of boundary or limit. This is knowledge about ourselves and it fascinates us. Even if or when the theory is abandoned as a part of 'scientific' explanation something in the change which it has made in our view of ourselves will remain for ever.

We may now turn with these very general considerations in our mind to the activity of the historian. Since we can only properly understand ourselves and our world, here and now, if we have something to contrast it with, the historian must provide that something. It is true that peoples and nations and cultures vary in the extent to which they wish to understand themselves in time in this way, but to claim that there has ever been a generation anywhere with no sense of history is to go too far. From this point of view therefore all historical knowledge is knowledge with a view to ourselves as we are here and now. But, and here is our second consideration, historical knowledge is also interesting in itself, objectively, 'scientifically' once more. It is in fact almost always of greater intrinsic interest than Jupiter's moons, or the wingspan of fly populations, because it is knowledge about people with whom we can identify ourselves.

Historical knowledge then, and the activity of the historian, need no apology. Without such knowledge we could not understand ourselves in contrast with our ancestors, and possessing it we also satisfy a spontaneous interest in the world around us and in the people who have been within it. Taken together, though with the emphasis on the first source of our interest, history often provides useful knowledge which we could not have in any other way. In order to know how to change and improve the National Health Service in our country, for example, it is necessary to know what it actually consists of and knowing that almost always means getting to know its history. So it is that the politician and administrator finds himself going through the story in chronological order; how before 1911 everyone in England had to pay for medical attention, although in New Zealand and in Germany health insurance was already in force; how in 1911 Mr Lloyd George got the first National Health Insurance act passed and how various acts succeeded it as the century went on, until in 1948 Mr Bevan and the Labour government . . . and so on, and so on. The same sort of chronological explanation is necessary, along with some considerations about geography and economics of course, to understand why Jugoslavia will not fit into the Communist Bloc, or why it is that the Elgin marbles are in the British Museum and no longer on the site of the Parthenon.

Historical knowledge for use might perhaps be regarded as distinct from historical knowledge acquired to understand ourselves in time and to satisfy our curiosity about our past. But these distinctions need be pressed no further for our present purposes, and we must recognize that the functions of the historian which are implied by these elementary considerations scarcely make it likely that his subject will be a progressive one. If this is what the historian has to do, it is not to be expected that what he is doing in England today should be very different from what he has always been doing, here and elsewhere. There cannot be a 'new history' in quite the sense that Einstein founded a 'new physics' nor indeed a new branch of historical study of quite the type of radio astronomy, which is a new and very recent branch of physics as a whole in virtue of its subject matter. Nevertheless the shift of interest towards inquiries of the sort which are reported with such brevity and sketchiness in this book, ought perhaps to be called a new branch of history.

The phrase 'sociological history' has been occasionally used here as its title, and for all its many associations, not all of them fortunate, it is probably the best for the purpose. This is mainly to register a distinction in subject matter, for confessedly historical writing has not previously concerned itself with births, marriages and deaths as such, nor has it dwelt so exclusively on the shape and development of social structure. But the outlook is novel as well as the material, at least in its emphasis. Perhaps the distinctive feature of the attitude is the frank acceptance of the truth that all historical knowledge, from one point of view, and that an important and legitimate one, is knowledge about ourselves, and the insistence on understanding by contrast.

From this flows an irreverent impatience with established conventions of the subject as it has been traditionally studied in our country. The search for contrasts in social arrangements leads one to the demand that English society shall not be seen for itself alone, but alongside French, German, Spanish, Dutch, Italian, Scandinavian society, as one variation on the Western European pattern. But even this cannot be wide enough. Russian and Eastern European societies, Asian, African and Oceanic societies too, are relevant to the study of our own, if contrast is what we are in need of. The object of the English historian of his own country may remain to get to know his own society, but now as one amongst others.

The search for contrast does not end even here. It is not simply geographical. We all know (and an exasperatingly imprecise thing it is to know) that in England and in Western Europe we live in an 'advanced' industrial society, to be further described as a 'capitalist' as opposed to a 'socialist' industrial society. There are in the contemporary world societies which are not industrial at all in the sense given to the word here. These are the primitive societies, as we somewhat patronizingly call them, of Africa, Asia, Australia, South America and Oceania. But what is 'industrialization', what are 'socialist' and 'capitalist' economies, what indeed is 'society' and what is objectively known and knowable about the constitution of societies and the ways in which they cohere, change, evolve, solve their conflicts and fight them out?

These are questions which have had to concern us in this essay, but they cannot be called exclusively or even predominantly historical questions at all, even if the historian has his responsibilities in helping to answer them. They are to some extent economists' questions, and so fall within the province of the most exact and advanced of the social sciences. For this we should be grateful. But too great a reliance on exclusively economic analysis has led in the past to all the sterilities of the economic interpretation of history. The complete description of questions of this sort is sociological as well as economic, and one of the important discoveries of the contemporary historian has been that he has carried on as if this were not the case.

History, we now begin to recognize with some dismay, has been written as if questions about social structure and types of society, questions about causation too, were fairly straight-forward and answerable by common sense and a little econo-mics, the more the better, but always fairly elementary. Historians have in fact tended up till now to look upon that area of inquiry which we have called sociological as if they knew it all already. This unfortunate tendency might be called 'naïf sociologism'.

We must not, after all, exaggerate the importance of the differences between the new historical criticism and the old; no doubt the distinction between naïf and sophisticated socio-logism, if that is what should now replace it, will look very uncertain to those who come after us. But the somewhat sudden recognition that historians have habitually attempted to solve complicated problems of social structure and social causation by guessing a little, with the help of a few insignificant statis-tics, has undoubtedly had a disconcerting effect. We have glanced back over our history books and found them full of the crudest sociological generalization, of highly unconvincing speculation on the nature of social development. This has led to scepticism, and it was inevitable that the new historical criticism should have begun by being negative. But we have chosen not to confine this essay merely to critical analysis, and to make an attempt at something more positive by the use of the method of overall contrast.

Some of the difficulties of deciding to compare rather than to recount, as historians ordinarily do, must have been evident throughout this essay, especially in the last chapter. So deeply embedded in the whole tradition of writing history is the feeling for development, process, evolution, for the necessity of knowing everything that happened in between, that the whole enterprise may seem wrong-headed, especially to those whose interests lie in the interval missed out here, the eigh-teenth and nineteenth centuries that is to say. To many it may seem unhistorical in the final sense, since it abandons the method of explanation by telling the story. Even the sym-pathetic critic may feel that it could only succeed at the very superficial and introductory level; directly there is time and available information to go at all deeply beneath the surface any impression that there could be two constants capable of entering into an intelligible contrast must soon disappear.

Perhaps this objection should be discussed a little further, for it is justified to a large extent. England in 1700 cannot be at all adequately described as wholly pre-industrial nor England in 1901 as wholly industrialized. A claim of this kind would have to assume in the first place that the expressions themselves have agreed and constant meanings, which they do not. Industrialization has been defined in almost as many ways as there have been historians and economists who have studied that elusive process. It assumes in the second place that the entity England was in fact without industry at the first chosen point and wholly industrialized at the second. There are many historians who could maintain that both these claims are quite without foundation, that the eighteenth century saw not the only but simply a particularly conspicuous 'industrial revolution', one of a series which goes far back beyond 1600 and still continues. Nothing can have been more obvious from the brief discussion of English society in recent times than that it has been in intensifying flux rather than in constant 'post-industrial' condition, and that many of the points of contrast with the world we have lost have made their appearance only very recently indeed.

It may be simple-minded, or even rather worse than that, to respond by appealing again to the reader's ordinary familiarity with his own surroundings, especially in respect of the scale of life. Still it was not found necessary to insist that the working man since 1901 has ceased to do his daily work in the circle of his family and has become almost entirely subject to the discipline of the factory and the office, to the necessity of going there and back to work every day, to all the experience known as mass living. Surely we know all this in a much more straightforward way than the historian seems to think that he knows how society works at any time he chooses to study it. Of course if this leads people to suppose that because we all know that economic organization is no longer almost entirely a familial matter, that therefore the family no longer plays any part in economic life, then it does become deceptive. Yet the self-evident importance of the overall comparison does justify its being drawn in heavy outline, and only a direct confrontation between our society before and after whatever it was that went on between 1700 and 1900 gives it sufficient

emphasis. It does enable us to understand ourselves by saying
with conviction: 'It might have been otherwise.'

The same point could be made for the other two heads which
were chosen for twentieth-century England, though here the
issues are more complex. When talking of the middle class in
the twentieth century it was not necessary to compare directly
the general similarities and differences between the ruling segment of the older world and the social and political establishment of the newer world, though some remarks had to be made
about the pattern of social mobility. But surely it does not
have to be elaborately reasoned that an *élite* minority cannot
nowadays live the whole political, intellectual and social life of
a whole country. We all know this already, in a way. We know
that representative chambers, parties, elections in our system,
the whole machinery of totalitarian politics elsewhere, have
had to come into being because élitist politics cannot work in
our world in the easy, spontaneous way described earlier on.
When it comes to authority in contemporary politics and to the
possibility of revolution, we may perhaps hesitate somewhat.
But we recognize easily enough the profound difference in
these crucial respects which has come with two very obvious
and evident changes. These are the departure of a common
religious belief shared by everyone, and the arrival of universal
literacy and access to the public, political world. These must
have much to do with the fact that revolutionism is now a
credible political belief and actual social revolution a possible
tactic. We all know also that the disappearance of servants
means more than an inconvenience to the rich.

Historical contrast if too blankly presented may obliterate
the subtler forms of change and survival. This was perhaps
apparent in what was said about the country house in the
politics of the old world and of the new, a topic which along
with the many others urgently requires a defter and more
informed analysis. Authoritarianism arising directly out of the
patriarchal family in the manor house may have departed from
the scene. But allegiance and submission to the father figure
continue to play their parts in the psychology of politics, even
if actual fathers now push prams and have thrown the rod
away. The Pope, as was said elsewhere in trying to make old Sir
Robert Filmer possible to believe in, is still Papa, and Stalin
died Little Father to the Russian people.

Contrast over time, furthermore, might conceivably be

allowed to divert attention from contrast over space, or rather cross-cultural comparison as the anthropologist might put it; understanding ourselves in time is after all understanding ourselves in one dimension only. It might be thought that it would be so much more illuminating to draw the comparison with the Trobriand Islanders, or the Nuer, or the Ainu of the Northern Island of Japan, vanishing survivals of societies wholly pre-industrial in everybody's sense and offering a much profounder depth of possible distinction. Only a glance or two has been made in this direction and the thorny problem of how to combine the different types of comparison, cultural and chronological, has been left on one side. Obviously there is much more to be said, and the beginnings of work on the feudal era in Europe as compared with contemporary African society may yet yield a great deal more than mere ancestor examination.

But it is an impressive fact that Louis Henry, when he made the first move towards a really scientific historical demography, the earliest element to appear in a properly sociological historical method, deliberately rejected contemporary underdeveloped societies in favour of the societies of our predecessors in Western Europe. He wanted to get to know what 'natural fertility' was and he decided that he would be more likely to find out from the village of Crulai in Normandy over the seventeenth and eighteenth centuries than from any twentieth-century primitive society, however benevolently administered and however carefully counted and registered. His reasons were entirely statistical nevertheless; no extra-European unindustrialized society yet keeps its *état civil*, as the French say, its births, marriages, deaths and so on, with the accuracy of the parish priests and parish clerks even of Stuart England. This being so, quantitative comparison seems unlikely ever to be as efficient for cross-cultural as it already is for chronological contrast.

Figures are not everything, even in our present mood of preferring any set of facts which can be counted over all those which arise from impressions, literary, legal and otherwise. The justification of the method chosen for understanding ourselves in time may seem to need sharper illustration. We may take it from the size, structure and function of the family.

The evidence about the household as it was in England before the industrial process began has been referred to on various occasions throughout this essay, though not presented in a systematic way.* It seems to make impossible any belief that the independent, nuclear family of man, wife and children alone in the world is an exclusive characteristic of industrialized society. When all allowance has been made for the very different assumptions about the household which then obtained, and the very different kinship relationships too, it remains the case that there slept together under each roof in 1600 only the nuclear family, with the addition of servants when necessary. Therefore in that vital respect our ancestors were not different from ourselves. They were the same.

Much so-called sociological history has been written as if the contrary were true, not perhaps by historians, too preoccupied with traditional activities, but by the sociologists themselves. Much of the alienation discussion of our time seems to suppose that the horror of industrialization was in part the result of separating the nuclear family from the kin group.

But there is more to it than a wrong account of how things have changed. Our whole view of ourselves is altered if we cease to believe that we have lost some more humane, much more *natural* pattern of relationships than industrial society can offer. When we inquire, for example, what we are trying to do for the lonely old people who are becoming so lamentably common as the twentieth-century decades go by, we find ourselves assuming that they must be restored to the family, where they belong. Perhaps none of those who write so urgently about these problems have a very clear notion of the situation which they are trying to restore. But few of them can have realized how inappropriate it is to think of restoration at all, in the sense of returning to the historical past. We have already talked of the identical error in relation to broken homes and the criminal tendency of our young people and shown that the problem of our ancestors in this regard may well have been worse, not better, than our own.

In fact, in tending to look backwards in this way, in diagnosing the difficulties as the outcome of something which has indeed been lost to our society, those concerned with social welfare are suffering from a false understanding of ourselves in time. Not completely false, of course; if that were so it would make nonsense of our general title. We have seen that in the traditional world the family did fulfil many functions

* *The author has in preparation a paper on this topic to be published in an early monograph of the Cambridge Group.*

which are left to very different institutions in our day, or which are not fulfilled at all.

But was it more 'natural' that this should have been so? Was *The World we have lost* a more appropriate one for human beings to dwell in? These are very vague and general questions, unlikely to be worth trying to answer in this book. But the point of importance to our argument is to have got into a position where such questions must arise. To recognize their urgency is also to begin to take a different view of our own place in time, and more than this. It may, perhaps ought, to change our view of what we should be trying to do. We can only begin to get into this position if we admit that historical knowledge is knowledge to do with ourselves, now.

Answering these questions does also yield objective knowledge about the past. The discovery that the society of pre-industrial England maintained the principle that each marriage meant a new household, and that the whole social structure can be ranged round that one critical feature, could justifiably be claimed as an addition to 'scientific' knowledge, much of it very remote indeed from simply knowledge with a view to ourselves now. It may make a great deal of difference to the work of the anthropologist, the sociologist, and the social sciences generally as well as to social history. The novelty of this discovery and the conviction that it belongs to a type of historical criticism previously unknown is suggested by the fact that the evidence on which it was based was not new, but always available in very obvious places.

This somewhat arrogant claim can perhaps be made most convincingly in respect of the liability of the peasants to starve, not exactly a part of the principle of the one-marriage house-hold but closely connected with it. Hundreds of parish registers have been published in England, more than in any other country. This has meant that millions and millions of entries from obscurely written, badly preserved documents have been painfully transferred into print at considerable expense for the use of thousands of persons bent on tracing their ancestry. Apart from the biographers, no other users have ordinarily been found for them, and as we have seen it has occurred to no historian up to now to try to see if the registers could tell us whether our ancestors did in fact some-times die of starvation. Only in the last year or two have they realized that they could be used for the purpose of family reconstitution, and then only as a consequence of the pioneering work done in France.

A romantic might say that this looks like a breach of faith with the Cowlmans and the Lancasters who, it will be remembered, were two of the tiny group of families so far known to have starved in England, in the year 1623 at Greystoke. Perhaps this infidelity is merely a part of the inevitable tendency to look on past individuals as important and worth investigating only if they show forth some political, economic, social or intellectual trend which the historian is concerning himself with. Still the indifference to questions such as these looks peculiarly inhumane, a failing which comes from too much concern with abstractions. But it is not for any generation of historians to condemn its predecessors too easily, for who can tell what blindness our successors will detect in us? The additions to the historical record which the close study of the contents of the humble parish registers will bring, may conceivably turn out to have their biological importance.

In order to undertake genetic analysis, it is necessary·to be able to study a community of specimens over a number of generations, the more the better. The great disadvantage of human beings for genetic study is that the generation is so long. With drosophila it is possible to observe the passage of ten generations in a matter of days. With humans ten generations would take some three hundred years to observe. Now three hundred years happens to be within the period during which the registration of births, marriages and deaths can be studied from this evidence, and in England we can go back two or three generations further.

It is difficult as yet to see how this opportunity might be used. If we refer to the example of the age at sexual maturity which has been discussed in the text, we can see how vague and confusing the evidence is likely to be, even on a point which in principle might be examined from the bare facts appearing in the parish registers and on the forms used for the reconstitution of families. No one would yet venture to suppose that the problem of distinguishing a possible genetic element in the fall of the age at menarche from the effect of improved diet and living conditions can be solved. Nevertheless the evidence exists to make some initial study of recent human biological history. It is necessary for biology even more than for sociology to understand its subject matter in time, over the generations.

The historian cannot hope to make his contribution to studies of this sort unless he is rather differently equipped than he has previously been. He must obviously be something of a statistician; at least he must have that statistical expectation and caution which so clearly distinguishes the inquirer after truth from the creator of impressions. He must have some economics, some sociology, even conceivably some genetics, as well as anthropology. But it would be wrong to think of the historian of the newer sort solemnly sitting down to acquire this extra-historical knowledge before he even begins to examine the evidence or to write about it. What must come into being is a working community where the historian is in the confidence of the economists, the statisticians and the others. Nevertheless the responsibility for enabling us all to understand ourselves in time must still rest where it has always rested, on the historian as an individual.

It is sometimes said that Clio the Muse is dead and that history is no longer written as literature. Perhaps the difficult situation we have been trying to explain is to some extent responsible. Once the historian brings himself to recognize anew that what he knows he knows with a view to himself as well as with a view to the past, this situation may change again. Herodotus had no doubt that what he wrote was for his contemporaries, relevant above all to his own generation. Neither had Lord Clarendon, nor Lord Macaulay. Macaulay indeed, and this is why he is now criticized, was perfectly aware that England under Victoria was the culmination of the story he was telling, and that the past had to be appreciated where it anticipated that splendid era, recounted as leading up to and evolving into it. Though we must be suspicious of the evolutionary, culminatory element in this attitude we must envy him the frankness with which he came out with the story as it looked to him. He might find it difficult to understand why we, his successors, are so much less attracted to the task of making literature out of how the past looks to us.

Certainly the imaginative reconstruction of a former society can only foster an interest in its people as people. The shortcomings we have mentioned have been called failures in sympathy as well as of method, and if the future is to see the historian in partnership with the other social scientists, it is important that he should never lose sight of his humanity. Naïf sociologism may indeed have come into existence because of an unwilling and largely unaware subservience of the historical imagination to the dogmatic social principles of an earlier generation. These principles dealt exclusively with those rise-of-a-class interpretations which have been criticized here, together with their wearisome insistence on cataclysm, crisis and revolution.

There has been a tendency in fact for English historians to give currency to certain features of Marxian historical sociology, which they have made no conspicuous effort to understand, perhaps because its political associations have been so inimical to them. Advantage was not taken in creating from it historical hypotheses at a time when it really was a novel and developing system. At the present time this half-recognized attachment stands in the way of a confessedly sociological historical criticism of the type we have tried to recommend. In such a new historical criticism the Marxian element in sociological thought because of its explanatory power will play a formidable part.

Perhaps too much fuss has been made here of what in the end will turn out to be just another swirl of opinion which is not simply historical. It could easily be shown that the interest historians are beginning to take in the contrast between English and European society before and after industrialization is also an interest recently acquired by politicians and economists, though their eyes are turned on 'underdeveloped countries' in the present world for the most part. Nevertheless I have no doubt myself that the sort of questions which arise out of an attempt to explore our own, contemporary, late twentieth-century relationship with what we have called the world we have lost could have arisen from no previously established form of historical inquiry. History, I believe, is about to claim a new and more important place in the sum of total human knowledge.

Notes to the Text

(All books published in London unless otherwise stated)

CHAPTER 1

1   See Sylvia Thrupp, *History of the Bakers' Company of London*, Croydon, 1933, p. 17, etc.

2   'No baker should sell bread in his own house or shop, but only in the open market, and only on Wednesday or Saturday.' This was an immemorial rule of the London bakers and was in full operation in Stuart times (see Thrupp, p.35), but it would be unjustifiable to assume that it was the practice in all trades and in all towns. Undoubtedly too some London tradesmen lived in houses apart from their shops. See *The Inhabitants of London in 1638*, edited by T. C. Dale for the Society of Genealogists, 1931.

3   For the structure of the family and the functions and duties of its members, see the considerable body of religious advice given by the clergy, generally the Puritan clergy, to their people and printed either as sermons or in the form of treatises on the family: for example, William Gouge, *Of Domesticall Duties*, 1622; William Perkins, *Christian Oeconomie*, 1609 (*Workes*, vol. 3, Cambridge, 1618); William Fleetwood, Bishop of Ely, *The Relative Duties of Parents and Children, Husbands and Wives, Masters and Servants* (1705) in his *Compleat Collection of Sermons*, 1737. Modern works are scanty, but two titles may be recorded here: C. L. Powell, *English Domestic Relations, 1487–1653*, New York, 1917, and R. B. Schlatter, *The Social Ideas of Religious Leaders, 1660–1688*, 1940.

4   Indenture between William Selman, Husbandman, his son Richard and Thomas Stokes, broadweaver, of Wiltshire, signed in 1705. We have found that the actual numbers of apprentices, formally so called, seems to have been very much exaggerated by historians, and by contemporaries too.

5   Paper for the Board of Trade, 1697, printed in H. R. Fox Bourne, *Life of John Locke*, 1876, vol. ii, p. 377 on.

---

6   See below, p. 93 for expectation of life.

---

7   Sir Thomas More's *Utopia* was published in 1516; Sir Wm. Petty's various works on *Political Arithmetick* appeared at different dates in the 1680's. Good examples of the intense curiosity of Stuart Englishmen about the social system and sexual arrangements of 'savages' in America, Africa and Asia are the reading habits and library lists of John Locke and also of Isaac Newton: see John Harrison and Peter Laslett, *The Library of John Locke*, Oxford, 1965.

---

8   Grimm's *Fairy Tales* were first issued in German in 1812–14, but were translated into English at once, to swell the repertory of such literature already becoming popular. It may be significant in view of the origin of Marxist social protest in the same country at the same time that traditional industrial life was romanticized on the widest scale in Germany.

---

9   For the movement of persons between settlement and settlement, see below Chapter VI, and the article there referred to: Laslett and Harrison, Clayworth and Cogenhoe, in *Historical Essays, presented to David Ogg*, edited by H. E. Bell and R. L. Ollard, 1963 (pp. 157–84).
The major source for Clayworth is *The Rector's Book, Clayworth, Notts*. Ed. Gill and Guilford, Nottingham, 1910.

---

10   See the remarkable listing of the inhabitants of this community in the *Newdigate Papers* at the Warwick Record Office, C.R. 136, vol. 12, p. 64 and on. It is to be noted that in this paragraph and elsewhere in this essay the words 'household' and 'family' are used interchangeably, as the men of the day used them. The technical distinctions made between them for sociological purposes will be discussed in reference to pre-industrial social structure in the larger work already referred to.

11   See John Aubrey, *Natural History of Wiltshire*, 1685, ed.
J. Britton, Oxford, 1847.

12   See *Selections from the Household Books of the Lord
William Howard of Naworth Castle*, Surtees Society, 1878.

13   On the county musters see E. E. Rich, in the *Economic
History Review*, Second Series, II, 3, 1950, and for a very
revealing record of one of them, John Smith of Nibley, *Men
and Armour for Gloucestershire, 1608*, published 1902.

14   Cromwell commanded 26,000 or 27,000 men at Marston
Moor, and this must have been one of the largest
organized crowds ever to have assembled before Napoleonic
times in England: the Queens transported about 15,000
troops across the Atlantic on each voyage in the 1940's.
The greatest strength of the armed forces was 70,000 for a
brief period under the Commonwealth, see C. H. Firth,
Cromwell's Army, 1902, p. 35.

15   There is a list of schools in W. A. L. Vincent, *The State
and School Education, 1640–1660, in England and Wales*,
1950; for the universities in Stuart times, see M. H. Curtis,
Oxford and Cambridge in Transition, 1558–1642, Oxford,
1959.

16   For the builders see D. Knoop and G. P. Jones, *The
Medieval Mason*, Manchester, 1933, and various articles
on this theme. For large-scale industry and its organization,
various articles by J. U. Nef, especially that in the
Economic History Review, 1934. For the miners, G. R. Lewis,
The Stannaries, 1908, J. W. Gough, *The Mines of Mendip*,
Oxford, 1930, and J. U. Nef, *The Rise of the British Coal
Industry*, 2 vols., 1932.

17   The numbers, size and organization of almshouses
instituted between 1480 and 1660 are amongst the subjects
dealt with for London and select counties by W. K. Jordan in
his three important volumes on philanthropy during that
period – *Philanthropy in England*, 1959; *The Charities of
London*, 1960; *The Charities of Rural England*, 1961. Few
seem to have contained more than a dozen or twenty

inmates, but in 1660 something like 1,400 people may have been living in such institutions in London.

---

18   At Ealing, in Middlesex in 1599 (see note 73 below), then a country village of course, no less than 60 per cent of all persons between the ages of fifteen and nineteen were in service. Servants numbered 109 in a population of 427, and were present in over a third of all households: two-fifths of these were 'servants in husbandry'. These detailed facts about the social structure have been confirmed for dozens of Stuart communities, perhaps to the fullest extent for Clayworth in Nottinghamshire: see the article by Laslett and Harrison (Note 9).

---

19   For the cloth-makers of Beauvais, see the classic work of sociological/historical description, Pierre Goubert, *Beauvais et les Beauvaisis*, Paris, 1960, Part I, Ch. viii, and for the actual size of undertakings see p. 284. The impression that in English towns employees were already walking in from the country to do a day's work is a general one gained from the community listings already referred to.

---

20   Richard Steele, *The Husbandman's Calling*, 2nd ed., 1672, pp. 76 and 86.

---

21   Karl Marx and Frederick Engels, Manifesto of the Communist Party, 1848, in *Selected Works*, Moscow, 1951, vol. 1, p. 35.

---

22   The tendency of recent economic historians, especially those with a Marxist bent, has been to distinguish *industrial* capitalism, the capitalism associated with large-scale enterprise which first appeared early in the nineteenth century, from capitalism generally. This goes some way towards the position taken up in the text, but continues to give exclusive emphasis to the ownership and disposition of the resources of production at the expense of the relationships, human and emotional relationships, between those engaged in work.

---

23   Richard Steele (see Note 20), p. 104.

CHAPTER 2

24   Some parsons and parish clerks, naturally, were more
generous, and others less generous, in distributing titles to
their entries and it would be foolish to expect any rigorous
consistency. We have used the burial entries as the most
revealing for the purpose, and results of such analysis (along
with those for marriages, see below) will be published in
due course. Here are three random examples: Manchester,
1653–5, 3·9 per cent of 2,380 death entries contained some
title like 'gentleman' or higher and the addition of those
marked *Mr* or *Mrs* brought the total up to 11·3 per cent. Of
those buried at Ludlow in Shropshire between 1632 and 1641
5·2 per cent bore some such title, and between 1599 and
1633 the proportion was 6·6 per cent at Wem in the same
county.

25   The Statute of Artificers, (5 Eliz. c 4), para. IV, quoted
from R. H. Tawney and E. Power, *Tudor Economic
Documents*, 1924 (1951) vol. I, p. 342, modernized.

26   Serjeant Thorpe, Judge of Assize for the Northern
Circuit, his Charge to the Grand Jury at York Assizes, March
20th, 1648, printed in *Harleian Miscellany*, vol. II, 1744,
p. 12.

27   King's table was printed by Charles Davenant in his
*Essay upon the Probable Methods of Making a People Gainers
in the Ballance of Trade*, in the year 1699. This version is reproduced here on pages 32–3. It differs in detail from that
which forms part of a manuscript treatise entitled *Natural
and Politicall Observations and Conclusions Upon the State and
Conditions of England*, by Gregory King, Esqr, Lancaster
Herald at Armes, A.D. 1696, along with other tables of
importance for the study of pre-industrial society.
In this work, which was never published in King's lifetime,
no explanation is advanced as to why the general distinction
was made, and very little evidence to justify any of the
statistical work is offered. We have found, however, that
King's figures are surprisingly accurate wherever we have
been able to provide independent checks on them. King's

manuscript treatise was printed from an original in the British Museum (Harleian MSS 1898: there are other manuscripts) in 1802 by George Chalmers as an appendix to an edition of his *Estimate of the Comparative Strength of Great Britain,* and again from the same source in Baltimore, U.S.A. in 1936 by George E. Barnett under King's title.

28   See the very important article of D. C. Coleman, 'Labour in the English economy of the 17th century', in the *Economic History Review,* new series, VIII, 3, 1956.

29   Sir Thomas Smith, The Commonwealth of England (1560's), published 1583, edition of 1635, p. 66.

30   William Harrison, Description of Britain, printed in Raphael Holinshed, *Chronicles of England,* 1st Ed. 1577.

31   Act of 12 Car. II, Cap. IX.

32   See for example the books of Christopher Hill, whose position in his recent and very stimulating general history of England in Stuart times, *The Century of Revolution,* Edinburgh, 1961, is rather different from that which he took up in 1949, when he made the following statement about events in England from 1640 to 1660: 'Very briefly summarized, our subject here is the story of how one social class was driven from power by another.' (*The Good Old Cause,* edited by C. Hill and E. Dell, 1949, p. 19.) Professor Brough Macpherson is responsible for the general reformulation of the position about capitalism (or the 'market society') and seventeenth-century English society. See his important book *The Political Theory of Possessive Individualism, Hobbes to Locke,* Oxford, 1962.

33   The position taken up here about class in relation to status is roughly that adopted by W. G. Runciman, *Social Science and Political Theory,* Cambridge, 1963, Chapter VII; compare R. Bendix and S. M. Lipset in their reader on this complex and difficult subject (*Class, Status and Power,* Glencoe, Ill., 1963), where the origins of this approach in the works of Max Weber are clearly set out. No more general claim is made for the definitions of class and status in the text than

that they seem to correspond to the uses made of the
concepts in the loose discussions of historians, particularly
Marxian and post-Marxian historians. For them only
action groups are by definition of importance because only
action groups can enter into historical events, such as
rebellion, revolution, or governmental action. Obviously if the
common work-situation of individuals be taken as the
critical characteristic of class, as for example by David
Lockwood (see *The Blackcoated Worker*, 1958), or if 'the
way a man is treated by his fellows' is taken to be its
essence, as it is by T. H. Marshall (*Citizenship and Social
Class*, Cambridge, 1950), it would be possible to identify many
social classes in Stuart England. But none of them, it is
claimed, was likely ever to come into relation with another, or
others, of them, in such a way that collective group
conflict, such as the Civil War of 1642–8, could possibly
have been created.

---

34 About 200 seems to be the number of such families
referable to England and Wales in such contexts as the
successive editions of Edward Chamberlayne's *Angliae
Notitia*, 1669, 1670, 1671, 1673 . . . 19th edition 1700.

---

35 The source of this remark is the statistical work of
Mr T. Hollingsworth of the University of Glasgow who has
made an analysis of the demography of the whole English
peerage since the fifteenth century, the full results of which
will be published in 1965. By 'commoner' here is meant
persons not born into a titled family; most noblemen and
noblewomen married plain gentlefolk if they did not marry
amongst themselves, but some married apparently below the
gentry line.

---

36 Sir Anthony Wagner, the present Garter King of Arms,
suggested these criticisms of the view that the emphasis on
the divide below the gentry was the distinguishing feature of
the traditional English social system. The assumption
that modern classes are descended in some way from the
Estates of the Realm is common amongst sociologists – see for
example the work by Bendix and Lipset quoted in note 33.

---

37 6 and 7 William and Mary, c 6; the demographic

importance of this act is discussed by David Glass in several articles. It is generally called the Marriage Duties Act and remained in force till 1705.

---

38   See note 31. In the twelve first companies (Goldsmiths, Drapers, etc.) the assessment went like this: Master £10 (equivalent to that for an Esquire), Liveryman £5 (equivalent to that for a gentleman; the liverymen were ex-masters or potential masters and of the same social standing), yeoman £3 (above a clergyman £2, but below a gentleman).

---

39   See W. Y. Tindall, *John Bunyan, Mechanick Preacher*, New York, 1934.

---

40   The families which Gregory King names as making up that half of the population which was 'decreasing the wealth of the kingdom' seems a rather miscellaneous assemblage: seamen, 'labouring people and outservants', cottagers and paupers, common soldiers and vagrants (see page 32). Evidently King was not anxious to be specific about the poor, and the major interest in these descriptions is what they did not include. Obviously King did not think that 'shopkeepers and tradesmen', 'artizans and handicrafts' were in permanent poverty since he places them above the 'decreasing' line, but this does not mean that the carpenters, bricklayers, masons, thatchers, weavers, coopers and so on were always out of poverty. It seems much more likely that they were in poverty at certain times of their lives, or in bad seasons, or for some weeks even in good seasons, but not perpetually dependent in the way that labourers, cottagers, paupers and the common soldiery were. This was the pattern of the industrial proletariat in the late nineteenth century and the early twentieth century when they were studied by Rowntree and Booth, see below Chapter 9.

The statement in the text is true if King's estimates are reliable. In an economy of the type he was describing any person in receipt of a transfer income from the wealthier people must surely be in need of such an income in order to subsist, and this is the sense in which it seems best to understand King's concept of 'increasing or decreasing' the national wealth. It is very difficult to believe that such

transfers were taking place in order to equalize wealth, or to
add to the incomes of those who already had enough to
keep them out of poverty. No doubt such transfers did
go on in favour of the craftsmen who were sometimes liable
to poverty but on balance they appear to have been
self-sufficient, which was perhaps why King did not think of
them as permanently among the decreasers.

41   William Harrison, Description of Britain, in Holinshed,
Chronicles of England, quoted in note 30.

42   William Lambarde, *Perambulation of Kent*, 1570,
published 1576, reprinted at Chatham, 1826, p. 6, modernized.

43   Thomas Westcote, *A View of Devonshire in 1630*, edited
by G. Oliver and P. Jones, Exeter, 1845.

44   Thomas Wilson, *The State of England, 1600*, edited by
F. J. Fisher, *Camden Miscellany*, 1936, p. 20.

45   See for example Sir John Doddridge, *Honors Pedigree*,
1652. The argument seems to have gone on since Elizabethan
times, and Sir Thomas Smith took the minority view that
apprenticeship did derogate from gentry.

46   See *The Visitation of London, 1633, 1634 and 1635*,
Harleian Society, 2 vols., 1880–83. On merchants who had
country houses at an earlier time, see Sylvia Thrupp,
The Merchant Class of Medieval London (1948) Ann Arbor,
Mich., 1962, and on city/country dynasties, Sir Anthony
Wagner, *English Genealogy*, Oxford, 1960, p. 141, etc.

47   Westcote (see note 43), p. 52.

48   *Some Considerations of the Consequences of Lowering of
Interest*, 1692, *Works*, 1801, vol. 5, p. 71.

CHAPTER 3

49   See A. M. Carr-Saunders, D. Caradog Jones and C. A.
Moser, *A Survey of Social Conditions in England and
Wales as illustrated by Statistics*, Oxford, 1958 (using the 1951
census), pp. 50–55.

50   The figure for London adopted here is once more King's
as given for 1688, and he is also the source for the
estimates of those living in the towns and in the villages. The
accuracy of his totals is exhaustively discussed by D. Glass
in 'Gregory King and the Population of England and Wales
at the end of the 17th Century', *Eugenics Review*, 1946,
and in 'Gregory King's Estimate of the Population of
England and Wales, 1695', *Population Studies*, 1950.

51   The Wingham area documents are in the Kent County
Record Office. The difficulty with them, as with all problems
of size of settlement, is the extent to which each named
place in fact represented an independent settlement, and not
just an arbitrary area which existed for some traditional
or administrative reason. Certainly the sixteen communities
with less than 100 people, nearly a half of the sample, look
as if they were large gentlemanly seats rather than
communities, though many of them no doubt were the remains
of once flourishing villages decayed by enclosure and
emparkment. The figures of 450 and 250 were obtained
by dividing the 4,100,000 which King gives as the population
of the villages and hamlets, first by 9,000 (the probable
number of parishes in the country outside the towns) and
then by 15,000 so as to allow for the possibility that up to
a half of all parishes in fact contained more than one
settlement (see below). We have compared these very
preliminary results with those obtained from 522 named
places selected at random from the census returns of 1801,
rural counties only. The mean size was in 1801, 422, the median
as high as 615, but only 35 per cent of persons lived in
settlements of less than 400, and 32·5 per cent in settlements
of more than 1,000. There is at the moment no way of
knowing whether the changes of the eighteenth century
left the rural settlements more or less as they were in the
seventeenth century, but it is not impossible.

52   See Glass in *Population Studies*, 1950, p. 341. The source
excerpted there is a manuscript notebook of King's called
by Glass the Kashnor Manuscript, and now in the National
Library of Australia. The table analysing the towns and
cities is on p. 2 of the manuscript and is reproduced by Glass
along with a paragraph of King's acknowledging the help
and collaboration of John Adams. Adams, so King declares,
worked at the Hearth Tax returns and Spelman's *Villare
Anglicum* to prepare his own *Index Villaris* – for both
these works see below. The table drawn up by King is in the
form of totals of *houses*, not individuals, for each town, and
in the text the figures have been converted into populations
by the use of the multiple 4.45 persons to a house, the
figure which Glass shows was the one used by King himself.

53   See Goubert's work on Beauvais and the Beauvaisis,
cited in note 19. On p. 255 he prints a list of the number of
feux in the thirty-five towns coming after the three greatest
from lists dating from 1713 and 1726. They have been
converted into the approximations given in the text by
multiplying by five. Rough as this work is, nothing at all
comparable is yet possible for England. Professor Goubert
tells me that in France the urbanized population was
nevertheless not so much greater in proportion than it was in
England.

54   See J. Carrière, *La Population d'Aix-en-Provence à la
fin du XVIIe Siècle, étude de démographie historique d'après le
registre de capitation de 1695*. Faculté des Lettres,
Aix-en-Provence, *Travaux et Mémoires*, *XI*, 1958,
mimeographed, from *La Pensée Universitaire*, 12 bis Rue
Nazareth, Aix-en-Provence. No English record of anything
like this extent has survived for so early a period and all
the facts in this study are of great social structural interest.

55   The Lichfield listing is amongst King's papers in the
Harleian Collection in the British Museum, no. 7022, folios
1–42; for comment see Glass in his article of 1946. This
listing still counts as the longest and most reliable for any
English community in Stuart times.

56   The figures for Norfolk parishes and for parishes in the
other counties referred to, come from Sir Henry Spelman,
*Villare Anglicum, or a View of all the Cities, Towns and
Villages in England* (1656), 2nd edition 1678. For Norfolk see
H. M. Cautley, *Norfolk Churches*, Ipswich 1949.

---

57   Social structural and demographic work has been done
on all these villages, of an elementary character except for
Colyton, where reconstitution of families on the French
model is in progress from the registers. The published
registers are also the evidence used for Widecombe (The
Devon and Cornwall Record Society, Exeter, 1938) and
Greystoke (transcribed and edited by A. M. Maclean and
published at Kendal in 1911), but more extensive sources have
been used for Cogenhoe, see article by Laslett and
Harrison cited in note 9.

---

58   For the influence of ethnic origin on the social system in
various areas of England see the work of George Homans,
English villages of the 13th century, Harvard, 1942, and *The
Frisians in East Anglia*, Economic History Review, 1957.

---

59   The most recent discussion of enclosure in the
voluminous literature on that subject is in G. E. Mingay,
English Landed Society in the 18th century, 1963, see pp.
179–88 and references. Recent writers seem unwilling to
comment on the actual amount enclosed by 1700, if only
because the precise area in, or potentially in, cultivation is so
problematic, but one-seventh is the traditional proportion
for about that date.

---

60   The facts about English settlements in Massachusetts
cited here all come from a study by S. C. Powell of the
townships of Watertown and Sudbury, Mass., and the
connections of those who established them with Sudbury,
Suffolk, and Weyhill, Hants, Shaftesbury, Dorset, etc.
Much of this important material with an interesting and
suggestive analysis was published as *Puritan Village, the
Formation of a New England Town*, Wesleyan University
Press, Middletown, Conn., 1963. The suggestion that the
model for the New England township is to be found in the

co-operative society of peasants in an open-field village was
made as early as 1910 by William Cunningham; see
Common Rights at Cottenham and Stretham, Camden
Miscellany XII and references.

61   See the article on the Gentry of Kent by Peter Laslett in
the *Cambridge Historical Journal*, 1948, and references.
    One of the great advantages of England as the point of
departure of the study of European pre-industrial structure is
the fact that it can be studied not only *in situ*, but also as
it became when removed, it would seem almost for
experimental purposes, 3,000 miles west across the sea into
the American wilderness.

62   See W. G. Hoskins, Galby and Frisby, *Essays in
Leicestershire History*, Liverpool University Press, 1950. Dr
Hoskins also presents the social history of the much
bigger village of Wigston Magna nearby (*The Midland
Peasant*, 1957) until late in the seventeenth century as one
dominated by substantial peasants and not by gentry.

63   For John Adams, see Dictionary of National Biography
and for his *Index Villaris* see Glass's article of 1950,
referred to in note 50. It was published in a revised edition in
1690 and again in 1700. In his original preface Adams said
that 'I have used all possible Care, Industry and Pains in
comparing the Villare Anglicum of Sir Henry Spelman (see
above note 56), and the printed Tables of Speed's Maps,
with the Maps themselves . . . regulating the whole by an
Abstract taken from the Books of the Hearth Office', and
Gregory King in the Kashnor Ms. (Glass 1950, p. 341)
repeats that this was what Adams did.

64   The county histories give numerous examples, e.g.
Hasted on Kent (see note 69).

65   For the distribution of the gentry in a midland county,
and their presence in the county town, Warwick, see
P. Styles, 'The Social Structure of Kineton Hundred in the
reign of Charles II', *Transactions of the Birmingham
Archaeological Society*, 1962. This is one of the very few studies
of an important subject, though see W. G. Hoskins on the

Caroline Gentry in *Devonshire Studies* (with H. P. R. Finberg), 1952.

---

66   This inquiry was part of what is known as the Compton Census, see article by Laslett and Harrison cited in note 9. The return for Goodnestone is in the Canterbury Diocesan Records and has been communicated by Miss Anne Whiteman of Oxford, who is making a study of this 'census'.

---

67   This is a fairly high proportion; compare 12·6 per cent in the town of Stafford, 1622; 16·7 per cent in 1676 and 15·8 per cent in 1688 at Clayworth in Nottinghamshire; 10·6 per cent at Harefield, Middlesex in 1698. The study of servants is one of the crucial issues in the early work on pre-industrial social structure and it is hoped to publish a full survey fairly soon; there seems to be a tendency for the proportion to fall where industry was developing.

---

68   The Goodnestone listing can be compared with the Kentish places of which we have detailed lists for 1705, see note 51; 'Goodnestone' actually appears amongst these later lists, but a much smaller community is obviously in question, which is one of the reasons why the 1705 'named places' have to be treated with caution. We have listings of communities in Nottinghamshire, Devonshire, Derbyshire, Middlesex, Staffordshire, Herefordshire, Wiltshire, Warwickshire, Essex and many other counties as well as Kent, all dating before 1710 and made for several purposes other than the Compton Census. Goodnestone has been chosen for the present essay, not because it is the most detailed of the listings, but because it illustrates the principles at issue very well.

---

69   Edward Hasted, *History of Kent*, Canterbury, 1782, vol. II, p. 815.

---

70   This is the village of Cogenhoe, and the document is described at length in the article by Laslett and Harrison referred to in note 9.

71 The great difference made to the social structure of a village community by a married parson is well illustrated by the position of the family of Christopher Spicer at Cogenhoe, whose establishment was the largest in the village from 1618–28, in the years when the manor-house was vacant; compare also the position at Clayworth, see ref. in previous note.

72 See above note 68.

73 Listing published by K. J. Allison, *Bulletin of the Institute of Historical Research*, 1963. A social structural analysis of this listing, one of the earliest in European history to give complete familial detail with ages, is in preparation.

74 See the article by Laslett and Harrison, reference in note 9.

75 A complete series of returns for London under the 1694 Act (see note 37), described in P. E. Jones and A. V. Judges, 'London Population in the late 17th Century', *Economic History Review*, 1935. This notable archive has still to be analysed for social structural purposes, but preliminary calculation shows that the proportion of servants could rise as high as 30 per cent of the whole population in such parishes as All Hallows, Honey Lane.

76 *Rural Economy in Yorkshire in 1641, being the Farming and Account Books of Henry Best, of Elmswell in the East Riding*, Surtees Society, No. 33, 1857, p. 93, modernized.

77 *The Towne Booke of Clayworth*, described in Laslett and Harrison, see note 9, is an example of this.

78 The document containing the listing for Goodnestone (see above note 66) goes on, very exceptionally, to provide these details.

79 See the Rector's Book of Clayworth (ref. in note 9) p. 43 and the parish register still in the parish, which records the christening of Elizabeth, daughter of Ralph and Anne Meers on June 10th, 1679. The couple had evidently married

outside the village. Their little girl died in the following
September. It is interesting that Anne should have had the
courage or the conscientiousness to bring the child to the
font after such a public rebuke, for it shows the hold the
church still had over the people. Even more noteworthy is
that Ralph Meers should have become a churchwarden
at Clayworth, although a labourer all his life.

80   See K. S. Inglis, *Churches and the Working Classes in
Victorian England*, 1963. The contrast between the
evidence presented there for the working-class suburbs
of Victorian England and the situation at places like
Goodnestone and Clayworth two centuries before is truly
astonishing. It has been doubted, however, whether church-
going was so faithfully maintained in Stuart times, amongst
the servants, labourers and paupers.

81   *Rector's Book* (see note 9), pp. 114 and 140; (135 Easter
Communicants, 1696, 126 Easter Communicants, 1701) and
other passages cited in the article by Laslett and Harrison.

82   Sources described in same article. It might be added that
there are occasional records of such meetings in school-
houses where these existed.

83   See the work by Powell, cited in note 60.

84   The records of the meetings of the justices of the peace
of the counties at quarter-sessions are full of references to the
granting, abuse and withdrawal of licences to keep ale-houses,
but the numbers of inns mentioned are very small, see for
a good example of this type of record, Lancashire
Quarter Sessions Records, Sessions Rolls 1590–1606,
edited by James Tait, Chetham Society, Manchester,
1917.

85   Gregory King preserved a copy of this listing of the
inhabitants of Harefield in 1699, and it is to be seen amongst
his papers in the Public Record Office, ref. T64/302.

86   It is recorded by John Aubrey, see his *Brief Lives*,
ed. O. L. Dick, 1949, p. 148.

87   For the Wawens, see Clayworth Rector's Book.

---

88   The Clayworth documents do not include the Wawen
estate records and we know nothing of how they ran their
land. The best example known to me of a landowner who
recorded his decisions and reflections on how much land he
would let, how much day-labour he would use and how large
a household he would keep and how much he would get done
for him by piecework is Robert Loder of Harwell, who had a
small gentleman's estate on the site of what is now the
Atomic Energy Establishment, and whose account book was
published in 1936 by G. E. Fussell, *Robert Loder's Farm
Accounts, 1610–20* for the Camden Series, vol. 53. Loder
keeps calculating that he would be better off if he did no
housekeeping, but nevertheless in some years had eleven
people in his family. The pressure on him to maintain his
establishment must have been very strong, for as all his
readers have noticed, he was hypersensitive to profit and loss.
His farming and household arrangements are far from clear,
unfortunately, and he would seem to have meant by keeping
servants 'at board wages', not only or even usually having
them with him for a whole year at a time, but having them
come and live for the ploughing, or the threshing, or the
harvest. Much work on the actual disposition of labour on
the land remains to be done.

---

89   E. Corbett, *A History of Spelsbury,* Banbury, 1962, p. 170.

---

90   In the Gloucestershire muster rolls of 1608, several
villages are given in which every male inhabitant of military
age is recorded as servant to the lord of the manor, for example
Postlipp, 'whereof Giles Brodway gent, is lord' and where
eleven 'servants to Giles Brodway, gent.' are the only names
mustered. There is no way of demonstrating that such
villages consisted of nothing but one great house, since
some of these men may well have been outservants and
householders: there were perhaps other male inhabitants
unfit for service. But the lord of the manor's establishment
was obviously the community for all practical purposes.

---

91   See Chapter 6, and the article by Laslett and Harrison,
ref. in note 9.

CHAPTER 4

---

92   The references here are to Romeo and Juliet, Act I,
scene ii, lines 8–11; scene iii, lines 69–73; The Tempest, Act I,
scene ii, lines 44 and 54.

---

93   Taken at random from vol. II of *Canterbury Marriage
Licences 1619–60*, edited by J. M. Cowper, Canterbury, 1894.
Another sample from the same source of a similar size yields a
mean age of all brides of 22·8, but of gentle brides (79 in all)
as low as 20·4: the ages of bridegrooms are much as in table
in text. It is possible that the Canterbury licences, though
they are the best we have found in print covering a
substantial period of years, do include some later marriages
as first marriages, which would naturally raise the resultant
mean age at marriage. But since the social status of
those married by licence shows an obvious tendency
to be higher (there is a noticeable excess of gentry
in the entries), and since those higher in the social scale
on the whole married younger than the rest, this bias is
perhaps compensated for. Some work has been done on the
age at marriage from these sources by other scholars
(notably by J. D. Chambers in his *Vale of Trent, 1670–1800*,
[1957], where marriage partners are classified by social
origin) and we ourselves have compared the results from
Canterbury with those obtained from Lincoln,
Nottinghamshire, Gloucestershire and elsewhere: the whole
class of record is usefully discussed by P. McGrath in his
note published in B. Frith's edition of *Gloucestershire Marriage
Allegations*, Bristol, 1954. We hope it will not be long before
we can supplement or replace these figures by much more
accurate ones taken from extensive family reconstitution on
the French model.

---

94   See note 35.

---

95   These figures are all taken from J. M. Tanner, *Growth
at Adolescence*, 2nd ed. Oxford, 1962. The known facts and
the then state of research on this intricate subject are
conveniently summarized, with references, in an editorial
entitled 'Early Maturing and Larger Children' in the *British
Medical Journal*, August 19th, 1961. The statistical basis

of all this work has sometimes been called into question
and it will be some time before reliable inferences can be
made. The sources for the little work we have done on
pre-industrial England are sketchy indeed. Nevertheless the
question of date of maturation is so important to the
whole subject of this book that it has seemed best to retain
the very speculative account of it given in the text.

96   Porter's play has been reprinted in the Malone Society
series, 1912, ed. W. W. Greg, see pp. 650–69 of vol. II
and Lyly's *Mother Bombie* in 1814, *Old English Plays*, ed.
C. W. Dilke, vol. I.

97   See the Diary of Robert Furse, printed in *Report and
Transactions of the Devonshire Association for the Advancement
of Science and Arts*, Plymouth, 1894, vol. XXVI, p. 181.

98   See B. S. Rowntree, *Poverty*, 1901, and the B.M.J.
editorial referred to in note 95.

99   This law is borne out by all the listings of communities
which we have so far examined. No instance of married
siblings making up one household has been found as yet, for
example, and the proportion of households containing
married children with their spouses is usually negligible.
A full analysis will be published in due course. See below for
some of the facts from Clayworth and Cogenhoe (see note 9)
and Chilvers Coton (see note 10).

100   See P. Willmott and M. Young, *Family and Class in a
London Suburb*, 1960, Table III, p. 37 and compare the
same authors' *Family and Kinship in East London*, 1957. The
figures and percentages are not, of course, strictly
comparable with those from pre-industrial England
quoted in the text.

101   See E. W. Hofstee and G. A. Kooy, 'Traditional
Household and Neighbourhood Group in Parts of the
Eastern Netherlands', *Transactions of the Third World
Congress of Sociology*, vol. IV, p. 75.

102   See for example Lancashire Quarter Sessions, ref. in
note 84, pp. 56, 143, 247, 260, etc.

103   Gregory King estimated that 2–2½ per cent of the houses
in the Hearth Tax returns were empty, but more than this
in London; Glass, article of 1950 (see note 50), p. 340.
Eight out of 117 houses in Harefield were vacant in 1699.
There were times when housing does seem to have been
short in the pre-industrial era, notably perhaps under
Elizabeth, when population was increasing.

104   S. C. Ratcliff and H. C. Johnson, Warwick Quarter
Sessions, *Warwick County Records,* 1939, p. 65.

105   Gregory King's figure is to be found amongst the
calculations in his papers now in the Public Record Office,
ref. T 64/302, pagination not given. Halley's table is
reproduced here from M. Greenwood, *Medical Statistics from
Graunt to Farr*, Cambridge, 1948, p. 44.
   British and Egyptian figures from *Demographic Yearbooks of
the United Nations*.

106   All the Clayworth documents have been used to
reconstruct this story, which is also told in the article by
Laslett and Harrison, see note 9.

107   At Clayworth in 1676, two-thirds of the solitaries were
widowed persons; in 1688 all of them were. In 1599 at
Ealing out of 7 solitaries 3 were widows; of the 26 solitary
persons at Lichfield in 1696, 14 were widows and 4 were
widowers; 8 of the widows were paupers.

108   Best, pp. 116–17, see note 76.

109   The proportions given in the text can be checked from
any detailed register though they are not entirely
confirmed by French historical demographers. At Manchester
of 397 marriages in the 1650's 132 (33·3 per cent) were
remarriages, where one partner or other had been previously
married and 46 (11·5 per cent) remarriages where both the
partners had been widowed. Of 305 brides marrying for
the first time 178 (58·3 per cent) had lost their fathers and of

279 similar bridegrooms, 136 (49 per cent) had lost their fathers too.

The Manchester registers for 1653–1665/6 were published in 1949, edited by J. Flitcroft and E. B. Leech for the Lancashire Parish Register Society. They are particularly detailed during the period of civil registration under the Commonwealth, 1655–7.

110 See Laslett and Harrison, article noted in note 9. It is unlikely that comparable figures will become available for any other community, but registers often note cases of repetitive marriage. The registers at Adel which contain ages at death for the earliest date known to us, were edited in 1895 by G. D. Lumb for the Thoresby Society.

111 These more sophisticated questions have been analysed for France by Louis Henry and others in the publications of *L'Institut National d'Etudes Démographiques*, Paris, Presses Universitaires, and in its journal *Population*. The definitive study of French peasant demography was published by Henry with E. Gautier in 1958, *Population de Crulai, Paroisse Normande, Etude Historique*. For an estimate of the importance of French historical demography for the study of English historical social structure, see the article by Laslett and Harrison, quoted in note 9.

112 Goubert, using the results and techniques of Henry and his collaborators, says that, in the relatively few cases where a union survived until the end of a woman's period of fertility, 'plus de 85 per cent ont été mères pour la dernière fois entre l'âge de 37 et l'âge de 46 ans; l'âge modal est le même que l'âge moyen, 41 ans . . . Dans notre ancien Beauvaisis (il est probable qu'on pourra écrire bientôt, dans notre ancienne France) les épouses ne donnaient des enfants que tous les deux ans, et souvent tous les trente mois'. (Work quoted in note 19, pp. 32, 33, 35.)

113 Louis Henry, *Anciennes Familles Genevoises* (publication of the Institute noted in 111), 1956.

114 This part of the text relies heavily on Goubert, see note 19.

115   Examples of such quotients at random: Widecombe-in-the-Moor 1634–73, 3·35; Ashton-under-Lyne, 1594–9, 4·8; 1600–09, 4·5; 1620–29, 3·33; 1630–39, 5·05; 1640–49, 5·1; Clayworth late seventeenth century, 4·87.

116   All these villages have been referred to in previous notes, except Buckfastleigh, the listing of whose inhabitants in 1698, including ages, is also to be found among the papers of Gregory King, British Museum, Harleian MSS 6832, fols. 132–43. It shows interesting differences in age structure from Lichfield.

CHAPTER 5

117   See Goubert (ref. in note 19) Chapter III, *Structures Démographiques*, and especially section 3, *Analyse des Crises Démographiques*, for an impressive exposition of this tendency in the Beauvais area, and for references to previous work in France, also superficially surveyed in the article by Laslett and Harrison (note 9), p. 172. The evidence from a dozen or more villages is presented in the volume of graphs appended to Goubert's work. In conversation Professor Goubert has told me that the one-crop, one-harvest, textile-producing character of the Beauvais region may be the reason for its particular liability to periodical starvation, which is not so easy to demonstrate in all areas of France.

118   Evidence for starvation in Scotland can be found in many sources, and is particularly well marked in the Register of the Scottish Privy Council, again at its most conspicuous in the early 1620's when the English evidence is clearest, see below. I am indebted to Mr Sidney Burrell for most of this information.

119   The manuscript diary of John Locke is in the Bodleian Library and this volume is MS. Locke f. 5, see pp. 19–22. His English has been modernized.

120   Though I cannot confirm Queen Elizabeth's visit to Worcester in 1588.

121   Best (see note 76) pp. 42–3.

122   The facts for Bethnal Green are summarized and
compared with those for Woodford in Willmott and Young,
Family and Class (see note 100) Chapter IV, showing that
middle-class parents, especially elderly ones, are as apt to
live close to their married children as working-class
parents. Though we have not yet examined the Lichfield
listing or any other listing in detail for this purpose,
and the difficulties of establishing kinship may make it
impossible ever to do so, it is my impression that the
town dwellers of pre-industrial England were no more liable
to live in kinship groups than town dwellers are today, and
perhaps less so. Since the peasantry lived in such small
settlements the issue scarcely arises with them. For the
Lichfield listings see note 55. The London documents noticed
in note 75 might yield more detailed results for certain
parts of that city.

123   John Graunt, *Natural and Political Observations upon
the Bills of Mortality, 1661,* etc., reprint edited by W. F.
Willcox, Baltimore, 1939, p. 33. For a definitive assessment
of the accuracy and value of Graunt's work, see D. V.
Glass, 'John Graunt and his Natural and Political
Observations', *Proceedings of the Royal Society,* B, vol. 159,
1963.

124   The account in the text is based on Goubert, see note 19.

125   Goubert, 76–7. In the original text the price of bread
is sometimes given in *deniers* and these have been
converted to *sols* at 10 *deniers* a *sol.*

126   The parish registers of Ashton-under-Lyne, Lancashire,
were published in 1927 and 1928 by H. Brierley. The
parish was already heavily engaged in textiles. Though
unfortunately marred by gaps, the registers contain
extraordinarily full information, especially for the
years 1590–1640, including abortions, suicides, etc. The
Yorkshire area mentioned covers the parish of Leeds and the
wapentakes of Morley and Agbrigg, whose vital statistics
are surveyed in a useful article by Michael Drake,

'An Elementary Exercise in Parish Register Demography',
Economic History Review, 1962, using calendar years not
harvest years, and births, not conceptions.

127 For Greystoke, see note 57. My attention was drawn to
these registers by Dr W. G. Howson of Lancaster, whose
article on 'Plague, Poverty and Population in Parts of
North-West England, 1580–1720', *Transactions of the Historic
Society of Lancashire and Cheshire*, 1960, is a most
suggestive and interesting one for the question of levels of
subsistence in England.

128 Statement of the Westmorland Justices quoted by
J. Thirsk, 'Industries in the Countryside', in *Essays in Honour
of R. H. Tawney*, ed. F. J. Fisher, 1961, Cambridge, p. 82. Mrs
Thirsk goes on to say of these northern counties: 'A crisis of
famine and consequent plague could easily be precipitated
by a harvest failure. The justices . . . of Westmorland . . . were
explaining the gravity of a crisis caused by the scarcity of
bread.' Howson talks of 'the culminating disaster of
1622–3' as affecting the whole north-west area.

129 For Colyton, its register and work in progress on it, see
note 57. Both in Devonshire and in Yorkshire several
registers have been examined which run unbroken from 1640
to 1660 and some show little sign of crisis in the mid-
1640's, as indeed many registers betray little disturbance in
the early 1620's.

130 For the mortality pattern of pellagra, see F. and
V. W. Sargent, Season, Nutrition and Pellagra, *New England
Journal of Medicine*, 1950.

131 I owe the extract from the Wednesbury register to
Mr J. F. Ede, of Wednesbury Boys' High School. The registers
of St Margaret's, Westminster, were published in 1914 by
A. M. Burke, and give causes of death from May 18th to
November 28th, 1557. The fact that 16 of the 181 so
accounted for were due to famine may call Graunt's confidence
into question.

132 This type of activity of English governments and city

fathers is well summarized in E. Lipson, *The Economic History of England*, 9th edition, 1947, vol. i, p. 302, etc., vol. ii, pp. 419–48.

133   For the movement between communities, see Chapter 6. Recent writers on the bubonic plague, which has always interested historians and on which there is considerable literature, are L. F. Hirst, *The Conquest of Plague*, Oxford, 1953, and J. N. Biraben in *Le Concours Médical*, Paris, February, 1963. Both authors seem to allow for the possibility that low nutrition may have increased susceptibility. In his analysis of demographic crises Goubert considers famine and pestilence alongside of each other, and this is becoming the convention – see Mrs Thirsk's statements in the article quoted in note 128.

134   See J. C. Cox, *The Parish Registers of England*, 1910, p. 175.

135   See A. C. Fraser, *Locke*, 1890, pp. 270–71.

136   By Biraben, see note 133.

137   See Goubert, pp. 59–67. But he reaches a very different provisional conclusion for Brittany (see note 117), which he now believes was worse off in the eighteenth than the seventeenth century.

138   For the Ashton-under-Lyne registers, see note 126, and for infantile mortality at demographic crises, Goubert, p. 54. The rise in this index at Greystoke, 1623–4 is naturally not very well documented.

139   See note 143.

140   The burial practices of earlier times are described in the rewarding work by J. S. Burn on *The History of the Parish Registers in England*, written by him in 1829 and revised in 1862. See pp. 127, 224 of the 1862 edition.

141   The figures from Crulai must be regarded as the most reliable for a rural community (see note 111), though that

for the Paris region is based on the largest sample (see Henry and Levy in *Population*, 1962). Goubert gives the Auneuil figure, and on p. 40 he prints the details of infant and child mortality for the village of St. Laurent-des-Eaux in mid-France, to demonstrate that the high rates round Beauvais were not exceptional. Paul Deprez presented the figure from Vieuxbourg to the International Population Conference in September, 1961.

142   The registers of Wem were edited for the Shropshire Parish Register Society by G. H. F. Vane and others, in 1908. The minimum here is the actual proportion of names which appear as buried within twelve months of baptism: the maximum is the same figure plus 'young children', who appear as buried but not baptized. The failure to record such babies ('chrissoms' or 'nuncupative', see above) in so many parishes in England makes our infantile mortality statistics suspect, but minimal comparisons have some utility.

143   For Graunt's exercises, see note 123. Unfortunately he breaks down his totals of burials under headings for the years 1629–36 and 1657–60 only. Since Graunt had a heading 'Abortive and Stillborn' his abortion figures are more straightforward. In our own day the estimated rate of spontaneous abortion is $7\frac{1}{2}$–11 per cent.

144   I.M. reckoned as for Wem, but no account taken of 'young children' since Parson Sampson was too meticulous a registrar to make it necessary. The crude index of cereal prices is made up of the total in shillings per quarter of the prices he records in his book (see note 9) for the wheat, barley and rye he sold, taking no account of the varying proportions these grains occupied in the food of the people or of substitution of cheaper for dearer grains when prices rose.

145   Rector's Book (see note 9) pp. 46–9. Harvest in 1678 was 'very sickly for servants'. Unfortunately the names of children born in 1678 and 1679 are missing, so we cannot recover infantile mortality. Professor J. D. Chambers of Nottingham, the authority on this area, believes that high mortality at Clayworth and elsewhere was 'more a

reflection of epidemics than of harvest conditions. . . . The standard of life was such as to enable the Nottinghamshire peasantry to withstand the worst effects of bad harvests' (letter of May, 1963).

CHAPTER 6

146 The intelligence quotient of the rural population has consistently fallen below that of the urban population as measured for schoolchildren, though very recently the correlation has been questioned. For a portrait of a contemporary village as a 'dying culture', see W. M. Williams, *The Sociology of an English Village: Gosforth*, 1956.

147 See J. Ruwet, in *Population*, 1954. Goubert records his dissent in his book on p. 51.

148 See for example the cases printed by Furnivall, reference in text on page 86.

149 This statement could only be demonstrated from a considerable body of evidence, which would be difficult to collect because chasms are so common in registers at that time. It is based on an impression of births of bastards in February and March 1660–61 which would betray irregular intercourse in May, 1660.

150 See his articles in the *Book Collector*, vol. 12, 1963, Libertine literature in England, 1660–1745.

151 Low fertility lasting until the early 20's is attested by the French demographers and is one of the facts which complicate the issue of the age at menarch; most evidence points to very regular conception within marriage, even if fertility was lower than it would be today without contraception. Neither difference from contemporary conditions would have obviated the birth of bastards on a large scale or the intrusion of strangers within families, if promiscuity or anything like it had been present.

152 See for example the statement about a wife's duties of

cohabitation in William Gouge (see note 3); unwillingness would lead her husband to the whorehouse.

---

153   The Ludlow Registers were edited for the Shropshire Parish Register Society by H. T. Weyman in 1915. 'Prostitutes' accounted for only a few (14·4%) of the bastardies, and the highest number to one girl was four. "Repeaters" account for 10% of bastards baptized.

---

154   Research on urban registers, especially the reconstitution of families, is exceedingly difficult because the populations of parishes tended to be so large and fluid.

---

155   In 1963 Jean Ganiage proved that contraception must be presumed amongst the peasants in three French villages in the 1780's, whilst at Crulai Henry believed it to be present soon after the Revolution arrived. See *Trois Villages d'Ile de France*, Paris, I.N.E.D.

---

156   Source described in 84, pp. 94, 107, 228, 238.

---

157   For registers concerned, see notes 111, 126 and 153; the Stoke-upon-Trent registers were published in 1914–17 by S. W. Hutchinson and E. P. Middleton, for the Staffs. Parish Registers Society, and those for Kerry in 1920 as vol. 39 of the Montgomery Collections. For the French figures, Goubert p. 31 and the article cited in note 141 above. Henry comments 'au XVIIIme siècle fort peu de paysannes avaient un enfant hors de mariage'.

---

158   The Westminster Registers (see note 131) have an editorial note on Bastardy: those of St Augustine's, Bristol, were edited by A. Sabin in 1956.

---

159   Ashton Registers (see note 126) p. 448, modernized.

---

160   These calculations will be found in an appendix to S. E. Sprott, *The English Debate on Suicide*, La Salle, Ill., 1961, though rates are there reckoned as proportions of total burials rather than as proportions of the population. I owe this reference to Mr Keith Thomas of St John's College, Oxford.

161   For registers concerned see previous notes: for Gosforth see note 146, and for the Wylye and Cartmel, see the registers edited by G. R. Hadow, etc., in 1913 and H. Brierley, etc. (Lancs. Parish Register Soc.) 1907, 1957. The Crulai rates have been calculated from Henry's monograph (see note 113) and those for the three villages from that of Ganiage (see note 155).

162   See *Marriage Contracts in the Reign of Queen Elizabeth*, Reports and Papers of Associated Architectural Societies for 1909, vol. XXX, pt. 1, paper for the Leicestershire Architectural Society, by A. Percival Moore. I owe this important reference to Dr Hoskins.

163   *A Mountain Chapelry*, being a guide to the parish of Ulpha, written in 1934 by H. L. Hickes, and revised and reprinted in 1950 and 1960 by B. S. W. Simpson.

164   Work cited in note 3, pp. 198–9, 202–3.

165   William Perkins (see note 3), p. 672.

166   *Marriage by the Morall Law of God Vindicated against all Ceremonial Laws of Popes and Bishops destructive to Filiation, Aliment and Succession and the Government of Families and Kingdoms*, 1680 (Wing 690). Under the powerful protection of the Earl of Shaftesbury he did publish a further portion the following year, calling it Book III, but concerned with the implications of his doctrine for politics, i.e. the superior claim of Charles II's bastard Monmouth to the throne over that of his brother, the future James II, the Catholic.

167   P. Girard and C. Piolé, *Aperçus de la Démographie de Sotteville-les-Rouen vers la Fin du XVIIe siècle*, Population, 1959. It should be noted however that a very high rate of pre-nuptial pregnancy, well up to English standards, has since been established for the three villages studied in the work of Ganiage described in note 155 above.

168   Laslett and Harrison, ref. in note 9.

CHAPTER 7

169   Max Weber, *General Economic History*, translated by
F. H. Knight, Collier Books edition, 1961, chapter 12,
especially page 132.

170   *The Pleasant History of Jack of Newbury*, in Deloney's
Works, ed. F. O. Mann, 1912.

171   E.g. by George Unwin, who recognized that the tale
was mainly mythological, but called it 'not unacceptable
as evidence', *Studies in Economic History*, 1927, p. 195.
A recent follower is S. R. Bindoff in his Pelican History,
Tudor England, p. 125.

172   *The Journeys of Celia Fiennes*, edited by Chr. Morris,
1947.

173   *The Law Book of the Crowley Iron Works*, edited by
M. W. Flinn, in 1957, for the Surtees Society. The full
document is in the British Museum, Add. MS. 34,555,
a tedious but extremely important body of evidence.

174   See Lewis Coser, *The Functions of Social Conflict*, 1956,
and especially the introductory chapter for the history
of conflict theory amongst the sociologists.

175   Peter Laslett, Foreword to J. H. Hexter, *Reappraisals
in History*, 1961.

176   Thomas Hobbes, *Behemoth, The History of the Causes of
the Civil Wars of England*, 2nd ed., 1682, opening sentence.

177   Max Gluckman has presented this phenomenon in a
succession of books and articles, of which perhaps the
most recent is the most important to our subject, *Order and
Rebellion in Tribal Africa*, 1963, see e.g. the essay there on
Succession and Civil War among the Bemba. Some interest
on the part of historians of what are still called medieval and
feudal institutions in Europe has been taken in
comparative studies of this kind, and the anthropologists
have reciprocated, but the historians of the 'Early

Modern' and 'Renaissance' period have not yet responded to any extent.

---

178   See *Class and Class Conflict in Industrial Society*, (1957), English edition 1959.

---

179   See note 175.

---

180   The story of Abigail is told in Peter Laslett, *Masham of Otes*, in *Diversions of History*, edited by Peter Quennell, 1954.

---

181   Richard Hooker, *Of the Laws of Ecclesiastical Polity* (1590's), ed. Keble, Oxford, 1836, vol. III, p. 411 (Book VIII i 2).

---

182   Bishop Fleetwood, *Sermons* (see note 3) pp. 232–3.

---

183   John Lilburne, *The Free Man's Freedom Vindicated* (June 16th, 1646), pp. 11–12, slightly abbreviated and modernized. See T. C. Pease, *The Leveller Movement*, Washington, D.C., 1916, p. 128.

---

184   John Locke, *Two Treatises of Government*, II para. 4, Laslett ed., Cambridge, 1960, 1964 p. 287.

---

185   James Tyrrell, *Patriarcha non Monarcha*, 1681, first pagination, p. 83. For this book and its relationship with Filmer and Locke, see work cited in 184, and for Filmer himself see Peter Laslett, *Patriarcha, and the other Political Works of Sir Robert Filmer*, Oxford, 1949.

---

186   See the famous Putney debates, edited by A. S. P. Woodhouse as *Puritanism and Liberty*, 1950 ed., pp. 53, 60 (Ireton's appeal to the 5th Commandment) and 61. In *The Case of the Army soberly Discussed* (Thomason Tracts E.396 10, July 3rd, 1647) it was argued that the law of nature giving all authority to the head of the family prevented 'the servants and prentices not yet free and children unmarried' then in the army from participating in such political activities.

187   Laslett, *The Gentry of Kent in 1640*, see note 61.

---

188   This book has Daniel King on the title, but he wrote only the dedication, see D.N.B.

---

189   Thomas Wilson, *The State of England, 1600* (see note 44), p. 24, modernized and slightly abbreviated.

---

190   Lancashire Quarter Sessions, 1591 (see ref. in note 84) p. 56. In his introduction to these records James Tait comments on the singular use of the word 'gentleman'.

---

191   See W. P. Baker, *Parish Registers and Illiteracy in East Yorkshire*, East Yorkshire Local History Series no. 13, 1961. (From the Society, 2 St Martin's Lane, Micklegate, York.)

---

192   For Crulai, see note 111 and for the growth of literacy in the eighteenth century see M. Fleury and P. Valmary, *Les progrès de l'instruction élémentaire de Louis XIV à Napoléon*, Population, 1957.

---

193   Lawrence Stone, *The Educational Revolution in England, 1560–1640*, Past and Present, 28, 1964, p. 43. I am indebted to the figures and the evidence presented in this pioneering study, but it will be clear that its conclusions about literacy and educational standards in Stuart England seem to me to be premature.

---

194   See previous reference. In 1962 Mark Curtis contributed to Past and Present, 23, 1962, a study of *The Alienated Intellectuals of Early Stuart England* analysing the surplus of educated clergy, an important development of his book on Oxford and Cambridge, see note 15.

---

195   E. P. Thompson, *The Making of the English Working Class*, 1963, p. 526.

Index

Index